My Walks around London

Flora Tristan's diary and observations on London life in the 1830s

By Flora Tristan

My Walks around London

Flora Tristan's diary and observations on London life in the 1830s

By Flora Tristan

First published in France, 1840 under the title "Promenades dans Londres" by Flora Tristan

© of this edition 2016 Trotamundas Press Ltd.

ISBN 978-1-906393-22-9

Published by Trotamundas Press Ltd
www.trotamundaspress.com
info@trotamundaspress.com

Table of Contents

	Introduction	i
I	The Monster City	1
II	On Climate	6
III	On the character of Londoners	9
IV	Foreigners in London	14
V	The Chartists	38
VI	A visit to the Houses of Parliament	53
VII	Factory workers	60
VIII	Prostitution	71
IX	Prisons	95
X	St Giles Parish	133
XI	The Jewish Quarter	141
XII	Stolen Scarves	146
XIII	Ascot Heath Races	149
XIV	Bethlehem (Bedlam)	159
XV	English Drama	167
XVI	Tribulations of Life in London	184
XVII	English Women	190
XVIII	Infant Schools	204
XIX	Robert Owen	224

SKETCHES

Clubs, Pockets, A Word on Art in England,
A Trip to Brighton, The Iron Dipper   244

INTRODUCTION

Flora Tristan (7 April 1803-14 november 1844) was an exceptional woman. She is probably better known as the grandmother of Paul Gauguin, but she deserves recognition for her own life and achievements.

She was born the illegitimate child of a Peruvian man in his fourties from a very wealthy and powerful family in Peru, Don Mariano Tristan y Moscoso and a young French woman, Thérèse Laisney, a seventeen year old of unknown origin. Don Mariano died suddenly in 1807 without a will, leaving his girlfriend and children in dire financial straits. They became a poor family and moved to the country. Flora's brother died soon after and Flora started to work when she was around 14 years old to help her mother, who was crushed by these misfortunes. When she was 17 years old, Flora married André Chazal, a young lithographer from a family of artists and craftsmen who was to be the father of her three children, including Aline, Paul Gauguin's mother.

Her marriage was an unhappy one from her own perspective and after leaving her husband, she decided to leave for Peru to claim her inheritance from her father. On arrival in Peru she claimed to be a single woman and through her family conections she had an entry to the world of political intrigue. During the Peruvian civil war of 1834 she entered the social struggle as a female Bolivar. Eventually she went back to Paris and published a book in 1838 about her life entitled "Peregrinations of a Pariah". In the book she described her Peruvian family in terms that made her uncle furious. Her uncle Don Pio, stopped Flora's allowance, banned the sale of her book in Peru and had it burned in the street. At the same time, her estranged husband also felt badly described in her book and decided to kill her and so he shot her in the back when she was leaving her lodgings. Fortunately she survived the attack and her husband was put in prison for twenty years.

Flora Tristan visited London a few times which she described as follows:

"Four times I have visited England, always with the aim of studying the manners and the spirit of the nation. In 1826, I found her very wealthy. In 1831, she was much less so, and moreover I saw that she was very troubled. In 1835, financial distress was beginning to be felt among the middle, as well as among the working classes. In 1839 I encountered extreme poverty in the London populace; passions were high and dissatisfaction widespread." Her book "Promenades dans Londres" was published in 1840. Although she was no trained scholar and almost without formal education, Flora was a natural writer and journalist and her book about London is one of the earliest and most courageous defences of women's rights. She eulogises Mary Wolltstonecraft: "This English woman is the first courageous enough to say that civil and political rights belong equally to both sexes.".

After her study of England she saw the need for organizing labor into an International Union and decided to tour France to promote this idea. While in Bordeaux she had a stroke and died there at the age of forty one. Four years later, on the anniversary of her death, ten thousand workers unveiled a memorial to Flora Tristan who was now recognised as an icon by the working class.

Her grandson, Paul Gauguin, son of her daughter Aline, introduced her to the twentieth century with the publication of his memoirs "Before and After" in 1918.

I

The Monster City

London, four times larger than Paris; London, where an eighth of England's population is found, two million souls, whereas Paris represents only one thirty-second of France; London, whose extravagant immensity a pedestrian could not encompass in a day's time; London, dismaying and magnificent accumulation of power ...

Aug. Luchet, FRÈRE ET SOEUR

... it is a great crowd without disorder, agitation without noise, enormity without grandeur!

Baron d'Haussez, LA GRANDE BRETAGNE

London! What an enormous city! Its great size, out of all proportion with the area and population of the British Isles, calls immediately to mind both the oppression of India and the commercial superiority of England. But its wealth, a result of the successful use of force and ruse, is ephemeral; it cannot endure without reversing those universal laws by which, when the time has come, the slave will break his chains, enslaved populations will shake off the yoke and knowledge useful to men will be broadcast so that ignorance too may be freed.

What then will be the sombre limits of the proud city? Will its gigantic proportions survive the foreign might of England and the supremacy of her commerce? Will her railroads, which radiate from the monster city in every direction, ensure her unlimited growth? These are the thoughts which fill one's mind when one sees the waves of people silently surging through the gloom of the long streets, the profusion of houses, ships and things; and one feels the need to devote oneself to a study of men of every class and their works of every description, in order to resolve the doubts which assail one's thoughts.

At first glance, the foreigner is struck with wonder at the power of man; then he is overwhelmed by the sheer weight of such vastness and is humbled by the thought of his own insignificant size. The countless vessels, boats, ships of every size and shape that, for mile upon mile, cover the surface of the river which is thus reduced to the narrow width of a canal; the imposing arches of bridges which one is tempted to believe were cast up by giants to join the world's two shores; the docks, immense warehouses which occupy twenty-eight acres of land; the domes, the towers, the edifices strangely deformed by the mists; the monumental smoke-stacks which belch their black smoke into the sky and reveal the existence of the great factories; the blurred look of the things around one; the confusion of images and sensations is both profoundly disturbing and overwhelming. But it is really at night that London must be seen! London, magically lit by its millions of gas lights, is resplendent! Its broad streets disappearing into the distance; its shops, where floods of light reveal the myriad sparkling colours of all the masterpieces conceived by human industry; a world where men and women come and go all about you; all these things produce, the first time, a state of intoxication! And by day the beauty of the streets, the number and elegance of the squares, the iron railings of sober design which seem to isolate each home from the crowd; the immense size of the parks and the felicitous curves which delineate them; the beauty of the trees; the multitude of superb carriages which roll up and down the streets, drawn by magnificent horses; all these splendid things have a fairy quality which dazzles one's judgement. Thus it is that the foreigner is invariably fascinated upon arriving in the British metropolis; but I hasten to add that the fascination vanishes like the dreams of the night or a fantastic vision; the foreigner soon recovers from his enchantment: he tumbles from the ideal world into the most arid egoism and the most materialistic way of life.

London, the centre of capital and business for the British Empire, constantly attracts new inhabitants; but the resulting advantages for industry are offset by the disadvantages caused by the vast distances: the city is several cities in one and it has grown too large for people to keep in touch or to get to know one another. How can one maintain close relations with one's father, daughter, sister, friends when, in order to pay an hour's call, one must spend three hours and eight or ten francs in cab fare to make the trip? The extreme fatigue of life in the city cannot be imagined by anyone who has not lived there with business to conduct or driven by the desire to see the city.

Ordinary errands involve distances of five or six miles; so that if one has several things to do, one must cover fifteen or twenty miles a day; it is easy to imagine the time lost in this way: on the average, half the day is spent striding through the streets of London. If moderate exercise is salutary, nothing kills the imagination nor paralyses the heart and mind like extreme and constant fatigue. The Londoner, when he returns home in the evening, exhausted from the day's coming and going, is not disposed to gaiety or wit, nor to cultivating the pleasures of conversation, music or dancing. The intellectual faculties with which we are endowed are destroyed by physical fatigue carried to the extreme, just as over stimulating these same faculties leads to atony of the physical powers: thus we see that the labourer, when he returns home from the fields after twelve hours of hard work, feels only the need to eat and sleep in order to repair his strength; his intelligence, however flexible it may be, lies dormant: such is the fate of the inhabitants of the monster city! They are forever broken with fatigue, their faces are marked by it, their character is embittered by it.

London is divided in three distinct parts: the City, the West

End and the suburbs. The City is the ancient town which, in spite of the fire under Charles II, has kept a great number of little narrow streets, crooked and poorly constructed, and the banks of the Thames are crowded with houses whose foundations are washed by the river. One sees then, apart from the new splendour, many vestiges dating from the Restoration, and the reign of William III is represented there in its entirety. There are a multitude of churches and chapels belonging to every religion, every sect.

The inhabitants of this part of town are considered by those of the West End to be of pure John Bull[1] stock. They are, for the most part, worthy merchants who are shrewd where their business interests are concerned and who care for nothing but those same interests. The shops, where many of them have made fortunes, are so dark, so cold, so damp that the West End aristocracy would disdain to have them as stables for their horses. Dress, manners and speech in the City are distinguished by forms, nuances, usages and locutions which West End fashion taxes with vulgarity.

The West End is inhabited by the court, the upper aristocracy, elegant commerce, artists, provincial nobility and foreigners of all countries; this part of the city is splendid; the houses are well built, the streets straight but extremely monotonous; it is there that one sees glittering carriages, magnificently dressed ladies, dandies capering on horses of great beauty, and crowds of valets dressed in rich livery and armed with long, gold or silver-headed canes.

The suburbs, because of the low rents, contain the workers, the prostitutes and the rabble of transients whom lack of work and vice of every kind force to lead a life of vagrancy, or whom poverty and hunger drive to beggary, theft and murder. The contrast found in the three parts of the city is the same that civilization presents in all great capitals; but it is more

---

[1]John Bull was the name given twenty years ago to the English people as a whole; nowadays it refers only to those still mired in the old customs, habits and prejudices of England.

pronounced in London than anywhere else. On the one hand there is the busy population of the city whose only motive is desire for profit, on the other there is the haughty, disdainful aristocracy who come to London each year to escape from boredom and make an unbridled display of wealth or to revel in their own superiority in contrast to the poverty of the people!... And finally, in the suburbs, there are the masses of workers so thin, so pale, and whose children look so piteous; the swarms of prostitutes with shameless gait and wanton glance; the bands of professional thieves; the troops of children who, like birds of prey, come out each evening from their holes and fall upon the city where they plunder without fear, perpetrating every sort of crime, confident of being able to escape from the police, who are insufficient to catch them in the vastness of the city.

II

On Climate

In London there are eight months of winter and four months of bad weather.

A Tourist

Never has a ripe fruit, plucked from an English garden, appeared on the table of its owner...

The grass of the meadows is cut green, grain is harvested green: no golden harvests, everything dries after cutting. No plant, no seed reaches its point of perfection, notwithstanding the appearance of lush vegetation. It is necessary each year to renew varieties and to import seed from the Continent, in order to prevent degeneration. Even wheat would degenerate if farmers did not bring in seed from the Baltic. From Sweden comes turnip seed, from Russia hemp seed, from France sainfoin, lucerne, clover, beans of various sorts, peas, etc., from Holland and the Low Countries all other garden vegetables.

Field Marshal Pillet,
L'ANGLETERRE VUE À LONDRES ET DANS SES PROVINCES

Vibrations are proportionate to the tension of strings, to the elasticity of resonant bodies; and life and movement to warmth, dryness, or moisture; cold and heat transform all beings: a great many differences of behaviour are explained by the diversity of climates. In the South, quick insights, the dazzling play of imagination; life is fast-paced, interrupted by long interludes of reverie and musing. In the North, the senses relay their perceptions one by one to the mind; investigation is calm, omits nothing; and action is slow, monotonous, but more steadfast; but from the Negro to the Laplander the scale is graduated: as one goes North, needs grow in importance; physical comfort and discomfort become almost the only motives of man; whereas in the South lavish nature allows the soul its own enjoyment; for this reason the awareness of life's blessings and misfortune is less acute, and the people are more accessible than in the North to the influence of religious thought.

To the mists from the ocean which constantly envelop the British Isles is joined, in English cities, the heavy, noxious atmosphere of the Cyclops' den. Forests no longer feed the domestic hearth; instead there is hell's own fuel, torn from the bowels of the earth. It burns everywhere, nourishes innumerable furnaces, usurps the horse's place on the roads and the wind's on the rivers and on the seas which bathe the Empire's shores.

To the enormous mass of soot-laden smoke exhaled by the monster city's thousands of chimneys is joined a thick fog, and the black cloud which envelops London admits only a wan daylight and casts a funereal pall over all things.

In London one draws gloom with every breath; it is in the air; it enters at every pore. Ah, there is nothing so lugubrious, so spasmodic as the look of the city on a day of fog, rain or bleak cold! When one is in the grip of such influences, one's head is heavy and aching, one's stomach has trouble functioning, breathing becomes difficult for lack of pure air, one feels an overwhelming lassitude; then one is seized by what the English call "spleen"! One feels deep despair! immense grief! without knowing why; bitter hatred for those one was accustomed to love the most, finally a loathing for everything and an irresistible desire for suicide. On those days, London has a frightening aspect! One imagines oneself to be wandering in the necropolis of the world, one breathes its sepulchral air, the light is wan, the cold is damp; and the long sombre rows of identical houses with their small windows and their black iron-work are like two rows of tombs which stretch to infinity and among which cadavers stroll awaiting the hour of their interment.

On these baneful days the Englishman, under the influence of his climate, is brutish with those who approach him; he is jostled and jostles with no word of pardon received or given; a poor old man falls in the street from starvation: the Englishman does not stop to help him; he goes about his business, anything else is of little importance to him; he hastens to finish his day's task, not in order to regain his home, where he would have nothing to say to his wife or children, but in order to go to his club where he will dine very well and quite alone, for he finds it tiring to talk; then he will drink and will forget, in drunken sleep, the day's ponderous boredom and its worries. Many women resort to the same method. The important thing is to forget that one exists; the English are no more drunkards by nature than the Spanish, who drink only water, but the London climate would drive the soberest Spaniard to drink.

Summer in London is scarcely more pleasant than winter: the frequency of cold rains, the heavy nature of an atmosphere charged with electricity, the continual variation in temperature bring on colds, colic, headache, so that there is at least as much sickness in summer as in winter.

There is something so irritating about the London climate that there are many Englishmen who cannot get used to it; and so it is a permanent subject of complaint and imprecation.

III

On the Character of Londoners

There must be some flaw in the character, in the domestic organization, in the habits of the English; for they are not satisfied anywhere: they seem to be tormented by a need for locomotion which propels them from city to country, from their country to others, from the interior to the coast. Whether or not they will be better off is of no significance, provided that tomorrow they are no longer where they are today. The variety, the diversion that other peoples seek in their imagination, they seek in going from one place to another. When they can no longer think of anywhere to go on land, they shut themselves up in the narrow confines of a yacht, and there they are exposed to the discomfort, the dangers of the sea, sailing with no destination, no fixed limit, no prospect of present enjoyment, nothing which promises memories, with no pleasure other than seeing an end to the one they profess to be enjoying. This mania is not peculiar to individuals; it is shared by a large number of families of every class, of every station, of every degree of wealth.

Baron d'Haussez, LA GRANDE BRETAGNE

There is such a great difference between the climate of England, particularly of London, and that of countries on the Continent located in the same lattitudes that, wishing to speak of the character of Londoners, I have no doubt noted those effects which properly belong to their climate. My intention is not to analyse the many and diverse influences which modify human individuality, to examine the degree of influence exercised by climate, education, diet, manners, religion, government, walks of life, wealth, poverty, the events of life, which cause one people to be serious, puffed up with heroism and pride, and another to be clownish, devoted to the arts and the enjoyment of life; which make the Parisian gay, sociable, open and brave, and the Londoner serious, unsociable, suspicious and timorous, flying like a rabbit before policemen armed with a little stick; why a certain wealthy Member of Parliament is venal, and a certain poet or artist possessing no property is incorruptible; why the rich are so insolent and the poor so humble, why some are so hard-hearted and others so compassionate. Such a study would be a lengthy one, for which the lives of several German philosophers would not suffice. I shall limit myself therefore to a rough sketch of the general character of London's inhabitants, while making no claim to the universality of the type. Of necessity, there are many who do not conform to type. The man of genius is always an exception, who owes more to his own nature than to outside influences. Therefore I leave a wide margin for exceptions and sketch only the ordinary physiognomy with which the monster city stamps, as with its seal, those who dwell in its bosom.

The Londoner is not very hospitable. The high cost of living and the formal tone which regulates intercourse prevent his being so. Moreover, his business takes up too much of his time, he has too little left to entertain his friends; so he issues no invitation nor shows any courtesy except as his own interest dictates; he is punctual where his business is concerned: the great distances make it absolutely necessary. The Londoner would fear the loss of public esteem if he arrived two minutes late for an appointment. He is slow to make a decision because he weighs the alternatives. It is, on his part, prudence and not hesitation; for, even more than to Englishmen of other ports, business on a large scale appeals to him; one might even say that he is a gambler in business matters. When he has made his decision, he is open and expansive; his complacency and helpfulness are almost always greater than merely business considerations would lead one to expect. He carries steadfastness in his undertakings to the point of stubbornness; he makes a point of honour of finishing what he has started; and neither loss of money, time, nor any obstacle can deter him.[1] In his family relationships he is cold and formal, requiring a good deal of deference, respect and consideration, and scrupulously returns the same deference, respect and consideration. With his friends he is circumspect, even distrustful, and yet he goes out of his way to make himself agreeable to them; but he rarely carries friendship so far as to put his purse at their disposal. With strangers he feigns a modesty which he does not possess, or puts on airs, which is ridiculous, to say the least. Toward his superiors he is compliant, fawning, and carries adulation to the point of servility toward those from whom he hopes to gain. With his inferiors he is brutal, insolent, harsh, cruel.

The Londoner has no opinions, no taste of his own: his opinions are those of the fashionable majority, his tastes, those established by fashion.

The servile conformity to fashion is typical of the nation. Nowhere in Europe are fashion, etiquette and prejudices of all sorts so slavishly followed. Life, in England, is surrounded by a thousand childish, absurd regulations as in monasteries; they are

---

[1]During the construction of Waterloo bridge, the shareholders responded to three appeals for funds, and dividends do not surpass 2 per cent on their investment. Nor did the accidents during construction of the tunnel discourage the shareholders.

troublesome in the extreme; if one happens to transgress them, Londoners are offended to a man! The offender is banished from society, excommunicated forever! The violent animosity against anyone who wishes to maintain his individuality inevitably suggests that envy, that mean passion of the human heart, is further developed in England than anywhere else. The vast majority are always far below mediocrity: they detest those who surpass them, who awaken them to their own nonentity; thus, one wounds English susceptibility whenever one deviates from the beaten path. A daguerreotype of a Regent Street or Hyde Park crowd would be remarkable for the artificial expressions, the slavish bearing, which are also to be seen crudely represented in Chinese paintings.

The Londoner professes the greatest respect for tradition and religiously observes time-honoured customs; he also complies with all that the prejudice of society and sect requires, and even though it often happens that his reason rebels, he submits in silence, and lets himself be bound by shackles which he does not have the moral strength to break.

His feelings of hatred for foreigners, especially the French, carefully fostered among the masses by the aristocracy, are fading day by day in spite of the efforts of the Tories to keep them alive. It is also good form among Londoners to appear to be free of them, lest one be mistaken for a London John Bull; however, be it business competition or envy, they are jealous of the French. Their hatred is revealed in every word with an intensity which their efforts to conceal it do nothing to diminish.

The dominant passion of the Londoner is luxury: to be well dressed, well lodged, to live in a style which puts him on a footing of respectability is the dream of his life, the goal of his ambition. In addition to this passion, there is another one of gigantic proportions: pride! to which he sacrifices everything — affection, fortune, future.

The Londoner has little room for affairs of the heart, he gives too much to pride, vanity and ostentation. He is habitually sad, taciturn and dull. His business excites his interest only through the greatness of the risks and the results; he is continuously seeking distractions, whatever the cost, but is rarely successful. When his profession and his financial situation do not present an insurmountable obstacle, he travels ceaselessly, never escaping his profound ennui, which so rarely lets a ray of light reach his soul. However, it can happen that sometimes this creature, whose sole destiny, it would seem, is "to be the recorder of human distresses", emerges from his taciturnity; then he goes to the other extreme: loud guffaws, wild outbursts, comical songs, and it is by fits and starts that he displays his unwonted gaiety. This contrast produces a painful impression.

Seeing the elegant comfort which the rich Londoner enjoys, one could believe him happy; but if one takes the trouble to study the expression on his face, one realizes from his features, which bear the stamp of boredom and lassitude, from his eyes devoid of any spark and wherein physical suffering can be read, that not only is he not happy, but the conditions in which he finds himself forbid his aspiring to happiness.

IV

Foreigners in London

Baron de Wormspire
You hesitate? No doubt when I have introduced myself ... I am Baron ...
Robert Macaire
Descended from the famous ...
Baron de Wormspire
Exactly.
Robert Macaire
His name has gone down in history.
Baron de Wormspire
Furthermore I am a Brigadier-General ... commissioned in the old days ... by the great man himself ... that is a title which means something, sir.
Robert Macaire
I am completely won over ...
Baron de Wormspire
Come now, my dear son-in-law, enough of this flattery. We who served him in the Grande Armée don't stand much on ceremony. We are rough and ready men.
Robert Macaire

FOREIGNERS IN LONDON

Oh the man is a jewel: open, sincere, what more could I ask for?

London, because of its commerce and its great wealth, attracts large numbers of foreigners, who are almost all engaged in business: some belong to the world of commerce, others to the world of intrigue.

I have been told that there are more than fifteen thousand Frenchmen living in London; there are also a great many Germans and Italians; since the recent disturbances, the Spaniards and Poles are flocking to London: I cannot supply exact figures for any of these emigrations. I shall say nothing of the other nations which all have their representatives in the monster city, as I have no information concerning them; but it is noteworthy that in England the multitude has never designated the foreigner by any epithet but that of "Frenchman", whatever part of the Continent he might be from. In the Orient as well, all Europeans are called "Franks" as if the name Frenchman, or free man, were one day to be adopted by all of Europe.

With the exception of refugees, all these foreigners have come on business: they include a large number of workers at various trades, decent people who work industriously to feed their families; then there are merchants engaged in wholesale or retail trade, artists connected with the various theatres, teachers, doctors, the diplomatic corps, and, finally, a floating mass of travellers who spend no more than a month or two in the country. As for those who have taken up residence and become what the English call "householders", the most umbrageous of Englishmen could find no reason to doubt their respectability, and so they enjoy the esteem which they deserve. The same is true of travellers whose reason for being in England is clear to all.

Foreigners who have no capital or credit enabling them to engage in commerce, and who have no profession or trade, must, like the others, find some way to live; and to reach that goal, they deploy by far the greatest ingenuity. What could be more ridiculous, more comical, than the means they use to worm their way into English society? No sooner have they discovered the great importance which not only the aristocracy and the world of finance, but also the middle class and even petty tradesmen attach to titles, than they unceremoniously deck themselves out in such titles as baron, marquis, count, duke, colonel, general and so on and so forth; they dress up their button holes with the Medal of the Legion of Honour or with the St Louis Cross; and, although decorations, uncommon in England, are worn only at court, the English are delighted to receive a Chevalier of the Legion of Honour. In their eyes, the Medal of Honour is still a sign of respectability. Alas, they are unaware that the lapel of informers proved to be its Golgotha!

It is amusing to see a commercial traveller, a barber's assistant, or some other individual with no breeding at all, signing the most illustrious names of France with an ease and aplomb that might lead one to believe that he has always gone under the name of Chevalier de Choiseul or Vicomte de Montmorency. The older ones were all at least field marshals in the Grande Armée and decorated by Napoleon himself! The young ones are invariably Carlists; they were, at the very least, colonels under Charles X, and they are unwilling to live in France because their king was driven out.

The mania for titles has even reached such extremes in London that kept women and even prostitutes make use of them as a stepping stone to fortune: the ladies style themselves the Marchioness of ***, Baroness ***, Countess ***; without compunction they make use of the coat of arms of the family whose name and title they have taken; seal their billets-doux with one of those magnificent seals of antique design with elaborate armorial bearings; their linen and silver bear the emblem of their house; even their lackeys, when they have any (which is extremely unusual), wear feudal livery. It is understandable that, in a country where appearances are all important, a prostitute decked out thus in aristocratic trappings must necessarily cut a certain figure ... and, sometimes make her fortune. Frenchwomen are clever and, living in the country renowned for advertisement and puffery, they quickly learn the procedure. You will hear Englishmen say, when speaking of a woman of the town: "Oh she is a lady of very good family, she is the niece of Count de la Rochefoucauld," or, "She is connected with the de Broglie family," etc. Only the English could be taken in by such humbug!

I observed in England a curious collection of barons, counts and marquis! Many of them are suspected of being in the pay of the French government (it is said that the police have republican refugees in London closely watched); the others are "fashionable gentlemen" who are quite simply trying to make their living.

All these noble lords talk of their feats of arms, pay court to the daughter of the house, sing duets, and all the while try to draw the father into a business scheme. Almost all these gentlemen possess secrets of the utmost importance for manufacturing!... One can transform "any sort of leaves" into tobacco; another can make excellent paper from an "unknown" pulp which "costs next to nothing"; and finally an even bolder one turns up and says: "My English friends, until now you have used the costliest means to obtain gas; I have been fortunate enough to discover new processes which would provide the shareholders with a return of 500 per cent! I can make gas from nothing! A little earth, a little air, that is all there is to it."[1]

Then there is the "monster filter" for providing the whole of the city of London with clear water. And what about the excellent beer containing neither hops nor barley? There are those who would free the English from the enormous duties which their government, in its love for freedom of trade, has imposed on wines. They can produce Bordeaux wines and Champagne at such modest prices that even the masses could afford them. They can make, without wine, vinegar as good as that of Bordeaux and brandy which is the rival of Cognac. My task would never end if I attempted to enumerate the countless marvels of which these gentlemen possess the secret.

---

[1]This story is literally true. A Frenchman managed to get paid a guinea a day for two whole years, continually promising the shareholders that he would make gas from nothing at all. It is the most original hoax I saw perpetrated in England; but it loses a great deal when written down: to appreciate it properly, one must hear the inventor tell the story himself and see him act it out.

The English are obliged to recognize that many more discoveries are made in France than in their homeland. French inventiveness has frequently provided England with the means of making millions. Without looking far afield, one may note that the dredging machine was invented, in the year VII, by a French engineer residing in St Germain; the process for the manufacture of continuous paper is Didot's, and the system for spinning linen is that of Girard. All these inventions were perfected and put into practice in England, from whence they have come back to us again. The English are so tenacious that by successive improvements they achieve success with inventions whose practical applications would have gone undeveloped in France. Girard's machines had been lying about for several years when the English adopted them, and soon, after a few improvements, the spinning of linen in England underwent such a development that it is on the point of ruining our linen industry, because of the absurd concession by our government to a government which makes no concessions and is forever trying to gull its rivals.

As a result, the English are fairly generally disposed to pay attention to the discoveries which the French claim to have made, because every day new chemical and mechanical processes reach them from France, as well as men of talent who help their factories confront the fearsome competition from the Continent. Such a disposition, as honourable as it is well disposed in our favour, is unfortunately exploited by charlatans, whose actions cause the French to be accused of bad faith and fraudulent schemes, are harmful to real inventors, explain why enterprising minds hesitate to devote themselves to attempting new things, and thus impede progress.

Ingenious discoveries often give rise to expectations of results which are not achieved in the first few experiments, without its being possible to doubt the good faith of the original inventor; the inventor, that emissary from Providence, as far removed from the charlatan as Rossini from a drummer, as far as Walter Scott's style is from the puff of a bookseller's advertisement. Thus if John Bull allows himself to be taken in, it is because he frequently has far too much confidence in himself; the charlatan could hardly deceive anyone knowledgeable in the field in which the so-called discovery has supposedly been made. John Bull makes up his mind without consulting anyone, because he has been cleverly persuaded that he knows enough about it to form his own opinion; he is motivated by three things so obvious that they cannot escape observation: pride, greed and gluttony. As the schemers of whom I speak do not have culinary artists at their beck and call, they cannot take advantage of this last weakness, but they very cunningly play on the first two; and when John Bull is exploited he rants and rails at those "rascally Frenchmen". In his witless anger, he lumps the entire nation together, calls them all scoundrels, etc., etc.; for John Bull has always come by his money so honourably that to deprive him of any of it is truly a crime worthy of God's wrath! The cries of the victims are rather like those of La Fontaine's raven who lost his cheese. If John Bull attached no importance to titles and honours he would never give his daughter in marriage, together with a large dowry, to an adventurer loaded down with titles, real or imaginary, with medals of various colours on his lapel. Gentlemen who are acquainted with France are not taken in; they know perfectly well that the French nobility bear no resemblance whatsoever to the self-styled nobles idling away their time in the streets of London.

It was considerations such as these that determined me to write this chapter on foreigners in London. It was my desire to show the English what we are really like, so that they might not be taken in by outward appearances; to show John Bull the difference between a knowledgeable man and a charlatan, between a man of true nobility and an adventurer, between the duke and his valet, the duchess and her soubrette, so that he might never give vent to his absurd recriminations, and that he might not in his anger cast aspersions on the entire nation, when he has only himself to blame.

In May 1839, there was an abrupt increase in the numbers of French in London; since 1830 such has been the case after every Paris uprising, whose eddies have always been felt in the monster city; moreover, a few Frenchmen, not many certainly, came over with Prince Napoleon-Louis Bonaparte. I mention it merely to show how ill-founded are the assertions by which *Le Capitole* would have its readers believe that its "prince" plays an important part in London.

Londoners, accustomed since the French Revolution to the presence of august emigrés and illustrious personages, appear perfectly indifferent and seem to attach no political importance whatsoever to the two "pretenders" currently residing in their city. The so-called Duke of Normandy who modestly takes the title of Louis XVII, can be seen walking (and for good reason) in Regent Street without causing the least stir; the unfortunate king consoles himself for the scorn of nations by ordering his domestics (two maidservants) to address his son as *Monseigneur le Dauphin* and his daughter as *Mademoiselle*. The other pretender is frequently seen in Regent's Park driving in a tilbury or riding horseback. Few people appear to know him. If you are with some fashionable Frenchman or Englishman, he will point him out to you, but the former will inform you: "*Tiens*, there is Prince Napoleon." The latter will say: "That gentleman over there is Napoleon's cousin." I had one young Englishman tell me, with perfect indifference: "That is Napoleon's son." What, indeed, does the degree of relationship matter? It is the name Napoleon, itself, which lives in the memory of men; each one feels that he was the man of his age, and that neither his genius nor his power can have any successor.

At a time when the multiplicity of opinions leaves one undecided as to what the majority believes, when political and religious apathy fosters the hopes of men of party and sect, certain people have judged it opportune to parade Napoleon before the public and have managed to create some stir by rattling the rusty arms of the Grande Armée. The French, passionately fond of glory, entertain themselves, in the midst of peace, with bellicose narratives and battles on the stage, but for all that, the government of the sword exercises very little appeal for them, because twenty-five years of peace have given them an extremely positive turn of mind. But if, as it appears, certain people are seriously thinking of founding a political party on memories of military glory, I too would like to express an opinion about the "great man". I will begin by stating that I have neither hatred nor enthusiasm for his memory; I do not think, as did Madame de Stael, that Napoleon is Robespierre on horseback. Both despots were necessary for different reasons. Mere agents of the great revolutionary event, neither one was conscious of his mission, and even when all was over and done, on the rock of St Helena, the ex-Emperor continued to believe in "human reason".

The events of the French Revolution are so great that men are crushed by them. The leaders disappear, however talented they may be, as soon as they obstruct the march of the revolution; it is God's will which directs it; men are powerless to guide it, to oppose it or to betray it; all serve it unknowingly, even when they seem to be striving toward a different goal.

Self-interest and the interest of the group have been, since men were brought together in society, the two driving forces of the struggle; there is no civil or religious turmoil, no war but what can be reduced to those two principles; but conflict brings them closer together and they have a tendancy to merge. The process is revealed to anyone who knows how to read in the book of human history.

France, rent by anarchy, accepted, on the 18th of Brumaire, the sword of Napoleon on the implicit condition that liberty be consolidated and peace be won; if the nation had wanted a return to despotism, there was no need to spill so much blood.

Men are eminent in the annals of mankind through the influence their works have had on the future of society, and through the domination they have exercised. Napoleon is the sovereign who carried to the greatest lengths the power of force over the people he dominated. The poor in their hovels and the rich in their palaces were in the grip of his power, and no one could escape it; but what of his endures? What institution of his has bettered the lot of humanity? What did he do that is of permanent utility? His codes which have been advanced as his claim to personal glory, are, in the judgement of all jurists, far inferior to the so-called "intermediate" legislation in existence when he took power. He substituted his prejudices, his tyrannical instincts for the liberal principles of republican legislation; he transformed marriage into servitude, and made of trade a suspect activity; he undermined equality; established the right of primogeniture; introduced confiscation, made non-disclosure of crime a crime itself; exempted the actions of the agents of authority from the jurisdiction of the courts; almost eliminated the jury; instituted evocations in the Council of State as well as provostal courts, and deprived the people of the right to appoint magistrates.

He filled all posts: mayor, deputy, rural policeman, notaries and clerks, judges in both courts of first instance and in courts of appeal, bishops and archbishops, prefects and kings; in short all authority emanated from his, and in his vast empire no profession or trade could be practised unless authorized; his army and the depositaries of his authority were under the surveillance of his secret police made up of an enormous number of agents. They were to be found in every regiment, in the palaces of ministers, and even at the tables of royalty. The press was censored, and espionage organized on such a large scale that not a single voiced thought could escape the knowledge of the Emperor.

Under his reign, censorship was everywhere! He treated the French like children who are taught what to say and think, and to this end he created a "director of public opinion". Suretyships, permits, licences, diplomas for the exercise of every profession, every trade, all date from that period; in some professions he even limited the number of people who might practise it; without a doubt the apprenticeship system was a regime of freedom compared to imperial inventions: the obstacles which citizens encounter because of what remains of those deplorable institutions may give them some idea of what it must have been like when no link in the chain had as yet been broken.

In that system, there is independence for no one. Napoleon decreed that some of the solicitors in Paris be eliminated. Under the Restoration we saw printers deprived of their livelihood by having their patents withdrawn, as if they were prefects. All professions which can be practised only by virtue of the permission of the authorities are still threatened by arbitrary decision; for if, in order to be a commercial broker, exchange broker, baker, butcher, etc., it is not enough to fulfil the fiscal conditions of suretyship or any other conditions required of such professions by law, it is perfectly obvious that the government, which cannot give anything gratis without being unjust to the masses, retains the option of withdrawing the privilege it has granted and can always open the profession, make it accessible to everyone and return to common rights which are violated by the creation of any sort of privilege.

The Revolution had introduced freedom everywhere; Napoleon left almost no activity in life free. The numerous decrees issued in administrative matters during his reign almost always tend to obstruct or restrict freedom. The Constituant Assembly's institutions were no more respected than those of the National Convention; the commune, the canton, the arrondissement, the department were stripped of their political rights, could no longer administer themselves, could exercise no surveillance over governmental administrators through freely elected assemblies, and finally the nation was entirely deprived of any effective control over the actions of government because of the suppression of any real franchise; even the Restoration, though supported by allied troops, was ashamed to make use of the electoral colleges and the election process established by Napoleon; it was unwilling, by calling upon a part of the nation to intervene in the actions of its government, to make a derision and absurdity of what it considered to be a concession of royal power.

Napoleon raised the French flag over the pyramids and the Kremlin; his sword served him well, he conceived ideas of great scope, yet nothing of his remains, unless it be oppression's deep scar! He shook Europe to its very foundations and sowed not one seed of liberty, nor of any useful institution.

The armies of freedom waged war upon kings! Napoleon waged war upon peoples! Those armies founded popular governments in Holland, in Switzerland and throughout Italy; Napoleon set up kings everywhere with power like his own. Supreme authority, such as Napoleon had designated, not subject to control, reaching everywhere, from which nothing and no one might escape, could not tolerate any vestige of freedom; the Emperor, therefore, followed a deliberate and consistent policy of destroying freedom, in whatever guise it might present itself, if it lay within his power to do so. He had to do it, it was necessary for his continuing existence, for the authority he wielded would soon have lost all power over men's minds if it had anywhere been possible to question the right of it, and the spirit of revolt would have spread from individual to individual. Napoleon's sway over the people was signalled by the destruction of the most ancient franchises; he bestowed upon the electors of Germany, along with the title of "king", authority which was irresistible in every respect. The cities lost their municipal administration, which was replaced by the new monarchs' delegates, and Napoleon at length proclaimed himself the great defender of royal power in Europe! He organized the Confederation of the Rhine, founded his protectorate over Switzerland, not so much in the interest of his military might as to contain the tide of the spirit of freedom.

The machinery of government and the political organization which Napoleon had given to Europe, though perceived by his reason as being no less inevitable than the result of a mathematical demonstration, were far from reassuring him as to freedom's ventures. According to Fontanes: "An invisible press would have thrown Napoleon into convulsions." And if he bore such ill-will toward England, it was above all because of the extreme licence of her newspapers. He was fearful of freedom in whatever corner of the world and in whatever station it might exist, as indeed one would have to be to think for an instant that England's aristocratic freedoms could infect the people and to ban English newspapers in France. "The kings of Europe will soon wish me back again," said Napoleon on St Helena; the phrase resumes the whole man! His whole political life is contained in it. If one reads Las Cases, O'Meara, Bertrand, Antomarchi, etc., one sees the same thought appearing again and again; no sooner is he informed of the Holy Alliance than he exclaims: "Aha! the Holy Alliance is an idea they stole from me." The words need no commentary. But quotations are superfluous, his actions are there for anyone to see, those actions are links in a chain, not a single one but what tends to repress all resistance, to instil passive obedience; if one delves into police annals one sees that the vast network, which extended everywhere, which encompassed everyone, was not enough to satisfy its inventor, he wanted more: to know the thoughts whose utterance he prevented, to spy out free ideas in order to snuff them out before they might grow; there was espionage everywhere: in the administration, the army, the church, the schools, and there was espionage abroad. Such espionage reveals better than anything else the Emperor's inner agitation and his awareness that he was powerless to crush the principle of revolution.

The adversary of freedom, he who is to slow its progress in Europe, is already apparent during the days of Vendemiaire as well as in the general of the Army of Italy and in the conqueror of Egypt. Throughout his career, his actions are in keeping with the goal he has set himself, and, the extraordinary being that he is, the personification of despotism, is fully revealed on St Helena. From atop the rock where they have chained him come his prophetic words: "The kings of Europe will soon wish me back again! ..."

Those peoples liberated by France, upon whom Napoleon imposed masters, and those whose irons he had forged, angered by such cruel deception and with hearts full of vengeance, answered the call of the kings, who were humiliated by the superiority of an upstart. Oh no! it was not the retreat from Russia which overthrew Napoleon, but rather the spirit of freedom which seized the first opportunity to shake off the yoke! If Napoleon had been the agent of the revolutionary principle, though his back were against the Pyrenees, he would have driven the royal armies back beyond the Borysthenes.

The Battle of Waterloo, even today so little understood, both by the victors and by those who lost, was, in my opinion, the second triumph of freedom!

Despotism was conquered, but its army had not abdicated at Fontainebleau, and freedom could not develop in the presence of the Praetoriens; if Napoleon had died on the island of Elba, his army would have been a blind instrument in the hands of those in power, and government by the king's will, announced by the Restoration, would have been re-established. After the Battle of Waterloo Louis XVIII, who was not lacking in good sense, understood perfectly well that he had no other forces at his disposal besides the allied troops, and that he could found his government only with the support of a substantial part of the nation; and that opened the way for the give and take of ideas, and the reign of public opinion was assured. The victory of Waterloo is essentially the triumph of freedom; the northern nations conceived of it as such; the petty kings of Germany were so alarmed at the hopes it fostered that they lost no time in granting charters to their people; and the Congress of Vienna took the precaution of investing the diet with high jurisdiction over those governments; later Austria, Russia and Prussia entered into an unholy alliance to stifle any attempt at emancipation.

Napoleon, on the 20th March 1815, evoked memories of national glory; he had ceased to pay lip-homage to liberty; he was aware that it was no longer possible for public opinion to believe in him. After the Peace of Amiens, he had re-established slavery in Guadeloupe and Cayenne, and had attempted by means of a sizeable expedition to reduce the Negroes of Santo Domingo once again to servitude. During the Hundred Days he abolished the slave trade in order to curry favour with England and re-established censorship and confiscation, while at the same time convoking the nation's representatives! If he had been victorious ...; but he could not have been victorious, for God cannot err. Clearly it was the last act of his performance; despotism could not triumph without belying the events which had brought about its downfall.

Bourmont's betrayal, Grouchy's error are the sorts of circumstances which reveal how insignificant is human knowledge! Napoleon at Waterloo seems to deploy all the resources of his military genius only to reveal to every beholder the judgment of Providence by which his cause is lost. He falls, and it is neither Blucher nor Wellington who brings him down; no, it is the angel who guards our freedoms!

The Prussian army, made up of volunteers, fought with the

spirit of men who have a stake in the outcome; brandy and fear of the lash took the place of enthusiasm for liberty among the English troops. Frederick's soldiers, fiercely courageous, believe only in destiny; the "untoward hero"[1] puts his faith in his powers of reason; and a great man in spite of himself, forever reaches the goal opposite the one he thought he was aiming for: Frederick's soldiers imagine that they have restored the lustre of Prussian arms; Wellington sees the English aristocracy assured of its omnipotence for all time, and the wealth of the Continent at the disposal of English merchandise. Blind instruments of Providence! How little they suspect that they have just overthrown the adversary of freedom and the obstacles which block the progress of the revolution! In England the aristocracy saw in the victory the guarantee of its dominance; industry saw the certainty of markets on the Continent, and the worker saw the assurance of high wages. Those results were short lived: peace and domestic tranquillity brought the establishment of important manufacturing in Germany; the German customs union was formed; in France and in Russia industry made enormous strides; whereas England has been reduced to going about begging for commercial privileges under the name of "treaties of commercial reciprocity", and now sees the power of her aristocracy threatened by masses of workers who have no work and nothing to eat.

The victory of Waterloo is then an act of Providence, an era of freedom for the people; its consequences free the Irish peasant and the helot of English factories; and in France, where the workers are more advanced intellectually than anywhere else, it has made the return of despotism forever impossible.

The mad undertaking by Charles X demonstrated to all of Europe that the triumph of ideas over force in France was definitive. The three July Days excited greater enthusiasm than

---

[1] The reader will remember that in Parliament the Duke of Wellington called the victory of Navarin an "untoward event". The noble lord is a master of misapprehension. What transpired on the occasion of the Reform Bill would be proof enough, even if the rest of his career did not furnish hundreds of examples.

the fall of the Bastille: kings too were more alarmed than at any other phase of the revolution and dared not take up the challenge.

Yet, after Waterloo, freedom having been denied to Italy and Germany, the secret societies of those nations saw no other way to achieve it than through the national unity of their respective countries. They called themselves *Young Italy* and *Young Germany*. Then memories of the Empire estranged them from France, but those memories faded in the face of July 1830. The attempts to gain political rights in Italy, the equally fruitless efforts in Germany, Poland's disastrous struggle, all combined to prove that freedom can exist only through the union of peoples, and that in this respect it must follow the example of despotism and form an alliance which is indeed holy in the true sense of the word. This truth was universally felt in the north as in the south and the secret societies took in common the name of *Young Europe*. Their hopes will be realized; my faith is upheld by three great events: the fall of the Bastille, Waterloo and the three July Days.

The opinion I have expressed about Waterloo will perhaps seem strange, yet I am not alone in professing it, but, for lack of space, I cannot give it the attention it deserves.

It is high time we returned to our barons and counts.

I used to frequent the house of a German, Doctor Warburg, a man of talent to whom we owe a great medical discovery; this worthy gentleman had just arrived from Demerary; he had spent fifteen years in that part of Guiana, where his love of natural history caused him to dwell almost constantly in the midst of the magnificent virgin forests which cover the land, observing and studying the animals, plants, etc.; it was for this reason that he was able to enrich science with new data and to discover in inexhaustible nature new methods of healing; but if his solitary life made him familiar with the ways of plants, animals and Indians, it left him in ignorance of the wiles of civilized man. The doctor is as the gods made him: he is as modest as he is talented; his discoveries are due to fortunate moments of inspiration, to chance encounters; that is how he would describe them; his simple trustfulness, his wide-eyed wonder were those of primitive man, not yet initiated into the fine art of self-praise and unaware of the immense resources of advertisement. Such a man was a gold mine for the French counts and barons! ... And so the doctor's house was always crowded. To tell the truth, the table was always set and all sorts of wines were served as well as excellent coffee.

When I was there, there was a crowd of Frenchmen flocking to make themselves agreeable to Mrs Warburg: they were the Marquis de Montauban, Baron de Chamoisi, Count de Crouy, Count Birague de l'Isledon, the Chevalier de Chateaubleu, Count Taffe, Doctor Conneau, Doctor Schulte, etc. All these gentlemen were received by "Prince" Napoleon, and several were "in his service". I am at a loss to say how he managed to surround himself with a dozen individuals whose names, when they are not downright peculiar, sound as if they were borrowed from novels of long ago. In truth, the little phalanx was composed of men of various nations: Frenchmen, Italians, Germans, Spaniards, Belgians, Portuguese, Swedes, Poles; there were no Englishmen among them; that is worthy of note, for even the animal beloved of gastronomes has no better nose for uncovering the truffle than the Englishman for seeking out the man who is rising in wealth or in power; if therefore the English have rebuffed the prince's overtures, it is because they latch on only to those who can help them along, and they have not sensed in Napoleon-Louis a man destined for great things, nor observed in him any of the conditions necessary to give political value to his name. These gentlemen in the service of "His Highness"[1] are not always on the best of terms with one another; each of them, endowed with varying degrees of intelligence, is motivated by self-interest and plays his role accordingly; as a result the play has neither harmony nor unity: the reader may judge for himself when he has seen the sketch drawn from life, that I am about to put before him.

---

[1] These gentlemen of Napoleon-Louis' little court address him as "Your Highness". I do not know if such adulation is obligatory, but the title also appears on the business cards of "His Highness" Prince Napoleon-Louis' barber.

The Marquis de Montauban, Colonel de Montauban, is what is generally described as a fine figure of a man: height, five feet six inches, slight of chest, a military bearing. His face gives no clue to his age; his small grey eyes are lively and bold, his smile crafty. His expression is that of a man perfectly satisfied with himself. The colonel is charming, especially after dinner. All the women are mad about him, as he himself will tell you, with the charm and credulity of a second lieutenant. Like good Frenchmen everywhere, he loves good French wine; as he owns country houses in Bohemia,[1] he demonstrates his ties with Austria through his libations of wine from Hungary or the Rhine, and simply because he likes it, he sips sherry with such enjoyment that it is a pleasure to see; it was while drinking that golden wine from pretty little cut crystal glasses that the Marquis de Montauban told me his story. The colonel told me that he was forty-two "and-a-half". That "and-a-half" struck me as priceless. At that rate, I thought to myself, he must have been only seventeen in 1814, and yet, at the time, he was already a colonel in the Grande Armée!

In 1815, after the return of Louis XVIII, he was banished; he was too much feared to be allowed to remain in France. He even found it quite difficult to obtain permission to reside in Frankfurt; there he lived the life of a lord and married a rich and beautiful English heiress. 1830 came along; the colonel found himself one day in Paris; he did not tell me what presentiment of glory brought him there in time to play a distinguished role in the events of the July Days; no matter, the colonel performed feats of valour and was wounded, which did not prevent him from leading the victorious bands. Appointed general of the Parisian troops at 1,500 francs per month and ten rations of forage, he set up his household in keeping with his new position, hob-nobbed with ministers, was received at court, etc.

Four months had passed since the three July Days; the colonel felt justified, considering his past services, in nourishing the

---

[1] Almost all these gentlemen around Prince Napoleon-Louis possess vast properties in Bohemia, Hungary, Transylvania, Illyria, etc., etc., etc.

highest hopes for his career, when suddenly he had a falling out with the Minister of War. There was talk of relieving him of his command; the Marquis de Montauban was not a man to give in easily; the matter was brought before the Council of State, where it is still pending. The colonel thereupon left an ungrateful government, returned to Germany, and later came to England to join Prince Napoleon. Colonel Montauban is endowed with a practical philosophy which allows him to rise above the reverses of fortune; he good-humouredly shrugs off the disappointment of thwarted ambition, leads a merry life, and divides his time among the ladies, horses, cards and politics.

I am not guilty of any indiscretion in relating the marquis's story, since he himself tells it in drawing-rooms all about town to anyone who cares to listen, but he does not stop there, and, though he is truly fond of the prince and sincerely devoted to him, he cannot go against his nature and speaks of his master's affairs as casually as he does of his own. In London, the marquis' listeners always knew that he would find some way to introduce his prince's name, sooner or later, into any conversation: it was because the prince was always uppermost in his mind and he was quite incapable of disguising his thoughts.

Many a time I have heard him hold forth, always in the midst of a large gathering and in the most amusing way, on the doughty gentlemen who "worm their way" into the prince's circle in the hope of "touching him for a few hundred" (the Marquis de Montauban is a military man, and although he is a man of the world as well, his language bears the stamp of his profession). Here, among hundreds I might choose, is one of the colonel's stories. Let us allow him to tell it in his own words.

Those humbug Frenchmen are real devils! Even I have to watch out if I'm not to be taken in by them. Have you heard about the famous conspiracy against the prince? No. Well, it's really extraordinary. One day I get a letter that says:

"If a stalwart Pole, who had the honour of serving in the

Grande Armée, can rely on the word of a French officer, I ask that you be at the Duke of York's Column tomorrow at noon, rain or shine, a relevation of the utmost importance awaits you ... The life of His Imperial Highness Prince Napoleon is at stake!¹
Signed a Pole"

A Pole! dear me, I said to myself, another humbug hoping to diddle me out of some money. What bores these Poles are! Those people are getting to be quite tiresome; to do you out of two or three shillings, they will concoct the most tedious stories, flood you with letters, and.... But, seeing that the Prince's safety was in question, I didn't want to leave any stone unturned, and at noon there I was at the appointed place. In spite of the driving rain and the icy wind, my man was waiting for me, huddled up against the base of the column.

The hero of the Grande Armée was wearing, if only for our meeting, worn out boots, threadbare clothes of black, and he didn't even have an umbrella to protect his hatbrim which looked to me to be pulling away from the crown. After the formalities, and civilities, my friend said: "Colonel, I have a dreadful secret ... to tell you ..." "Speak up, man, but be brief; a public square is no place for a long speech." The chap was not in the least disconcerted, and he continued with admirable aplomb: "Colonel, I am Polish!" Well, well, I thought, what a surprise ... "I am an exile! I am a victim of the tyrant! And besides, Sir, I am married, my wife is ill, my aged father is bed-ridden and I have five children."

I am so used to hearing what all these bully exiles have to say that I understood at once what sort of a man I was dealing with. Aha! I thought, here we have a chap who is going to ask me for ten shillings; how amusing! "My dear Sir", I said, "I assume you

---

¹It is my intention to repeat the story just as it was told me, without changing a single word, I also feel the need to assure the reader of my great esteem and affectionate sympathy for the Polish refugees; I have met several in London whose laborious life attests to the energetic temper of their souls; but it may be that there are others who have allowed themselves to be brought down by misfortune.

didn't bring me here in this weather to talk about you: I am in no humour to tolerate being dragged out under false pretences ..."

"Colonel," replied the hero unperturbed, "I am going to inform you of the matter concerning the Prince ... but first I wanted to tell you that I need the Prince's signature and yours in order to obtain a subscription which will enable me and my family to escape from poverty." Thereupon the fellow drew from his pocket a long list and requested me to sign my name, to pledge three pounds sterling and to take the list with me and have it signed by the Prince with a pledge of six pounds sterling.

I confess that, of all the tricks played on me by those Grande Armée humbugs, this one appeared to me a wee bit obvious. If, at first, I was annoyed at being put upon, the turn the meeting was taking restored my good humour, and I was looking forward to having a good laugh at the whole thing. I felt that the chap, who had had the temerity to draw a gentleman out in such weather to get him to sign a subscription for three pounds, while standing under an umbrella in the middle of the street, must have invented quite a story concerning the projected assassination of the Prince, and I was not about to miss out on the creation of such a fertile imagination.

"Very well," I said, "I shall take your list and have it signed by the Prince and his friends; but, out with it, what's this about a conspiracy?"

"Here is the situation. It so happens that, by the merest chance, I have discovered that there is a scoundrel here sent by Louis-Philippe to assassinate the Prince!"

"Really! And do you know how he intends to go about performing the horrible deed?"

"The man has a subtle poison in his possession. He carries it always with him, hidden under his fingernail; he is to approach the Prince when he passes in the street, and he will then thrust his fingernail into the hand of the Prince, who will immediately fall dead in the street!"

"And are you acquainted with this man?"

"Yes, indeed."

"What is his name?"

"*Fleury.*"

The assassination story was so absurd that I had to make an effort not to burst out laughing. "Very good", I said, "I shall inform the Prince of your important revelation. Write down the name and address of the assassin." Ah, and then he put the crowning touch on his little deception. He wrote down in my notebook: Monsieur Guillot, Tottenham Court Road, No. 42.

"*What? What do you mean, Guillot? You just told me his name was Fleury.*"

"*Oh! I beg your pardon, I'm a foreigner and as all your French names sound alike to me ...*"

Well, this time I had had enough. To mistake Guillot for Fleury struck me as just too incredible!

Madame, you have just heard the first part of the story, let me give you the second.

I left my Polish chap, and as I was not far from the Prince's house, I went straight there, feeling the need, I must confess, to have a good laugh with him. When he saw me come in, all soaked and bespattered from head to toe, the Prince, who is the soul of kindness, said to me: "Good heavens, my dear Colonel, what a sight you are! What is so urgent that you must venture out in this weather, and on foot?" "Your personal safety, Sir." "My safety? And who threatens my safety?"

Unfortunately I was not able to keep a straight face: as you know, I love a good laugh, which does not prevent me from standing my ground on the battlefield; and too I have known the Prince since he was a child, and feel quite at home with him.

"*Your safety is threatened by a monster named Guillot, a fearsome poisoner who is intent upon taking your life!" And so saying I fell back upon the sofa and burst out laughing.*

As I said a moment ago, the Prince is very kind, I might even say too kind; for fear of offending, he puts up with any number of people around him ... but then, who does not have his weaknesses?

There was that day, as usual, a gathering of good Napoleonists who come every morning to make up to the Prince, smoke his tobacco and to drink his tea and his cognac. My laughter infected the Prince, who joined in, but it scandalized a number of other gentlemen. They disapproved of my displaying such hilarity in speaking of a projected attempt on His Highness' life. I must explain that each of those gentlemen around the Prince is forever engaged in finding ways to monopolize the Prince's confidence: this aim, which all have in common, is a frequent cause of jealousy, and to achieve it there is no petty scheme which they will not resort to.

When I was able to talk once again, I told the Prince of my curious meeting and the dreadful plan of the so-called Guillot; at the end I drew from my pocket the list given to me by the veteran of the Grande Armée; the whole thing was laughable, a matter of sending the unfortunate Pole a couple of guineas and enjoying the joke; that had been my sole intention in telling the story; but Monsieur de Persigny, His Highness' private secretary, companion, friend, confidant, personal advisor, etc., took it into his head to take the Pole's story seriously. As everyone knows that Monsieur de Persigny is really the master where the Prince's affairs are concerned, as soon as he had expressed his concern over the story, the assembled toadies, who had laughed at first, were of the same opinion as the Prince's advisor; we quarrelled, I lost my temper, and to prevent things from reaching a worse pass, I left quite upset.

As I've told you, the Prince is fond of me, and Persigny may do what he will, he'll not change that.

The Prince wrote to me, asking me to come back as usual, but I was vexed and wouldn't go back; five or six days had elapsed when the Prince called on me. "I've come after you," he said, "I've too few friends for you to deprive me of my best one. Let us forget the quarrel of the other day, come and dine with us, and shake hands with Persigny who is my friend and yours as well."

I am easy to get along with, I have never held a grudge against anyone. When I arrived at the Prince's, I shook hands with Persigny and we dined quite merrily. Harmony had been restored, not a word had been said about the story of Guillot; we had gathered in the drawing-room and were smoking excellent cigars and drinking good French coffee, when in comes Monsieur de Chamoisi, shouting and waving his arms like an actor on the stage:

"*Your Highness, we've got him! we've got him! we've got him!*"

I knew immediately from the expression on Persigny's face, and even on the Prince's, that it was about Guillot.

"*But, whom are you talking about?*" *said the Prince with embarrassment.*

"*The assassin, Your Highness.*"

"*Ah you've got him,*" *I said,* "*Guillot or Fleury?*"

But old Chamoisi knew what he was about, he was not to be disconcerted.

"*Sir,*" *he replied sharply,* "*the assassin is called both Guillot and Fleury, you ought to have been shrewd enough to guess as much, even without definite information ...*"

I had no desire to reopen the discussion; seeing that everyone was ill at ease, I picked up my hat, left the room and asked the Prince to join me in his study. "*Sir*", *I said,* "*I am certain that this assassination business is nothing but another pretext to wring money out of you, as has happened so many times before; what's more it can only make you look an ass, which, in your position, is a serious matter. Now that I have given you fair warning I shall have nothing more to do with it except to sit back and laugh.*"

I'll not try to describe all the tomfoolery occasioned by the fascinating Mr Guillot: first of all, Monsieur de Chamoisi led off with a request for twenty-five pounds to find the assassin, then he asked the Prince for forty pounds to track down Guillot who had supposedly escaped, then, once he was found, forty pounds to have him arrested, and finally after several months of manoeuvres, counter manoeuvres and 100 pounds in expenses, they claimed they had discovered for a fact, who knows how, that Guillot had returned to France to report on his mission.

There you have, Madame, one of the hundreds of pranks to which the Prince is exposed every day because he is such an easy target.

To appreciate the story fully, one ought to hear it from the Colonel himself, with his intonation, his gestures and his laugh which is so hearty, so warm and so infectious.

To sum up, if the Colonel does not possess the gravity seen today in officers fresh out of military school, one can say of him that he is a jolly good fellow, handy with a sword, the sort of man who would not hesitate to lead an assault. Moreover, he has a good heart, likes to be of service, freely gives his money, when he has any, to the poor Frenchmen starving in London. The only fault with which one might reproach him, is the looseness of his language which people indulged in once upon a time, but which is not suitable for our age when everything is taken seriously. The Marquis de Montauban would sacrifice his best friend for the sake of a good joke.

My conversations with the Colonel taught me more about the Prince and his entourage than I would have learned in six months time had I been a frequent caller at the house of "His Highness". I think it is quite clear that the people around him are cleverer at getting money out of him than in pointing out to him the only path by which he can achieve distinction. If I had had occasion to speak with Monsieur Napoleon-Louis Bonaparte, I would not have addressed him as "Your Highness" or by any other title, nor would I have called him the "great nephew of the great man". Ah how deplorable it is to persist in playing a part for which one is not suited, and how stupid to insist upon being a "prince" in spite of destiny!

V

The Chartists

Put your trust in God and keep your powder dry.

O'Connell

Chartist mottoes as they appear on their banners at meetings:

It is better to die by the sword than by hunger.
Patience and Perseverance, we will win our rights.
He who would be free must know how to give the sign.
Universal suffrage.
The scorned producers will take the law into their own hands.
One day of freedom is worth an eternity of servitude...
We live to die of hunger!
Freedom, — whatever the cost!
To be free or not to be!
All men are men; who then is anything more?
Turn your ploughs into swords; your bill-hooks into pikestaffs.
Let the weak say: "I am Strong!"

THE CHARTISTS

Can the true soldier be made an instrument of oppression?

Whatever influence fanaticism and the hypocrisy it imposes may still have in the British Isles, religious beliefs nevertheless have only a secondary influence on the formation of parties. Everyone is jealous of his sect, as he is of his freedom of opinion, and resents being forced to pay priests in whom he does not believe; but religious hatreds are dying out, in spite of all that is done to revive them, and it is primarily through material considerations that one must seek an understanding of the diverse parties.

My readers will all have heard of *Whigs* and *Tories*, and of *Reformers*, *Conservatives*, *Radicals* and *Chartists*. All these political groups are at war with one another; but the great struggle, the struggle which is destined to transform the social order, is that which pits property owners and capitalists — who control everything, wealth and political power, and for whose benefit the country is governed — against the workers of city and countryside, who have nothing, neither land, nor capital nor political power, yet who pay two-thirds of the taxes, furnish recruits for the army and the navy, and whom the rich, whenever they see fit, keep on the verge of starvation to get them to work for cheaper wages.

Land in the United Kingdom is divided among a very small number of families, the result of feudal laws which govern the transference of property. Large farms are now the rule, cultivated fields have been given over to grassland, and the commons have been divided up exclusively among landowners. The inevitable result of all this has been the utter impoverishment of the country labourer, and as administration, law enforcement, civil and criminal justice are all in the hands of the landowners, the labourer has consequently been reduced to nothing more than the slave of the landowner, a slave more wretched than the negro or the serf, whose masters never allow them to perish of starvation or to die in prison for having killed a partridge or a hare.

The division of labour pushed to its extreme, the mechanization of all production processes, the greatest source of power, which is always in the hands of the capitalist, are three great revolutions in manufacturing which will bring about significant revolutions in the political order among peoples. Individual manufacturing is gradually disappearing: there is now almost nothing destined for man's use which is not produced by machinery in large factories, and the work requires so little skill of the worker, that it can be done by anyone at all.

At first, workers benefited from the progress of industry; the quality of the work and the low cost led to an increase in the number of consumers, and wages went up; but with the advent of peace, competition began to develop on the Continent, and the English manufacturer began to combat it with the enormous capital he had amassed: he accumulated large quantities of merchandise in his warehouses and in the English depots throughout the world, and successively reduced the worker's wages.

In such a state of affairs, the English worker is entirely at the mercy of the capitalist manufacturer; the latter can fill his orders for a long time to come without bowing to the worker. The profits of manufacturing are thus all for the manufacturer, and the worker gets nothing but a subsistence wage for his fourteen hours of work.

The Radicals call for the abolition of the Corn Laws; but the workers call only for universal suffrage, because they are well aware that, participating in the making of laws, they would soon achieve the abolition of duties on corn and all kinds of provisions, as well as the right to form unions in order to fight the capitalists.

The most formidable association yet formed in the United Kingdom is that of the Chartists. I am dismayed to see that O'Connell, either because of religious fanaticism or in order to maintain his dictatorship intact, prevents Irish workers from fraternizing with their brothers in England; yet their suffering stems from the same causes; oppression weighs equally on all, whether the workers bear the yoke of the English or of the Irish aristocracy, whether they pay tithes to the protégés of the one or of the other, whether they weave cotton cloth or linen; in a word, all men who are excluded from the voting process must be

THE CHARTISTS

Chartists, for they are judged without being heard and without an advocate to plead their cause. The Chartist league must one day be the league of twenty million inhabitants against all the privileged class in the United Kingdom. The association's ramifications extend everywhere: in every mill, every factory, every workshop Chartist workers are to be found; there are Chartists in country cottages; and this holy alliance of the people, who have faith in their future, grows greater and stronger with each day. Expenses are met through monthly dues; all operations are centrally controlled, and never has there been a human organization so strong.

Although the league derives great power for action from being well organized, its strength lies in its unity of purpose. All, without exception, want the suppression of aristocratic, religious or mercantile privileges; all want equal taxation and equal civil and political rights; all know that in order to attain their goal, a tyrannical aristocracy which uses its usurped power solely for its own selfish ends must be driven out, that its power must be taken away and restored to those it oppresses and who have strength and intelligence on their side.

No half-measures can hope to satisfy the Chartists; they will never put their trust in a party whose object is to transfer to shopkeepers the privileges of the aristocracy, for they would find such an extension of privilege nothing but an aggravation of oppression. The workers, to whom shopkeepers, bankers and merchants, and landowners as well, owe their wealth; the workers, who have lifted England's fortunes to such heights, are the pariahs of English society; mention is never made of them in Parliament, unless it be to propose laws that interfere with their freedom; it is therefore their firm conviction that any measure not based on equality of political rights could be only another disappointment.

Under the rule of universal suffrage would anyone profess the intention of forcing up the price of bread in order to starve the workers? Would there be any prohibitions against the importation of almost every type of provisions? Would the things consumed by the poor be taxed three times as much as articles destined for the rich? If all could elect their representatives, would the administration of justice be so odious? Would we see the sons of lords fined insignificant sums for violation of women or for having beaten their inferiors so as to endanger their lives, while the indigent plebeian is punished without mercy for slight offences and, unable to give bail, languishes in prison while his family starves? Would fines be set so that the minimum equals the wages a worker can earn in the space of several weeks, and the maximum is half the daily expenses of a rich man? Would there be more arrests for infringing the game-laws than for all misdemeanours and felonies combined? Would squads be assigned to the country to wage battle on poachers and avenge the death of a few pheasants? Would the King's Bench have pronounced that, in the case of enclosure or alienation of commons, landowners alone are entitled to an indemnity, and that the poor who have built cottages on those lands may, without compensation, be driven away, along with the cow and the pig they have raised? If the people, from whom the army and the navy are recruited, were represented in Parliament, would soldiers and sailors still be driven by the lash, would commissions in the army continue to be sold, would violence be used to get sailors into the service of the state for lower wages than they would otherwise be able to earn, and during the long years between impressment and the hospital at Greenwich would they have to forgo any hope of rising even to the rank of midshipman?

At the sight of working-class movements, the aristocracy sounded the alarm and attributed spoliatory intentions to the popular masses. The workers aspire to the reign of justice and must consequently be viewed as despoilers by those who owe their wealth to privilege: it is malicious outcries of this sort that are responsible for the repugnance and the real or feigned terror they inspire. Those workers who actively participate in the workings of the association are all the elite of their class; the leaders are educated men, full of zeal and love for their fellow men. The workers have no dream of agrarian laws, nor of taxes on machines, nor of minimum wages; they think that they are oppressed, both by duties on materials, and by the capitalists: they refuse to be reduced any longer to being ruled by those who employ them; they want to work for their own sake and to have laws which do not prevent workers from organizing into unions; they would like to follow the example, in manufacturing, of those Italian and Greek sailors who hold shares in the boats they sail on, and who are thus supplanting, in the Mediterranean, the mercantile marine of the other nations. Their claims, which others have basely striven to denounce, are clearly founded on the idea of justice whose divine imprint is in our souls. A well-run union of workers, exploiting whatever industry it might be, ought to obtain more credit than an individual manufactory of equal importance; for, in the first case, the risks of manufacturing are shared by all the members of the union, whereas, under individual exploitation, one or two persons take all the risk upon themselves.

The lords of industry have accurately assessed the reach of these ideas, and they have calumniated workers who profess the intention of joining together to compete with them; there are, however, exceptions whose attitude does them honour. A number of manufacturers are sufficiently enlightened to sense that the workers' cause is their cause, and that it would be equally advantageous for factory owners and for workers to form societies in co-operation.

The national petition, the text of which I shall submit to the reader, is addressed to Parliament in the interest of manufacturers as well as of workers; it calls for universal suffrage as the sole means of preserving the nation from the egoism inherent in any aristocracy, no matter how broadly based.

National petition by the undersigned for universal suffrage, etc., June 14th 1839

"Unto the Honourable the Commons of the United Kingdom of Great Britain and Ireland in Parliament assembled, the Petition of the undersigned, their suffering countrymen.

"Humbly Sheweth,

"That we, your petitioners, dwell in a land whose merchants are noted for enterprise, whose manufacturers are very skilful, and whose workmen are proverbial for their industry.

"The land itself is goodly, the soil rich, and the temperature wholesome; it is abundantly furnished with the materials of commerce and trade; it has numerous and convenient harbours; in facility of internal communication it exceeds all others.

"For three-and-twenty years we have enjoyed a profound peace.

"Yet, with all these elements of national prosperity, and with every disposition and capacity to take advantage of them, we find ourselves overwhelmed with public and private suffering.

"We are bowed down under a load of taxes; which, notwithstanding, fall greatly short of the wants of our rulers; our traders are trembling on the verge of bankruptcy; our workmen are starving; capital brings no profit, and labour no remuneration; the home of the artificer is desolate, and the warehouse of the pawnbroker is full; the workhouse is crowded, and the manufactory is deserted.

"We have looked on every side, we have searched diligently in order to find out the causes of a distress so sore and so long continued.

"We can discover none in nature, or in Providence.

"Heaven has dealt graciously by the people; but the foolishness of our rulers has reduced the goodness of God to no effect.

"The energies of a mighty kingdom have been wasted in building up the power of selfish and ignorant men, and its resources squandered for their aggrandisement.

"The good of a party has been advanced to the sacrifice of the good of the nation; the few have governed for the interest of the few, while the interest of the many has been neglected, or insolently and tyrannously trampled upon.

"It was the fond expectation of the people that a remedy for the greater part, if not for the whole, of their grievances, would be found in the Reform Act of 1832.

"They were taught to regard that Act as a wise means to a worthy end; as the machinery of an improved legislation, when the will of the masses would be at length potential.

"They have been bitterly and basely deceived.

"The fruit which looked so fair to the eye has turned to dust and ashes when gathered.

'The Reform Act has effected a transfer of power from one domineering faction to another, and left the people as helpless as before.

"Our slavery has been exchanged for an apprenticeship to liberty, which has aggravated the painful feeling of our social degradation, by adding to it the sickening of still deferred hope.

"We come before your Honourable House to tell you, with all humility, that this state of things must not be permitted to continue; that it cannot long continue without very seriously endangering the stability of the throne and the peace of the kingdom; and that if by God's help and all lawful and constitutional appliances an end can be put to it, we are fully resolved that it shall speedily come to an end.

"We tell your Honourable House that the capital of the master must no longer be deprived of its due reward; that the laws which make food dear, and those which by making money scarce, make labour cheap, must be abolished; that taxation must be made to fall on property, not on industry; that the good of the many, as it is the only legitimate end, so must it be the sole study of the Government.

"As a preliminary essential to these and other requisite changes; as means by which alone the interests of the people can be effectually vindicated and secured, we demand that those interests be confided to the keeping of the people.

"When the state calls for defenders, when it calls for money, no consideration of poverty or ignorance can be pleaded in refusal or delay of the call.

"Required as we are, universally, to support and obey the laws, nature and reason entitle us to demand that in the making of the laws, the universal voice should be implicitly listened to.

"We perform the duties of freemen; we must have the privileges of freemen.

"WE DEMAND UNIVERSAL SUFFRAGE.

"The suffrage, to be exempt from the corruption of the wealthy and the violence of the powerful, must be secret.

"The assertion of our right necessarily involves the power of its uncontrolled exercise.

"WE DEMAND THE BALLOT.

"The connection between the representatives and the people, to be beneficial, must be intimate.

"The legislative and constituent powers, for correction and for instruction, ought to be brought into frequent contact.

"Errors which are comparatively light when susceptible of a speedy popular remedy, may produce the most disastrous effects when permitted to grow inveterate through years of compulsory endurance.

"To public safety as well as public confidence, frequent elections are essential.

"WE DEMAND ANNUAL PARLIAMENTS.

"With power to choose, and freedom in choosing, the range of our choice must be unrestricted.

"We are compelled, by the existing laws, to take for our representatives men who are incapable of appreciating our difficulties, or who have little sympathy with them; merchants who have retired from trade, and no longer feel its harassings; proprietors of land who are alike ignorant of its evils and their cure; lawyers, by whom the honours of the senate are sought after only as means of obtaining notice in the courts.

"The labours of a representative who is sedulous in the discharge of his duty are numerous and burdensome.

"It is neither just, nor reasonable, nor safe, that they should continue to be gratuitously rendered.

"We demand that in the future election of members of your Honourable House the approbation of the constituency shall be the sole qualification; and that to every representative so chosen shall be assigned, out of the public taxes, a fair and adequate remuneration for the time which he is called upon to devote to the public service.

"Finally, we would most earnestly impress on your Honourable House that this petition has not been dictated by any idle love of change; that it springs out of no inconsiderate attachment to fanciful theories; but that it is the result of much and long deliberation and of convictions, which the events of each succeeding year tend more and more to strengthen.

"The management of this mighty kingdom has hitherto been a subject for contending factions to try their selfish experiments upon.

"We have felt the consequences in our sorrowful experience — short glimmerings of uncertain enjoyment swallowed up by long and dark seasons of suffering.

"If the self-government of the people should not remove their distresses, it will at least remove their repinings.

"Universal suffrage will, and it alone can, bring true and lasting peace to the nation; we firmly believe that it will also bring prosperity.

"May it, therefore, please your Honourable House to take this our petition into your most serious consideration; and to use your utmost endeavours, by all constitutional means, to have a law passed granting to every male of lawful age, sane mind, and unconvicted of crime the right of voting for Members of Parliament; and directing all future elections of Members of Parliament to be in the way of secret ballot; and ordaining that the duration of Parliaments so chosen shall in no case exceed one year; and abolishing all property qualifications in the members; and providing for their due remuneration while in attendance on their parliamentary duties."

The principles upon which this petition is based are so in keeping with feelings of universal justice that they cannot be refuted: and so those to whose advantage the country is governed, who owe their income to monopolies, who receive large salaries or benefit from sinecures, proclaim that the working class seek to abolish property, as if property could be justified by usurpation and as if it could recognize any legitimate titles other than labour; but such impassioned accusations have about as much effect as the cries of popery with which certain fanatics among the Tories' attempt to stir up the masses. England currently presents a strange anomaly; prejudice is dying out among the popular classes, religious and national hatreds are vanishing, whereas in the upper regions the aristocracy, alarmed by the progress of enlightenment, clothes itself in impenetrable darkness, reverts to the unenlightened Middle Ages, evokes memories of Crécy and Agincourt, the ghosts of Henry VIII and Queen Mary, and at a time when the people are starving, would embroil itself in religious controversy; it would ressuscitate those aberrant eras when men slaughtered one another for empty theological cavil. And these are the men who profess to guide the nation!

As for the Whigs, they are still in the age of Louis XIV: witness how they insist that one royal family rather than another govern a kingdom. They appear to assume that the prevailing opinion in Europe is dictated by its kings, who, it is further assumed, are not powerless without the consent of their people. What a pity! They are blind to the fact that national prejudices are disappearing, that peoples are uniting ever more closely with each day, that the interest of the masses predominates over every issue on the Continent as well as in England! Nor do they see that any war other than a popular one would fail in every country in Europe and bring down the aristocracy which had provoked it!

The newspapers were so full of the Chartists, I had heard them spoken of in so many different ways that I was eager to know more about them. The Tories described them as atrocious scoundrels; the Whigs, with their customary fatuity, consider the Chartists to be outrageously impudent; and finally the Radicals, who pin their hopes upon the Chartists, informed me that they were the saviours of their country. So many contradictory opinions made me extremely desirous of seeing the leaders of the great popular movement for myself and of attending a session of the central committee. I had no faith in the impassioned testimony of factions and intended to arrive at my own opinion of the Chartists after due consideration, and to see if they were really blood-thirsty monsters, madmen undermining the people's cause, or heaven-sent men of genius come to deliver England from slavery. One of my friends, himself a close friend of two of the leaders, came to fetch me, and we went to Fleet Street to the hall where the National Convention held its meetings. The entrance has, of course, often been an object of raillery for the Tories of the

House of Lords; they are so clever! In truth it is not very impressive: in one of the dirty, narrow little passages in Fleet Street there is a public house of mean appearance; inside the tavern a waiter will ask you if you would like a mug of beer; by the tenor of your reply he will know why you have come, and if you give him the password, he will take you through a back room, across a small courtyard and down a long corridor to the meeting hall; but what does it matter where the meetings are held? Was it not in crypts, in vaults and caverns that the first apostles gathered together the Christians? And their words carried more force than the power of the Caesars, for they were inspired by faith and the wooden cross in their hands bore the word *Redemption*!

My companion announced that he wished to see Messrs O'Brien and O'Connor; the two gentlemen appeared; I was introduced to them and admitted to the hall — where no one may enter unless he is sponsored by two members. Such careful precautions do not prevent spies from slipping in amongst the gathering.

I was immediately struck by the expressive faces; in previous English gatherings I had seen nothing but a wearisome uniformity devoid of any character which would recommend them to the memory, just as if they had all been cast in the same mould. Here, however, every face presented a well-defined individuality; there were approximately thirty or forty members of the National Convention, and about as many sympathetic spectators. The latter were from the working classes; almost all of them were young. I noticed four or five French workmen and two working-class women. Unlike the House of their Lords, here there were no interruptions, no whispering, no private conversations. Everyone paid close attention, following the discussion with interest. The speaker would occasionally, according to the English custom, introduce a joke which would evoke peals of laughter. O'Connor is a fiery and energetic speaker; he inspires his listeners, who are carried away by his brilliance. O'Brien is remarkable for his clear thinking, his lucidity, his self-control and his knowledge of past events. Doctor

Taylor is enthusiastic and fiery; he is the Mirabeau of the Chartists. These three men, together with Lovett, may be considered the present leaders of the people; but immediately below them there are important positions occupied by men of considerable talent. I was particularly struck by three young men at the meeting, of whom the oldest was scarcely twenty-six. One of them, Dr Stephens, has a charming face; everything about him suggests a man suited by temperament for a studious life and who is exhausting himself by dint of work; he is firm in his opinions and preaches and defends them with the energy of a man convinced of the importance of ensuring that they prevail. He is never at a loss for words, he expresses himself well with ease and his exceptional intelligence grasps every nuance. This young man has a brilliant future before him, for God has given him all the necessary talent to be the apostle of the people. Palmer, who next caught my attention, is from the ranks of the people. His tall stature suggests strength, he is well proportioned, there is something proud and even menacing in his appearance. His face is remarkably handsome! He is an example of the Irish type of masculine beauty[1]: fine regular features, thick black hair, a rather dark complexion, dark blue eyes darting fire, an energetic and passionate mouth and chin, and there you have a portrait of the young man. His expression is so martial, so determined, I would even say so awesome, that it is impossible to look upon him without thinking of carnage.

It is evident that this child of unhappy Ireland is aware of his human dignity, that his soul rebels against the yoke. Ah you may take my word for it, that youth will do great things in the popular revolution, if Providence wills that it take place within the next ten years. His strength is mighty and with his implacable hatred he will pursue the lords as Marius pursued the Roman senators. His language has not received the polish of education; nevertheless I was able to observe, during the course of that same meeting, the impression produced by the words pouring from his heart, and the deference with which his opinion was greeted. A

---

[1] He is Irish

THE CHARTISTS

rather puerile discussion had arisen between Mr O'Connor and a quibbling old lawyer; several members had tried to appeal to the old pettifogger's common sense, but to no avail, for he was so accustomed by habit to plead the pro and contra, to prove at great length that which is incontrovertible and to slide lightly over that which is undecided, to approach a question by turns from every side, that he could not be silenced and continued to drown everyone in the torrent of his words.

The young Irishman rose and said in a full and sonorous voice which seemed to swallow up the old lawyer's ramblings: "Sir, we have not come here to argue about words, but to examine important things: our time is precious, we must spend it on actions and not on idle phrases." Those few words, from the mouth of that young man, produced an effect which I can scarcely describe; everyone there gave a sign of approval. For once, the old lawyer was at a loss for words, he was on unfamiliar ground; the young Irishman went straight to the point, and the veteran of the bar had either forgotten that approach or thought it beneath him.

The third Chartist who captured my notice was Irish as well. Picture a pale, thin young man with a sickly complexion, one of those feeble creatures for whom life is endless suffering, who, since they live through their imagination, forsake real life for fantasy and starve while dreaming of enchanted palaces; one of those poetic souls which think only of progress and are happy only through the happiness of others. One can see that the poor child believes in devotion, in womanhood, in God. He is twenty years old. The immensity of his love embraces all humankind, his face is radiant with hope, his confidence knows no bounds, he has not yet learned to recognize the various masks behind which self-interest hides. Unaware of rivalry's desperate struggles and the hatreds which envy inspires, the unfortunate young man rushes headlong into the abyss known as society. What disappointments await him! What painful torments! Each time my gaze fell upon that frail creature, I was reminded of Camille Desmoulins, of Madame Roland and Saint-Just who fell victim to evil passions in our civil disorders.

I came away from the gathering extremely edified, extremely satisfied. I had seen order prevail in the deliberations, and I saw a good augury in the talent, sincerity and devotion of the men whom God has brought forth to lead this people.

VI

A Visit to the Houses of Parliament

> *Members of Parliament appear in the most careless attire: frockcoat, boots, their hats on their heads, an umbrella under their arms. They pay scant attention to most of the speeches.*
>
> Baron d'Haussez, LA GRANDE BRETAGNE

In France freedoms are present in customs long before they become part of law. Napoleon and the Restoration's repeal of those laws which had inaugurated the emancipation of women was futile. Their tyranny has awakened resistance everywhere: woman is proving that her intelligence is on a par with that of man, and the public is becoming more enlightened. In England, intellectual progress is powerless to widen freedom's sphere; freedom has never made any advance there, except on the heels of revolt, and while women authors light up the British horizon with their brilliance, not only do laws and prejudice subject women to the most dreadful servitude, but the House of Commons, which claims to represent the *whole* nation, if not in reality, at least symbolically, and whose Members kneel to receive the orders of a woman, carries inconsistency to the point of forbidding women to attend its sessions.

Thus, in this land of freedom, if one is to give credence to parliamentary chatter and to the bombast of journalists, in this country that purports to be free, half the nation are not only deprived of civil and political rights, they are moreover, in various circumstances, treated as slaves: woman can be bought and sold, and the legislative assembly closes its doors to her. O shame, shame on a society which persists in its barbarous ways! What absurd pride on the part of your English society which aspires to impose its principles of freedom everywhere! Come now, where is there a country less free than England? Is not the Russian serf happier than the Irish peasant, than the helot of the factories? In what corner of the earth does woman not have more freedom than in the British Isles?

The prohibition against attending the sessions of the honourable Members of Parliament made me all the more desirous to do so; among my acquaintances there was a Member of Parliament whom I saw with some regularity, a Tory, but on the whole quite reasonable: he was well travelled and claimed to be free of prejudice. In my simple ignorance I believed that he practised what he preached; I proposed to him, as a perfectly natural thing, that he lend me a suit of clothes and take me with him to a session. My proposition had the same effect on him as, in the good old days, a sprinkling of holy water on the devil! To lend men's clothes to a woman in order to sneak into the sanctuary of male power! oh what an abominable scandal! what shamelessness! what monstrous blasphemy! My Tory friend turned pale with fright, red with indignation, he rose, gathered up his hat and cane, and without looking at me, announced that he could not see me again. His last words were: "Woe to him who creates a scandal." I answered him with the following verse: "Woe to him who lets himself be scandalized."

The incident revealed to me the limitless power of prejudice in England. However, I realized that the bigwigs are not taken in, that it is just another example of hypocrisy, and that the upper classes voluntarily submit only because prejudice, like religious dogmas, is a means of domination: blind submission to its demands is the mask now worn by the aristocracy, which goes so far as to bestow its esteem upon those who uncover some feudal practice of the Middle Ages, long forgotten except in dusty chronicles.

Women's will and God's will work to the same ends; this is so often seen to be true that it must be taken as a sign of the future emancipation of woman. My resolution was not in the least shaken. Obstacles appear to me as so many challenges and only increase my determination. I realized that I could not depend on any Member of Parliament, whatever his breed, nor on any Englishman. I approached in turn several attachés of the French, Spanish and German embassies. I met with refusals everywhere, not for the reason advanced by the Tory, but for fear of compromising themselves by offending public opinion. Strangely enough, I finally met a Turk, a prominent person whom his government had sent to London, and who not only approved my project but helped me to carry it out: he provided me with the necessary clothes, his pass, his carriage and the pleasure of his company. How gratefully I accepted his offer!

We set a day; I went to his lodgings with a Frenchman who was in on the secret and I put on a sumptuous Turkish costume. The clothes were much too large and too long for me and I felt very ill at ease in them; but the end would have to justify the means.

London and its buildings are so well-lighted that one can see better at night than during the day. I got out of the carriage at the door of the House of Commons. Our dress attracted attention; everyone was looking at us, following us, and I heard people around me whisper: "The young Turk appears to be a woman." Since in England everything is done with punctilious formality, the usher asked the real Turk for his pass, took it to show to I know not whom, and left us waiting for more than ten minutes. There was a crowd of curious men and women three deep all around us; they had come to the last of the public rooms in order to enjoy the interesting spectacle of watching their representatives pass by. Two or three ladies stared at me and said quite audibly:

"There's a woman in Turkish clothes."

My heart was beating wildly, in spite of myself my cheeks were aflame, I was on tenter-hooks during the long wait, because I feared that a public outcry might prevent my going in. However, my demeanour inspired respect, I overcame my agitation and I was to all appearances calm; for such is the influence of clothes that by putting on the Turkish head-dress I had taken on the solemn gravity common to Moslems.

Finally the usher came back and told us that we could go in.

We immediately dashed up the little staircase on the left and took our seats in the last row so as to have no one behind us. But then our costumes drew everyone's attention and soon the room was buzzing with the report that I was a woman in disguise. I learned, that evening, more about men of the English upper class than I would have during a ten-year sojourn in London in ordinary circumstances. I cannot express how impolite, rude, and I would even say, brutal they were towards me.

Although the Turk and I had, to all appearances, the composure of true Ottomans, it was easy to imagine the extreme embarrassment and uncertainty we must be feeling. And yet, without any regard for my being a woman, a foreigner and in disguise, all these "gentlemen" ogled me, discussed me in audible tones, made a point of passing close to me, staring me brazenly in the face; then they would stop behind us in the little staircase and speaking in a loud voice so that we could hear them, would say in French: "What is that woman doing in the Chamber? What motive could she possibly have for attending the session? She must be French. French women have no respect for anything. Really, it's indecent! The usher should eject her." Then they would go and speak to the ushers who would turn and look at me. Others went running to tell Members of the House who then left their seats to come and have a look at me. I was on pins and needles! How ill-mannered and inhospitable! But enough of painful memories, let us describe the Chamber.

The appearance of the hall could not be meaner, more bourgeois, more worthy of a nation of shopkeepers. It is rectangular, small and very inconvenient; the ceiling is low; the upper galleries jut out and partially hide the side sections, the benches are of wood painted a walnut colour. Nothing in the hall gives any indication of its purpose; it could be for anything at all, could, in a village, serve as a church, and would not be inappropriate for a meeting of grocers; it is without dignity either in its architecture or in its decoration. The gas lighting is sumptuous, and it is the only thing worthy of praise.

The honourable Members of Parliament loll on the benches, like so many tired and bored men; several of them are completely stretched out and actually asleep. The English, who are always zealous martyrs to the rules of etiquette, who attach so much importance to dress that even in the country they do not fail to change three times a day, who are so stiff and who take offence at the slightest social blunder, at the least oversight, affect in the Chamber nothing but contempt for the courtesy which good manners require. It is good parliamentary form to come to the session bespattered with mud, an umbrella under one's arm, in morning dress: or to come on horseback, to enter the Chamber with spurs on, riding whip in hand, and dressed in hunting clothes.

Insignificant people, of which there are so many in the British Parliament, hope in this way to give the impression of having important business, or having just come from some fashionable pastime, and although, I assume, none of these gentlemen would venture to visit any of his colleagues without taking his hat off, each one of them makes a point of keeping it on in the Chamber. To tell the truth, they demand no more courtesy from others than they have toward one another! No one in the galleries takes off his hat. In France this mark of respect is required in all public meetings; one must assume that in England the House of Commons does not believe itself entitled to it.

When a Member speaks, he takes off his hat, leans on his cane or umbrella, puts his thumbs in his waistcoat or in his watch pocket. In general, orators are very long-winded, they are accustomed to not being listened to at all, and appear to be not particularly interested themselves in what they are saying. Of course, a deeper silence prevails there than in our assembly: most of the Members are either asleep or reading their newspapers. We had spent more than one hour in the hall, two orators had spoken in turn without attracting the slightest attention, and I was beginning to feel quite tired. I did not understand English well enough to follow the discussion, and had I understood it better, the monotonous voices of those wooden figures would not have jarred any the less on my nerves. We were just about to go to the House of Lords when O'Connell stood up, whereupon everyone awoke from his parliamentary torpor; those who had been lying down sat up, rubbed their eyes and snapped to attention, the others left off reading their newspapers and all whispering stopped. Their pale and impassive faces took on an expression of rapt attention.

O'Connell is a short fat man, thickset and common looking; his face is ugly, all wrinkled, red and pimply. His gestures are jerky and rather commonplace, his clothes complete the picture. He wears a wig and a broad-brimmed hat, his umbrella has become a part of him, it never leaves him, and resembles by its size those carried by the kings of the Congo. Seeing him on the street one would take him for a coachman in his best Sunday clothes, but I hasten to say that under that coarse exterior there is a being full of spirit and poetry, heaven-sent to Ireland! Seeing him walking in the street one would never believe that there goes the champion of the people!...

The people's spokesman is, in appearance, no way different from the people themselves, and that partially explains the power he exerts, for, in this corrupt society, elegant manners cast suspicion on pureness of heart and sincerity. When he champions the cause of the people or speaks in the name of his religious beliefs, he is stirring and superb! He makes the oppressor quake! His ugliness disappears, and his countenance is as impressive as his words. His small eyes flash, his voice is expressive, clear and sonorous, his speech is forceful, it goes straight to the heart and arouses the most violent as well as the sweetest of emotions; at meetings, he stirs up at one and the same time anger, tears, enthusiasm and revolt! I can think of nothing so marvellous as this man. If Queen Victoria could rely on such a powerful auxiliary ... she would complete in a few years what Louis XI was not able to do during his whole reign, and her emancipated people would bless her name.

We went on to the House of Lords. There also they guessed my sex; but the manners of these gentlemen were quite different from those I was exposed to in the House of the representatives of shopkeepers and financiers. They did not crowd around me to get a better look, they exchanged amused whispers, but I heard no improper or discourteous remark. I saw that I was in the presence of true gentlemen, tolerant of ladies' whims which they felt honour-bound to respect. The refined manners and courtesy of the English nobility, haughty though it may be, are not to be found among the lords of finance or in any other class.

As we entered, the Duke of Wellington was speaking; his delivery was cold, colourless and languid. His words were received with some deference, but they failed to produce any effect. Lord Brougham proffered two or three broad jokes which were greeted with guffaws by their lordships.

The Chamber of Lords is scarcely any better than that of the Commons; it is built on the same plan: massive architecture without adornment.

The lords behave with no more decorum that the Members of the House of Commons. They too keep their hats on, but in their case it is not lack of manners, but pride of rank, and they require spectators and witnesses, even Members of the other House, to bare their heads. After Lord Wellington had finished speaking, he stretched out, nay sprawled on his bench with his feet up on the bench above so that his legs were higher than his head; a truly grotesque position.

I came away from the two Houses far from edified by the spectacle they had offered me and most certainly more shocked by the behaviour of the gentlemen of the House of Commons than they had been by my attire.

VII

Factory Workers

Alerte, alerte, alerte, enfants
De la grande patrie,;
Soldats de l'industrie,
Garde à vous, à vos rangs!
 Va, c'est en vain
 Qu'en son dédain,
 L'oisif raille
 De qui travaille;
 Toi seul es roi,
 Réveille-toi,
Producteur, impose ta loi,
Montre par la pratique,
Au siècle écrivailleur,
L'avenir pacifique
Qui s'ouvre pour le travailleur.
Alerte, alerte, alerte, etc.

APPEL

(a song by Vinçard, worker and follower of Saint-Simon)

Workers nowadays are the pariahs of society; no mention is ever made of them in Parliament, unless it

FACTORY WORKERS

be to propose measures that impinge upon their freedom and interfere with their pleasures.

LONDON AND WESTMINSTER REVIEW

Slavery appears in the early stages of all society; the harm it engenders makes it fundamentally transitory, and its duration is in inverse proportion to its harshness. If our fathers had treated their serfs with no more humanity than manufacturers in England treat their workers, slavery would not have endured throughout the Middle Ages. The worker, under English rule, no matter what his trade, leads such a dreadful existence that the Negroes who have left the sugar plantations of Guadalupe and Martinique in order to enjoy English "freedom" in Dominica and Santa Lucia return, when they can, to their masters. Far be it from me to entertain the sacrilegious thought of attempting to defend any kind of slavery! I only wish to demonstrate by this fact that the worker is more harshly treated by the law than the Negro by the whim of his French master. The slave of English property has, in order to earn his bread and pay the taxes imposed on him, a far more burdensome task.

The Negro is only exposed to the whims of his master, whereas the life of the English worker, his wife and children are at the mercy of the manufacturer. Should the price of calico or any other product drop, immediately those affected by the drop, spinner, cutler, potter, etc., lower wages in concert, without any thought as to whether the new wages they have decided upon are sufficient to feed the worker; they also increase the working hours. For piece-work, they demand better quality work but for less pay, and work which does not meet all the requirements is not paid for. Cruelly exploited by his employer, the worker is also squeezed dry by the tax collector and starved to death by the landlords; he almost always dies young; his life is cut short by excessive work or by the nature of his work. His wife and children do not survive him for long; harnessed to factory work, they succumb for the same reasons; if they are not employed in the factories in winter, they starve to death on the street corner.

Division of labour, which has been pushed to the extreme and has brought tremendous progress to manufacturing, has destroyed intelligence and reduced men to mere cogs in the machinery. If at least a worker was trained to perform the various steps in one or more manufacturing processes, he would enjoy more independence; his master's cupidity would have fewer means of tormenting him; the organs of his body would retain enough energy to combat the harmful effects of an occupation he would be engaged in for only a few hours at a time. Tool grinders in English factories do not live beyond thirty-five years of age; the use of the grinding stone has no pernicious effects on our workers in Châtellerault, because grinding is only a part of their trade; and takes up only a small amount of their time, whereas in English workshops, tool grinders do nothing else. If the worker could work at various aspects of manufacturing, he would not be overwhelmed by his own insignificance, by the perpetual inactivity of his mind, while doing over and over again the same things all day long; strong spirits would not become necessary to arouse him from the stupor in which the monotony of his work plunges him, and drunkenness would not add the final touch to his misery.

Without having visited the manufacturing towns, without having seen the workers in Birmingham, Manchester, Glasgow, Sheffield, in Staffordshire, etc., one cannot get a true idea of the physical suffering and moral degradation of this class of the population. It is impossible to form an opinion about the lot of the English worker from that of the French worker. In England, life is half again as expensive as in France, and since 1825 there has been such a drop in wages that almost without exception, to support his family, the worker is obliged to ask the parish for assistance; and since parishes are hard-pressed because of the amount of assistance they give, they determine the share to be given in proportion to the wages of the worker and the number of his children, not according to the price of bread but according to the price of potatoes; for the English worker, bread is a luxury! The elite among the working class, excluded from parish assistance because of their wages, are scarcely better off. The average wage they earn, I am told, does not exceed three of four shillings a day, and they have on average four children. By comparing these two figures to the cost of living in England it is easy to understand their distress.

Most workers have no clothes, no bed, no furniture, fuel or nourishing food, and often not even potatoes to eat! ... They are confined for twelve to fifteen hours a day in low rooms, where they breathe in, with the foul air, fibres from cotton, wool, linen, particles of copper, lead, iron, etc., and frequently try to compensate for an insufficient diet by excessive drink: in consequence, the wretches are all sickly, rachitic, debilitated; they are thin and stooped, with weak limbs, pale complexions and lifeless eyes; it is as if they were all suffering from consumption. I know not whether the painful expression to be seen on the faces of almost all the workers should be attributed to permanent exhaustion or to the dark despair which feeds upon their souls. It is difficult to get them to meet your glance, they constantly keep their eyes lowered and will only look at you furtively, with sly sidelong glances[1] which give a stupid, savage and thoroughly vicious expression to their cold, impassive faces impregnated with profound sadness; English factories are unlike ours in that no singing, chatter or laughter is heard. The master wants no reminder of the world to distract, for a single minute, his workers from their task; he demands silence, and a deathlike silence reigns, such is the power of hunger that the master's word becomes law! There exists between the worker and his employer none of the ties of familiarity, courtesy and interest to be seen in France: ties which lull the hatred and envy which the disdain and hard-heartedness of the exacting, luxury-loving rich foster in the hearts of the poor. In English workshops, the master is never heard to say to the worker: "Hello, Baptiste, old man; well, well, and how is your wife doing? And the little one? Indeed, that's

---

[1]This look, which I also noticed in America among the slaves, is not, in the British Isles, peculiar to factory workers. It is found everywhere among those who are dependent, subservient; it is one of the distinguishing characteristics of twenty million workers. There are nonetheless exceptions, and it is almost always among women that they are to be found.

splendid. Let us hope that its mother will soon be better; tell her to come and see me as soon as she is up and about." Any master would think it demeaning to talk to his workers in this way. In every factory owner the worker sees a man who can have him thrown out of the shop where he works, so he slavishly doffs his cap to every factory owner he meets; but the latter would feel compromised if he returned the courtesy.

Since I have become acquainted with the English working class, slavery is no longer, to my mind, the greatest human misfortune; the slave is sure of his daily bread as long as he lives and he is sure of being cared for when he is ill; whereas there is no bond whatsoever between the worker and the English master. If the employer has no work to offer, the worker starves; if he is ill, he succumbs on his wretched cot unless, on the point of death, a hospital will take him in: for it is a special favour to be admitted to one. If he gets too old, if he is crippled in an accident, he is dismissed and takes to begging stealthily for fear of being arrested. This situation is so horrible that in order to bear it, the worker must be possessed of superhuman courage or total apathy.

Cramped premises are common to English factories; the space alloted to the worker is parsimoniously measured out. The yards are small, the stairways narrow; he is obliged to sidle around the machines and the looms; it is easy to see, upon visiting a factory, that the builder has given no thought to the comfort, well-being, or even the health of the men destined to occupy it. Little attention is paid to cleanliness, the most effective means of assuring salubriousness; the machines are as carefully painted, varnished, cleaned and polished as the yards are filthy, full of stagnant water, the floors dusty, the windows dirty. In truth, if the buildings and the workshops were clean, tidy and well-kept as are the factories in Alsace, the tattered clothes of the English workers would seem all the more hideous. It matters little whether it be negligence or design, this lack of cleanliness nonetheless adds to the worker's ills.

England has no greatness left except in her industry, but she is a giant in respect to the instruments devised by the mathematical genius of modern times, magical instruments which petrify

FACTORY WORKERS

everything around them! The docks, the railroads, the enormous dimensions of factories give an idea of the importance of British commerce and industry.

The power of the machines and their universal application are astonishing and stun the imagination! Human science incorporated into a thousand shapes has taken the place of the functions of the intellect; with machines and the division of labour, only motors are needed, reasoning and reflection are useless.

I have seen a steam engine with the strength of 500 horses![1] Nothing is more formidable than the sight of the motion imparted to these iron masses whose colossal proportions frighten the imagination and seem to surpass the power of man! This motor of hyperbolical power is located in a vast building where it runs a considerable number of machines which work iron and wood. Its enormous polished iron bars go up and down forty or fifty times a minute and impart a backward and forward motion to the tongue of the monster which seems to suck in everything in order to swallow it up, the awesome groans it utters, the rapid turning of the enormous wheel which emerges from the abyss to plunge immediately back again, never revealing more than half of its circumference to the eye, fills one's soul with terror. In the presence of the monster one sees nothing else, one hears nothing but its breathing.

Upon recovering from your stupefaction and your terror, you look around for man; he almost escapes notice, reduced to the size of an ant by the dimensions of all that surrounds him, he is busy placing under the cutting edge of two large blades, shaped like the jaws of a shark, enormous iron bars which the machine cuts with the precision of a Damascus blade slicing a turnip.

---

[1] I saw it in Birmingham. The owners of the factory assured me that the power of this steam engine could be estimated as that of 500 horses; it turns more than 200 pulleys, and runs saws, metal cutters, flatting mills of all sizes, an assortment of machines for making zinc spoons, etc. A six pence coin was set under a press to give me an idea of its power and I watched as a narrow band of silver paper forty-two yards long and thin as the skin of an onion emerged from the machine.

If at first I felt humiliation at seeing man thus annihilated, working as if he were a machine himself, I soon realized the enormous improvement which, one day, would result from these scientific discoveries: brute force would be eliminated, physical labour would be performed in less time, and man would have more leisure to cultivate his mind. But for these great advantages to materialize, a social revolution is necessary. It will come to pass! for God has not revealed these admirable inventions to man in order to reduce him to being the helots of some manufacturer or landowner.

In London, beer and gas are two important items of consumption. I visited the superb Barclay-Perkins brewery which is most certainly worth seeing. The establishment is very spacious; no expense has been spared in equipping the factory. I could not find out the number of gallons of beer that it produces each year; but judging by the size of the vats, it must amount to an enormous quantity. It was in one of these vats, the largest, it is true, that Messrs Barclay-Perkins gave, in honour of one of the English Royal Highnesses, a dinner for over fifty guests. The vat is ninety feet high. Wherever steam can be used, man's strength is excluded. The most striking thing about the brewery is the small number of employees needed for such an enormous operation.

One of the large gas plants is located in Horseferry Road, Westminster (I have forgotten the name of the company). One must have an admission ticket to visit the factory.

In this manufacturing palace the abundance of machines and of iron borders on profusion, everything is made of iron: the ramps, the posts, the stairs, some of the floors, the roofs of the sheds, etc.; it is apparent that no effort has been spared to assure the sturdiness of the buildings and equipment. There were vats of cast iron and of zinc as tall as a five storey house and proportionate in width. I would have liked to know how many thousands of tons they can hold; but the foreman who was accompanying me was as reserved on this point as the Barclay-Perkins' foreman had been concerning the number of gallons of beer. In other words, he uttered not a word.

We visited the vast furnace room. The two rows of furnaces on each side were fired up; the effect was not unlike the descriptions which the poets of antiquity have given us of Vulcan's forge, except that the Cyclops were animated with a divine spark, whereas the dusky servants of the English furnaces are joyless, silent and benumbed. There were about twenty men fulfilling their task slowly and perfunctorily. Those who were not doing anything stood motionless, their eyes fixed on the ground, they had not the energy even to wipe off the perspiration streaming from every pore. Three or four of them looked at me with vacant eyes, the others did not even turn their heads. The foreman told me that stokers were selected from among the strongest, but that nevertheless they all became consumptive after seven or eight years of toil and died of pulmonary consumption. That explained the sadness and apathy apparent in the faces and in every movement of the hapless men.

They are expected to perform tasks beyond the limit of human endurance. They are naked except for scanty cotton drawers; when they go out they throw a coat over their shoulders.

Although the space which separates the two rows of furnaces appeared to me to be fifty or sixty feet wide, the floor was so hot that the heat immediately penetrated through my shoes, so much so that I was obliged to hop from one foot to the other as if I were standing on burning coals. I was helped up onto a large rock, and, although it was up off the floor, it was *hot*. I could not remain in this inferno; the air was unbreathable, the gas fumes were making me giddy, the heat was suffocating. The foreman led me to the far end of the furnace room to a balcony from where I could see everything without feeling so much discomfort.

We walked all through the factory. I stood in admiration before all those machines, before the methodical perfection with which the work is done. However, the precautions which are taken do not entirely prevent accidents from happening, there are a good many of them which have disastrous effects, injure the men and sometimes kill them. Oh! dear God! can progress be achieved only at the cost of the lives of a certain number of individuals?

The gas produced in this factory goes through pipes to light that part of the city from Oxford Street to Regent Street.

The air one breathes in the factory is truly pestilential! At every moment one is assailed by noxious fumes. I came out from the shed I was under, hoping to breathe purer air in the yard, but I was pursued everywhere by the foul exhalations of gas and the smell of coal, tar, etc.

I must also add that the place was extremely dirty. The yard, full of stagnant water and piles of refuse, is witness to the extreme neglect in matters of cleanliness; to tell the truth, the nature of the materials from which gas is obtained is such that constant attention would be required to maintain cleanliness, but two men would suffice for the task, and, with the slight increase in cost, the establishment would be healthier.

I was suffocating and impatient to flee the evil-smelling place when the foreman said to me: "Stay a few minutes longer, you will see something curious: the stokers are going to take the coke out of the furnaces."

I went back to my perch on the balcony: and from there I saw one of the most awesome spectacles that I had ever beheld.

The furnace room is on the second floor, beneath it is the cellar destined to receive the coke; the stokers, armed with long iron pokers, opened the furnaces and pulled out the coke which fell in flaming torrents into the cellar. Nothing could be more terrible, more majestic than these mouths vomiting flames! Nothing could be more magical than the cellar suddenly lit up by the burning coals which were rushing down like a waterfall cascading from the heights, and similarly engulfed in the abyss! Nothing could be more terrifying than the sight of the stokers, streaming with perspiration as if they had just come out of the water, and illuminated from all around by those dreadful sheets of fire whose tongues of flame seem to be darting out to devour them. Ah no, it would be impossible to see a more awesome spectacle!

When the furnaces were half empty, men would stand on vats situated in the four corners of the cellar and throw water onto the coke to extinguish it. Whereupon the aspect of the furnace room changed: there came from the cellar a funnel of thick, black, burning smoke which rose majestically and escaped through the roof which had been expressly opened to let it out. I could hardly make out the mouths of the furnaces through the cloud which made the flames look redder and the tongues of fire more frightful; the stokers had turned black from head to toe, and the poor wretches, who might be taken for devils, merged into this infernal chaos. The smoke took me unawares and I was only just able to climb down from my vantage point.

I waited until the end of the operation, wishing to know what would become of the poor stokers. I was surprised to see that no women arrived. Heavens! I thought, do these workers then have no mother, no sister, wife nor daughter waiting at the door to wash them with warm water, to wrap flannel shirts around them, to give them a nourishing and fortifying beverage to drink, and a few affectionate, loving words which comfort, encourage and help man to bear the cruellest misfortunes. I waited anxiously: not a single woman appeared. I asked the foreman where the men, drenched in perspiration, were going to rest themselves.

"They will throw themselves down on a bed which is under that shed," he said coldly, "and after a couple of hours they will begin to stoke again."

The shed, exposed to every wind, provides protection only from the rain; it is freezing cold. In one corner there is a mattress of sorts that cannot be distinguished from the coal which surrounds it; I saw the stokers stretch out on the mattress, which was as hard as a rock. Their only covering was an extremely dirty coat, so impregnated with perspiration and coal dust that one could not guess its colour. "That is how", the foreman said, "the men become consumptive, by going from hot to cold without taking any precautions."

This last observation by the foreman had such an effect on me that I left the factory in a state of exasperation.

So, men's lives can be bought, and when the required task is one that will lead to their death, the manufacturer's obligation goes no farther than raising wages! But it is even worse than the slave trade! ... I can think of no enormity more monstrous except cannibalism! Factory owners may, with impunity, dispose of the youth, the vigour of hundreds of men, buy their existence, and sacrifice it in order to make money! and all this for a wage of seven or eight shillings a day!

To the best of my knowledge not one owner of a factory, similar to the one I have just described, has had the humanity to fit up a room decently heated, provided with tubs of warm water, mattresses, woollen blankets where the stokers could go and wash as they come out of the furnace room, where they could rest, warmly covered, and where the temperature would be more in keeping with the one they have just left. Truly, it is a shame, a disgrace for a nation to let the sort of things I have just related happen.

In England, when horses arrive at the relay, a blanket is immediately thrown on their backs, they are wiped down, their feet are washed and they are taken to an enclosed stable provided with nice, dry straw.

Several years ago the relays were shortened after it was recognized that the excessive distance between them shortened the lives of the horses; yes, but a horse costs the owner between forty and fifty pounds, whereas the nation furnishes industrialists with men for *nothing*!...

VIII

Prostitutes

There is no country, no city or town where this evil is so systematically, so openly or so extravagantly carried on, as in England and her chief city.

Report of Mr Talbot, the Secretary of the London Society for the Prevention of Juvenile Prostitution.

Now, I appeal to any reasonably intelligent being to tell me whether or not, in the interest of present and future generations, it is useful to study and observe prostitutes, and whether he who devotes himself to that research, who does not shrink from its loathsomeness, who sacrifices his time, his fortune and his labour to it, truly deserves the scorn which prejudice, begot by ignorance, has kept alive to the present day. As for myself, seeing things, as I believe I do, in their true light, and realizing that the esteem in which an undertaking is held is not always in proportion to the benefits derived from it, nor to the difficulties it may entail, I rely on the judgement of reasonable men who see and appreciate the intent, and though I respect the prejudices of others, I deplore their blindness.

Parent-Duchatelet,
DE LA PROSTITUTION DANS LA VILLE DE PARIS

Never have I been able to see a prostitute without being moved by a feeling of compassion for our societies, without experiencing contempt for their organization and hatred for rulers who, strangers to decency, to any respect for humanity, to all love of their fellow creatures, reduce her whom God created to the lowest degree of abasement! Lower than the level of beasts.

I can understand the brigand who robs passers-by on the highways and surrenders his head to the guillotine; I can understand the soldier who forever risks his life in exchange for a mere penny a day; I can understand the sailor who exposes his to the fury of the sea; all three find in their livelihood a dark and terrible poetry! But I cannot understand the prostitute — surrendering her very self, annihilating both her will and her feelings, surrendering her body to brutality and sufferance, and her soul to contempt! The prostitute is for me an impenetrable mystery ... I see in prostitution a frightful madness, or it is so sublime that my mortal self cannot comprehend it. To face death is nothing; but what a death awaits the prostitute! She has betrothed herself to suffering, pledged herself to abasement, physical tortures unceasingly repeated, moral death with every moment and self-contempt!

Yes, it is either sublime, or it is madness!

Prostitution is the ugliest of all the sores produced by the unequal distribution of wealth. The human race is defiled by this abomination which, much more damningly than crime, bears witness against the organization of society. Prejudice, poverty, serfdom all combine their pernicious effects to produce this revolting degradation.

Yes, if you had not made of chastity a virtue and required it of women but not of men, women would not be spurned by society for having yielded to their hearts, and young girls who have been seduced, deceived and abandoned would not be reduced to prostitution. Yes, if you permitted women to receive the same education, to practise the same trades and professions as men, poverty would be their lot no more frequently than for men. Indeed, if you did not force women to submit to the abuses of paternal despotism and the indissolubility of marriage, they would not be confronted with the only alternative: to submit to oppression and infamy!

Virtue and vice imply the freedom to do good or evil. But what kind of ethical notions can be expected of a woman who is not her own woman, who owns nothing and whose life-long training has taught her to counter arbitrariness with deceit and coercion with seduction? Brought up in the art of seduction, is she not, when tormented by poverty and seeing all wealth in the hands of men, inevitably driven to prostitution?

Put the blame therefore on the social order and let women be exonerated. As long as she is under the yoke of men or of prejudice, as long as there is no professional education for her, as long as she is deprived of her civil rights, there can be no moral law for woman. As long as she can obtain wealth only through the influence she exerts on men's passions, as long as she can have no title to anything, as long as she is divested by her husband of all the property she has acquired through her work or that her father has given her, as long as she can enjoy freedom and make use of her posssessions only by remaining unmarried, there can be no moral law for woman. We can even say that until woman is emancipated, prostitution will grow ever greater.

Wealth is more unevenly distributed in England than anywhere else; prostitution must therefore be greater in that country. English law puts no restrictions on the right of making one's will, and because of the aristocratic prejudice prevalent in the lord's manor as well as in the humblest cottage, every family has its designated male heir. Girls are consequently given only small dowries, unless they have no brothers.

And yet, there is very little employment open to those women who have received a little education. What is more, fanatical, sectarian prejudice closes all houses to girls who have been deceived and seduced, and often they are even driven from under the paternal roof. Most of the rich landowners, manufacturers and factory managers make a sport of seducing and deceiving these poor girls. Those capitalists and landowners have enriched themselves at the expense of the proletariat, who exchange fourteen hours of work for a bit of bread, but the use they make of their fortunes does not begin to compensate for all the evils and disorders caused by the accumulation of wealth in their hands. Their wealth almost always feeds their pride and intemperance, and it provides for excesses and debauchery. Thus the people, already perverted by horrible poverty, are also corrupted by the vices of the rich.

Girls born into the lower classes are driven to prostitution by hunger. Women are excluded from farm work, and when they do not have work in the factories, their only resources are servitude or prostitution.

Come, all my sisters, night is descending,
Love is our trade, and the task is unending.
Walk the dark streets, for 'tis our sacred mission
Wives to replace and heal conjugal scission.[1]

There are so many prostitutes in London that they are to be seen everywhere at all hours. They are plentiful in all the streets, but at certain times of the day they come in from outlying districts where most of them live, and flock to the streets and into the theatres where crowds gather. They rarely receive men in their own quarters; the landlords are opposed to it, and their lodgings are too meanly furnished. The women bring their "captures" to houses intended for their trade. These houses are to be found here and there in all districts without exception. According to Dr Ryan, there are as many of them as there are gin palaces.[2]

Around seven or eight in the evening and accompanied by two men armed with canes, I went to visit the new district on either side of the long, broad street called Waterloo Road, at the end of Waterloo Bridge. This district is populated almost entirely by

---

[1] Auguste Barbier, *Lazare*
[2] *Prostitution in London*

prostitutes and people who live off prostitution. It would be extremely dangerous to walk there alone in the evening, It was a very warm evening; the women were looking out of windows or seated at their doorsteps, laughing and jesting with their fancy men. They were half-dressed; several were bare to the waist. They were revolting, disgusting, and the cynical and criminal expressions on the fancy men's faces were frightening.

The fancy men were in general very good-looking, young, tall and strong; but from their coarse and common look one had the impression that they were animals with no other instinct but their appetites.

Several came up to us and asked if we wanted a room.... As we answered in the negative, one, more shameless than the others, said to us threateningly: "What are you doing in this part of town then if you don't want a room to go to with your missus?" I confess I would certainly not have wanted to run into this man alone.

We walked about all the streets near Waterloo Road and sat down on the bridge to watch another spectacle. Around eight or nine o'clock, the Waterloo Road women pass by in groups on their way to the West End. They carry on their trade during the night and come back around eight or nine in the morning.

The women scour all the promenades and streets frequented by the public; those which lead to the Exchange, when it is open, the approaches to theatres and other public places; at half-price time they invade all the theatres and take possession of the foyer where they receive as if in their own drawing rooms (See chapter XV). After the theatre, the women go to the "finishes". These are low taverns or large and luxurious public houses where people go to finish off the night.

Finishes correspond to the English way of life as the beer hall does to German customs and the elegant cafe to French life. In the one sort, clerks and tradesmen drink ale, smoke cheap tobacco and get drunk with women in dirty clothes. In the other, fashionable people drink cognac punch, wines from France and the Rhine, sherry and port, smoke excellent Havana cigars, laugh and disport themselves with well-dressed and beautiful women.

But in both, the same debauchery is to be found in all its brutality and horror.[1]

The scenes of debauchery which take place in finishes had been described to me, but I could never bring myself to believe them. This was my fourth trip to London, and I was determined to see everything. I therefore made up my mind to overcome my repugnance and go myself to one of the finishes to judge to what extent I was to believe the various scenes described to me. The same friends who had accompanied me to Waterloo Road offered again to be my guides.

What goes on in these places ought to be seen. It reveals England's moral state better than anything one could say. These luxurious taverns have a look all to their own. The habitués of these palaces seem to be creatures of the night. They go to bed when the sun begins to lighten the east and awaken when it sets. From the outside, the gin-palaces appear to be shut up; they give the impression of silence and sleep. But scarcely has the doorkeeper opened the little door reserved for the initiates than one is dazzled by the brilliance of hundreds of gas lights. On the second floor there is a huge saloon divided into two lengthwise. On one side there is a row of tables separated by wooden partitions, as in all English restaurants. On each side of the tables there are sofa-like benches. On the other side there is a platform where the prostitutes display themselves in their finest attire.

---

[1]There are, in various parts of the monster city, splendid saloons where as many as two hundred richly dressed prostitutes assemble. These places are visited by fashionable and wealthy young men who select women there. The saloons adjoin taverns which become the source of immense wealth. These are not exclusively confined to the West End of the city or to the area of London beyond Temple Bar. They are known elsewhere under the name of long rooms; they are found particularly on the banks of the Thames where there are a great many sailors. Some of the long rooms can accommodate five hundred people.

The prostitutes are lined up in these houses like cattle at Smithfield Market until visitors, sailors or others, come and choose their women. After making their selection, they enter another spacious apartment in the establishment where, after copious libations and dancing, the woman leads the man to her room; there he continues to imbibe poisoned drink until he falls into a stupor; and then he is fleeced, robbed and beaten by the bullies. (Dr Ryan, *Prostitution in London*, p. 189).

Their words and glances are calculated to arouse men. When one responds they lead the amorous gentleman off to one of the tables laden with cold meats, hams, fowls, pastries, and all kinds of wines and cordials.

The finishes are temples raised by English materialism to their gods! The servants who minister unto them are richly dressed; the owners of the finishes respectfully greet the *male* guests who come to exchange their gold for debauchery.

Around midnight, the habitués begin to arrive. Several of these taverns are meeting places for society; it is where the elite of the aristocracy gather. At first the young lords lie on the sofa-like benches, and they smoke and jest with the women. Then after several libations, the alcoholic vapours of champagne and madeira go to their heads. The illustrious scions of English nobility, the honourable Members of Parliament take off their coats, waistcoats and braces. They make themselves at home in a public tavern as if they were in their private boudoir. There is no reason for them not to feel quite at home; after all they pay a high price for the right to show their contempt. As for the contempt they inspire, they could not care less. The pace of the orgy increases; it reaches its peak between four or five o'clock in the morning.

It takes a good deal of courage to sit through it all, a silent spectator of what goes on!...

What a noble use these noble English lords make of their immense wealth! How handsome they are, how generous, when they have lost their senses and offer fifty or a hundred guineas to a prostitute if she will lend herself to all the obscenities conceived by intoxication...

There are all sorts of entertainments in the finishes. One of the most appreciated is to ply a woman with drink until she falls reeling to the floor, and then to make her swallow vinegar mixed with mustard and pepper. The mixture almost invariably produces horrible convulsions. The unfortunate creature's gasps and contortions provoke laughter, and the honourable society is enormously amused. Another much appreciated entertainment in these fashionable gatherings is to throw a glass of anything at all on the drunken woman lying senseless on the floor. I have seen satin dresses whose colour could no longer be ascertained; they were merely a confusion of filth. Countless fantastic shapes were traced in wine, brandy, beer, tea, coffee, cream and so forth — debauchery's mottled record. The human creature can sink no lower![1]

The sight of such satanic depravity is revolting and alarming. The atmosphere is nauseating. The air is heavy with foul vapours: the smells of meat, drink, tobacco smoke and others even more fetid. They catch in your throat; your temples throb; you are seized with dizziness. It is horrible!... However, the prostitute's only hope of success is to go through this experience *every night*, because she has no hold whatsoever on the sober Englishman. The sober Englishman is chaste to the point of prudishness.

It is usually seven or eight in the morning before people leave the finish. Servants go and fetch cabs. The men who can still stand up look for their clothes, gather them up and go home. As for the others, they are dressed by the waiters in whatever clothes happen to be at hand and are carried to cabs; the drivers are given the addresses of the baggage entrusted to their care. It often happens that no one knows the person's address, so he is left lying on the straw in a back room. This room is called the drunkards' hole. He stays there until he recovers enough of his senses to say where he wants to be taken.

---

[1] In that same finish I saw four or five magnificent women; the most striking was an extraordinarily beautiful Irish woman; though an habituée, her entrance into the room caused a sensation and a buzz of excitement. As for myself, my eyes filled with tears. What a beautiful creature! Had she been Queen of England, people would have come from the ends of the earth to admire her!

She arrived toward two in the morning, dressed with an elegant simplicity which only served to heighten her beauty. She was wearing a gown of white satin, half-length gloves revealing her pretty arms; a pair of charming little pink slippers set off her dainty feet, and a kind of diadem crowned her head. Three hours later, that same woman was lying on the floor *dead drunk*! Her gown was revolting. Everyone was tossing glasses of wine, of liqueur, etc., over her handsome shoulders and on her magnificent bosom. The waiters would trample her under foot as if she were a bundle of rubbish. Oh, if I had not witnessed such an infamous profanation of a human being, I would not have believed it possible.

It goes without saying that the prices in these taverns are exorbitant. Consequently, the drunkards leave with empty pockets, lucky if the cupidity of their temptresses has spared them their watches, gold eyeglasses or other valuables.

In this intemperate city, prostitutes of all classes have a short life span. Whether she likes it or not, the prostitute has to drink alcoholic beverages. How could anyone's constitution withstand such continuous excesses? Half the prostitutes in London do not hold out for more than three or four years; a few manage to resist for seven or eight years, but that is the outside limit which few attain, and fewer still exceed. Many die in hospitals from shameful diseases or pneumonia. When they cannot be admitted, they die in their frightful hovels, deprived of food, medicine, care and everything else. A dying dog gets a kind look from his master, but the prostitute ends up in the gutter, and nobody gives her a compassionate glance.

There are in London from 80,000 to 100,000 women — the flower of the population — living off prostitution. Each year, 15,000 to 20,000 of these unhappy creatures waste away and die a leper's death, forsaken by all.[1] Each year, an even greater number come to replace those whose terrible existence is ended.

In order to explain the tremendous extent of prostitution, we must keep in mind the huge increase in wealth that has taken place in England in the past fifty years. And we must remember that among all peoples and in all periods of history, appetites and wealth have gone hand in hand. Among the English, Mammon has become so powerful that he has overthrown all others. There is no Englishman whose dominant thought is not the making of money. Younger sons of the richest families find themselves obliged to make their fortunes, and no one is satisfied with what he has.

The love of money, embedded in young men's hearts at an early age, destroys family affection and all compassion for the

---

[1] The Bill which requires death to be recorded is quite recent, and there is as yet insufficient information to determine exactly the mortality rate among prostitutes.

troubles of others. It leaves no room for love. Love is of no importance in their lives. It is not for love that they ruin young girls. It is not for love that they get married. The young man marries a dowry, neglects his wife and goes and squanders her money in gambling houses, clubs and the finishes of the West End. How repulsive is this wholly materialistic life of selfishness and self-gratification! Has society ever presented such a hideous face? Money is all that makes it go round; wine and prostitutes are its only pleasures.

In London all classes are deeply corrupted. Vice comes to them early and in old age outlasts their jaded senses. No family has escaped the diseases caused by debauchery. The pen recoils from describing the disorders, the depravity to which are drawn these sated men who, with listless souls, withered hearts and uncultured minds, have only their five senses left. Confronted with such depravity, St Paul would have cried: "Anathema upon fornicators!" and he would have fled the island shaking its dust from his feet.

The Londoner has no commiseration for the victims of vice. The prostitute's fate inspires no more pity than the Irishman's, the Jew's, the proletarian's or the beggar's. The Romans were no more insensitive to the fate of the gladiators who perished in the arena. Men, when they are not drunk, spurn prostitutes; they would even beat them if they were not afraid of the scandal, of the consequences of a battle with the fancy men, or of the police.[1]

---

[1] While I was in London, a merchant of the town, sick with an evil disease, thought he could trace the source of his trouble to a prostitute whom he knew; he summoned her to a house of assignation: there he raised her skirts over her head and tied them with a rope, enclosing her upper body as if in a sack; and then he whipped her with switches, and when he grew weary of beating her, he threw her out in that state in the middle of the street. The unfortunate woman, deprived of air, was smothering; she struggled, cried out, rolled in the mud. No one would come to her aid. In London, one does not get involved in what transpires in the street; "that's not my business," the Englishman will tell you without pausing, and by the time his words reach your ears, he is already ten paces farther along. The prostitute, lying on the pavement, had ceased to move, she was on the point of expiring when a policeman happened by, went up to her and cut the rope binding her clothes. Her face was purple, she had stopped

Respectable women are harsh and contemptuous of the unfortunate creatures, and, unlike the Catholic priest, the Anglican clergyman does not bring solace to all who suffer. The clergyman has no mercy for the prostitute. He will give a pompous sermon on charity and Jesus' warm feelings toward Mary Magdalen, the prostitute, but he does not shed a tear for the thousands of Magdalens who die every day, dreadfully poor and forsaken by all. What do such creatures matter to him? His duty is to deliver an able sermon in church on a certain day at a certain time, and that is all. In London the prostitute's only right is to be admitted to the hospital, if there is an empty bed.

National pride makes us desire that the country in which Providence caused us to be born should surpass all other nations. This malevolent feeling toward other countries which is the bitter fruit of past rivalries, constitutes the greatest obstacle to progress. It often keeps us from recognizing the causes of the evils foreigners point out to us. We become angry and challenge them to furnish proof of facts that are as obvious as fog on the Thames. It is because there are as yet few people enlightened enough to understand that all nations have common interests, and the foreigner who does not approve of us is looked upon as an enemy who insults us.

Prostitution exists everywhere, but in London it is so prevalent that it has become a monster ready to engulf everything. I realized that most people would refuse to recognize the truth, and that my description would be taxed with gross exaggeration. Therefore I decided to gather proof and authoritative testimony which would confirm what I had seen with my own eyes.

---

breathing, she had been asphyxiated. She was taken to the hospital, where timely assistance restored her to life.

The author of this execrable assault was called before the magistrate and sentenced, *for indecent behaviour on a public thoroughfare*, to *a fine of 6 shillings*.

In a nation of absurd prudishness, it is evident that the price of *outraging public decency* is not very dear. And the astonishing part is that the magistrate saw nothing in the act but a *misdemeanour to be punished*. Yes, in this country of so-called freedom, the law is for the strong, and the weak cannot invoke its protection.

I had read Mr Parent-Duchatelet's book, and I knew that even if it was impossible to be mathematically exact in evaluating a situation for which no statistics exist, nevertheless one could get very close to the truth by prolonged observation. I asked if there had been any English philanthropist sufficiently devoted to humanity to dedicate his life to the study of prostitution in London, as Parent-Duchatelet had, with such indomitable persistency, studied prostitution in Paris. I was told about Dr Ryan, whose book on prostitution in London was stirring up outrage and recriminations.

Dr Ryan is the author of several other works of recognized merit; his large following is an indication of his capabilities. He had no need of this publication to assure his reputation. His publication of a book which was to arouse the indignation of the hypocritical guardians of English morality and to outrage the upper classes whom it unmasked, was an act of supreme courage on his part. Dr Ryan knew his countrymen and was aware of the consequences of his book, but being a man of great courage and capable of rising above the clamour of a corrupt world, he boldly revealed the facts and pointed his finger at the corruption and depravity rampant in the monster city.

Dr Ryan's book *Prostitution in London* was published just last year. It contains information on the subject as precise as the present state of the English police permits. In support of the facts he presents, Dr Ryan quotes from the reports submitted to the parliamentary committees in 1837 and 1838 by the Society for the Supression of Vice; the Metropolitan Police reports for 1837 and 1838; the 1836, 1837 and 1838 reports of the London Society for the Prevention of Juvenile Prostitution; the reports issued by the secretary of that same society, Mr Talbot, those submitted to Parliament by the Commissioner of Police, as well as those of the Home Secretary for 1837 and 1838.

These documents reveal that in 1793, Mr Colquhoun, a very able Magistrate of Police who had studied the problem extensively, put the number of prostitutes in London at 50,000. However this is just an approximation, because even though the police are much better organized nowadays, they have no way of

PROSTITUTION

arriving at an exact figure. Since 1793 the population of London has doubled. It is reasonable to suppose that vice has increased in a greater proportion, in view of the fact that the distribution of wealth is no more equitable than before, that employment has not kept pace with the population, that salaries have decreased, and that, furthermore, the government has made no real improvement in the condition of the proletariat.

Dr Ryan, from information gathered from Police Magistrates Prichard and Talbot, who are secretaries of the two associations mentioned above, estimates that there are about 80,000 to 100,000 prostitutes in London, and that half of them (two-thirds according to some) are under twenty years old.

We can only guess at their average life span, because up until 1838 there was no law in England which made it mandatory to register deaths. Mr Clarke, the last Lord Chamberlain, puts the life of a prostitute at four years; others put it at seven years. The Association for the Prevention of Juvenile Prostitution estimates that 8,000 prostitutes die in London each year.

As a result of his research Mr Talbot believes that there are 5,000 houses of ill repute — no fewer than the number of shops where gin is sold. Dr Ryan thinks that there are in London 5,000 people, both men and women, employed in procuring girls for the houses, and 400 to 500 "trepanners" who set traps for girls of ten or twelve and entice or drag them by force to those frightful dens. He estimates that 400,000 persons are involved, directly or indirectly, in prostitution, and that £8 million is spent annually on this vice in London.

The Society for the Prevention of Juvenile Prostitution was founded in May 1835. In its address to the public it exposes the depravity of London's lower classes. It asserts that there are schools where young people of both sexes are trained in thievery and in all kinds of vice, that prostitution and theft are openly encouraged by those who profit from it. The Association also maintains that crime is systematically organized. And finally it warns that, of all the crimes committed with impunity in broad daylight in the London streets, the most execrable are those whose purpose is to feed this infamous traffic. There are indeed a great number of men and women whose business is the selling of girls of ten or fifteen whom they have entrapped. The children are lured, on plausible pretexts to storehouses or lewd houses where they are held prisoner for a fortnight or so. Their parents will never see them again.

In May 1836 the Society's committee remarked in its account of its stewardship that: "Although the metropolis too frequently presents scenes of open and undisguised vice, distressing to every moral and religious person, yet no picture is perhaps more revolting than the frightful increase of juvenile prostitution. Under the shadow of night, and even at midday the streets are perambulated by unhappy children, decoyed from the paths of virtue and from the protection of their parents, by miscreants, for the mere purpose of gain, and who though the authors of their destruction, yet remain unpunished."

Among the young girls whom the committee aided during its first year of operation, I notice the case of a thirteen or fourteen year old girl. The slave trader who had suborned her and who was holding her was brought to trial and he was acquitted! As a matter of fact, in the Association's report for 1837 and 1838, several similar cases are mentioned, and the traffickers in human flesh got off with *a few months* in prison.

After having related several of the means employed to ensnare children whom it has succoured, the committee adds: "To detail the numerous artifices employed to draw unwary children of both sexes into this vortex of misery would be impossible, they are so complicated and varied; the committee will therefore only allude to the treatment experienced by these unfortunate creatures after having been trepanned. As soon as the female is decoyed to one of these dens, she is no longer allowed to wear her own clothes, which become the prize of the keeper. She is decked with second-hand trappings, once the property of some wealthy lady. The habitués are alerted, and when she ceases to draw custom to the house, she is sent into the streets, followed by a child hired for the purpose, or by the master or mistress, so that she cannot run away: if she tries to do so, she is accused of having stolen from the master of the house the clothes she wears on her back; then a policeman arrests her, sometimes he takes her to the station, but more often than not he returns the runaway slave to her master in return for a reward. Once back in the infamous house, the poor girl is the victim of unrestrained and wanton barbarity; deprived of her clothes, she is compelled to wander about the house during the day, *entirely naked* so that she cannot escape, and she is frequently even denied food. At night, her trappings are restored to her and she is sent into the streets, always under the watchful eye of a spy. Failing to bring home nightly a certain number of the other sex, she is severely punished, and she is not permitted to appropriate one penny to her own use."

Houses of prostitution are illegal in England, but proof of their existence is hard to come by. Shame would prevent those who frequent them from testifying in court. The police are unable to enter the premises unless some disorder or other is taking place, and cannot verify offences. Parish officers can close them only when neighbours lodge a complaint that the houses are disturbing the peace.

In any case, legislation against prostitution is absurd since it is an inevitable result of the organization of Western society. Governments must strive instead to eradicate its causes and to regulate its practice.

In the reports for 1837 and 1838, the Society's committee gives an account of the charges it has brought against brothel keepers and procurers. But the penalties for keeping such houses and for suborning and corrupting children of from ten to fifteen years old do not exceed one year's imprisonment and are more often than not from one to six months. Sometimes the charges are even dismissed because the little children of both sexes found in the houses "have, of their own free will, consented to enter or to remain on the premises." Such are the laws that protect the proletarian's family! As for the children of the rich, they are constantly watched over and are rarely exposed to such enticements.

Depravity is so widespread and the price obtained for children so high, that no ruse is overlooked in order to procure them. In 1838 the Society's committee called upon patriotism, virtue, religion and humanity to witness "the shameless efforts which are made to recruit victims for debauchery. Scarcely can one walk down a street without coming upon some storehouse used for this infamous traffic. Agents are employed in countless ways for the purpose of entrapping the unwary and innocent. The suburban villages, the bazaars, the parks, the theatres, continually furnish new victims. Your committee have authority for stating, that the keepers of brothels and procurers are frequently in the habit of obtaining females from the workhouses and penitentiaries."[1]

In spite of the mask of hypocrisy they continue to wear in the hope of perpetuating fanaticism among the people, the upper classes have shown little disposition to support the efforts of the Society for the Prevention of Juvenile Prostitution. On the other hand the Society for the Suppression of Vice, in all its thirty-seven years of existence, has been concerned only with the proper observance of the Sabbath and the prohibition of fortune-telling and the sale of improper publications. It is hardly surprising that the Society has always received support and encouragement from every quarter. One can very well sleep through the minister's sermon on Sunday, put away one's Aretino and still keep one's vices. What is more, by supporting an association which claims to be working for the suppression of vice, one gains a reputation for virtue, a reputation dear to the heart of every English Tartuffe.

The committee of the Society for the Prevention of Juvenile Prostitution said in May 1838: "While carrying forward the operations of the Society, the members of the committee have had to encounter obstacles of no ordinary character, arising from the almost universal apathy and indifference prevailing upon the subject. They have been met in their course by the sneers and contempt of the profane and immoral; the censures and condemnation of those who believe that licentiousness is necessary to the well-being of society, the supineness and negligence of the religious; nowhere have they encountered aid or encouragement; but amidst the buffeting of all, they have been enabled to persevere, supported by a consciousness of the

---

[1]*Prostitution in London*, p. 146

importance of the objects they have in view, and by the sympathies and kindness of their subscribers."

English depravity has begot nothing more heinous than the monsters, male and female, who travel the length and breadth of England and the Continent in search of children. They set traps for them and spirit them away, or with vicious lies they nourish false hopes which enable them to take the children from the very arms of their parents. In London the children are sold to that oh-so-virtuous aristocracy and to the *nouveaux riches.* Some of these agents hob-nob with the respectable classes of English society. Connected with the West End slave trade, they are sent to various towns and villages in Holland, Belgium, France and Italy. They negotiate with the parents. They hire the daughters as milliners, seamstresses, music teachers, lady's companions, servants or something of the sort in order to lull suspicion. Sometimes they go so far as to give the parents a quarter's wages payment in advance. When they have procured a certain number of young girls, they return to London.[1]

In 1837, the Committee of the Society for the Prevention of Juvenile Prostitution instituted proceedings against Marie Aubrey, a Frenchwoman, who was obliged to abandon her infamous commerce and escape to France to avoid several months in prison."The house in question was situated in Seymour Place, Bryanstone Square. It was an establishment of great notoriety, visited by some of the most distinguished foreigners and West End society, and carried on in a style little short of that observed in the richest and noblest families. The house consisted of twelve or fourteen rooms, besides those appropriated to domestic uses, each of which was genteelly and fashionably furnished. The saloon, a very large room, was elegantly fitted up; a profusion of valuable and splendid paintings decorated its walls, and its furniture was of a costly description. A service of solid silver plate was ordinarily in use when the visitors required it, which was the property of Marie Aubrey. At the time the prosecution was instituted there were about twelve or

---

[1]*Prostitution in London,* p. 181

fourteen young females in the house, mostly from France and Italy. There was a medical practitioner in the neighbourhood who was employed as agent. It was his duty to attend the establishment. He was frequently sent either to France, Italy, or the villages near London, to procure females. Aubrey had lived in the house a number of years, and had amassed a fortune. Shortly after she left, the inmates were sent away, and the house is now shut up and the furniture disposed of. Upon receiving a fresh importation of females, it was the practice of this woman to send a circular, stating the circumstance, to the parties who were in the habit of visiting the establishment. At the present time there are in the metropolis a great number of young females from France and Italy, and other parts of the Continent, a large proportion of whom have been decoyed from their homes, and introduced into the paths of iniquity by Marie Aubrey or her infamous agents. There are a number of houses of this description at the West End now under the cognizance of the Society, and whose circulars are in its possession, who adopt this plan, and, by means of the Court Guide and twopenny post, are forwarding notices of their establishments indiscriminately to all.

"The Committee desire to lay before this meeting the means adopted by the agents of such abominable characters as Marie Aubrey. As soon as they arrive on the Continent they obtain information respecting those families who have daughters, and who are desirous of placing them in respectable situations; they then introduce themselves, and by fair promises induce the parents to allow their children to accompany the stranger to London, with the understanding that they are to be engaged as tambour workers, or in some other genteel occupation. A sum of money is left with the parents, as a guarantee for the due performance of the contract, with an agreement that a certain amount shall be forwarded quarterly. While they remain in the house they are first taken to, the money is duly forwarded, and their parents are thus unconsciously receiving the means of support from the prostitution of their own children; if they remove, letters are sent to their friends to apprise them that their daughters have left the employ of their former mistress, and the money is accordingly stopped; they fail not to inform the parents that they have obtained other respectable situations, and are doing well."[1]

The profound corruption of the wealthy classes and the high prices they are willing to pay encourage and protect this infamous trade. Mr Talbot says that in the West End seraglios, newly arrived slaves will fetch from twenty to one hundred pounds sterling. When one thinks about the luxury of these houses, the enormous expenses they incur, the agents' travelling expenses, the price does not seem inflated. When these young girls no longer attract the customers' fancy, they are passed on to inferior establishments, and after a year or a year and a half the hapless girls die in a hospital or are left to shift for themselves in the streets.

The demand for children is so great that traps are laid everywhere to capture them and to catch unawares those who look after them. Females, says Dr Ryan, hang about the offices of public conveyances to offer lodgings to young girls coming to London to find a place; others visit the workhouses and hospices under the pretext of engaging servants and frequently succeed in having children entrusted to them: these women are well dressed and their manner inspires confidence; in the bazaars they strike up conversations with shopgirls, they frequent milliners' shops and all the places where women are employed and entice the young apprentices away with a thousand tricks; their employers send them sometimes as far as eighty miles from London in search of their prey.

"The other modes by which infamous houses are supplied," says Mr Talbot, "as death, disease, or demand requires, is, that the keepers employ agents, women of about eighteen years, to perambulate the streets, and decoy any children they may meet with, under pretence of taking them to see a relative, or going a pleasant walk, or inviting them to a theatre, or getting them a place of service. The most subtle artifices are employed on these occasions, both by day and night. The Sabbath is a favourite day

---

[1]*Prostitution in London*, p. 153

with these wretches, and they watch young children to Sunday schools, and entice them to their haunts; nay, I believe children have been actually taken from the schools in the sight of teachers and companions, they having no idea of so shocking a system being in operation. As soon as the children are secured, they are *sold*, and their ruin sealed, perhaps, by some hoary-headed debauché at an enormous price."[1] Mr Talbot relates numerous instances which have come to his knowledge of children of ten or eleven violated in lewd houses. These crimes occur frequently and are so rampant that the masters of such establishments contract with coachmen who supply, *at so much per head*, children between ten and fourteen, whom they have decoyed to London under various pretexts. These coachmen have often appeared before a police magistrate for crimes of the sort; but due to the law's imperfection, when they are punished, they get off with only a light sentence.

"Testimonies in my possession," says Mr Talbot, "show that a great many brothel keepers lure young boys to their establishments. This goes on all the time, and I believe I am correct in estimating that 2,000 out of the 5,000 brothels encourage the prostitution of young boys."

"*Sunt lupinaria, nunc inter nos, in quibus utuntur pueri vel puellae!*[2] Mr Talbot mentioned localities," says Dr Ryan, "which of course, cannot be printed.

"These most infamous and horrible dens, are mostly supplied by children and young persons, who are observed gazing at the windows of the improper printshops, and as much as 10 pounds was expended to secure one boy."

Since the police cannot enter any house unless it is evident from the noise within that a disturbance is taking place, most of the houses of ill repute are dangerous places, with the exception of those concerned with establishing a reputation in the fashionable world. They harbour swindlers and thieves of all

---

[1] *Prostitution in London*, p. 182
[2] *Prostitution in London*, p. 198. I transcribe the latin of Dr Ryan, which, for decency's sake he did not translate.

kinds. Brothel keepers are often brought before the judge for fights, disturbances and theft. Thieves come to hide out in these dens and share the spoils of their crimes. Brothel keepers traffic in stolen goods and come to the aid of thieves when they are arrested. They give money to subvert justice and often succeed in having thieves acquitted. Most of the fancy men are among the ranks of their regular visitors; they spend the night, and are ready at the slightest signal to pounce on a victim and to fleece or assassinate him.[1]

Dr Ryan speaks of an area in London called the Fleet Ditch, where almost every house is an infamous den. Through it runs an aqueduct of large dimensions which empties at a considerable distance into the Thames. Murderers and bandits of every sort who live in those houses, precipitate the bodies of their victims into the aqueduct without the slightest chance of discovery. "I have been informed," adds Dr Ryan, "that there are two influential men in the City of London, who let two houses in the vicinity, not in reality worth 30 pounds a year each, at 2 pounds a week each as common brothels! The rental of such houses varies from 100 pounds to 500 pounds a year, and a premium from 100 pounds to 300 pounds is asked for the goodwill of a first-rate establishment." Dr Ryan further relates the story of two gentlemen who were prevailed upon to spend the night in a brothel situated in an infamous square and who in the morning had to put up a fierce struggle against their sirens' bullies.[2]

Apart from the disorderly houses, which are found in every street in London, where prostitutes bring the men they accost in the streets and where some of them live, there are in some quarters lodging houses, kept by receivers of stolen goods, resorted to by thieves of every kind. Several of these houses contain fifty beds occupied by persons of both sexes. Into some of these houses boys only are admitted, to prevent their being controlled by persons stronger than themselves. These children are in no way inferior to any thief in skill, presence of mind and

---

[1] *Prostitution in London*, pp. 176-192
[2] *Prostitution in London*, p. 177

knowledge of their business. The keeper wishes to reap as much as possible of the boys' plunder, and he will not admit men who might rob the boys. However, women are not excluded — or more correctly, girls of ten or fifteen, for it is seldom that the female companions of thieves live to be women. The little girls are admitted as the mistresses of the young boys who introduce them. Dr Ryan says that the scenes of profligacy that occur in these dens are indescribable and would be incredible if described.[1]

Almost all the boys between twelve and fifteen who are in prison have had connection with lewd women, and their mistresses come daily to visit them, passing themselves off as their sisters. Mr Talbot estimates that there is a constant turnover of 13,000 to 14,000 young prostitutes in London. He says that during a period of eight years, 2,700 girls, aged ten to fifteen, came to Guy's Hospital with venereal disease, and that a far greater number of children of the same age had been turned away for want of accommodation. "In one day," he says, "I have seen as many as thirty of them turned away from one hospital, although they were in such a direful state that they were scarcely able to walk ..." Dr Ryan also says that a great number of applications are made every day at the Metropolitan Free Hospital by girls of twelve to sixteen who have syphillis.[2] "I have been often shocked," continues the doctor, "by the large number of children who present themselves at hospitals and other public charity to which I have served as physician, for advice for venereal diseases."[3]

There are five organizations in London that lend assistance to prostitutes who wish to quit their horrible profession.[4] But the

---

[1]*Prostitution in London*, p. 201
[2]*Prostitution in London*, pp. 185, 186
[3]*Prostitution in London*, p. 186
[4]The Magdalen (1758); The London Female Penitentiary (1807); The Guardian Society (1812); The Maritime Penitent Refuge (1829); The London Society for the Prevention of Juvenile Prostitution (1835).

As for the Society for the Suppression of Vice, founded in 1802, its particular objects are five; to wit:
1. The prevention of the profanation of the Lord's day.
2. The suppression of blasphemous publications.

efforts of these societies are generally misguided, and their means are too limited to do very much good. The total number of prostitutes to whom these five shelters offer refuge annually does not exceed 500. Five societies can assist and find work for only 500 of these unfortunate women! The only society which attacks depravity at its source is the Society for the Prevention of Juvenile Prostitution. That society does what it can within the existing laws, but in spite of its zealous efforts it has very little power to halt crime because of insufficient support and because of insufficient legislation. Therefore a brothel keeper who has ensnared and led astray children of ten or fifteen in order to sell them to the depraved, will, if the charges are not dismissed, get off with *eight or ten days* in jail, whereas a woman of the poorer classes or someone of similar circumstances, arrested for selling fruit, or anything at all on the street, will be sentenced to thirty days in jail! However a few days in prison are only a light sentence for a brothel keeper. He is dead to all feelings of shame; his associates do not esteem him the less; on the contrary he finds them sympathetic. They do what they can to shorten his imprisonment, and to prevent his getting bored, they come and keep him company. On the other hand, thirty days in jail almost inevitably mean total ruin for virtuous young girls guilty of minor infractions. But who cares about the proletarian's child, his wife or his daughter? It is to the shopkeeper's interest that nothing be sold in the streets. Keepers of shops and brothels have *political rights*; they are *voters, jurors*. The proletarian, his wife and his

---

3. The suppression of obscene books, prints, etc.
4. The suppression of disorderly houses.
5. The suppression of fortune tellers.

The Society is actively concerned with little more than promoting the observance of the Sabbath. To the Society's way of thinking, idleness on the seventh day of the week, time spent in the taverns, are the only manifestation of religion among the masses. They also combat obscene books and pictures, and that, in truth, is their only useful pursuit. The abduction of eight or ten thousand children sacrificed yearly to the vices of opulence does not command their attention in the least. The Society enjoys great favour among the aristocracy and the Anglican Church, and if they do not single out fortune tellers, it is probably because the latter have found favour among the clergy.

children almost always become dependent on the parish. Obviously the sacrifice of 8,000 to 10,000 children to the lust of the wealthy fits into Malthus's system to reduce population, and from this point of view a brothel keeper is a *respectable man*, a man useful to his country!

IX

Prisons

In England, imprisonment is not a penance, but a repressive punishment having as its goal to inflict upon the guilty the punishment he has brought upon himself and to draw from it a stern lesson for the guilty party and an example for any who might be tempted to imitate him.

Moreau-Christophe, RAPPORT SUR LES PRISONS DE L'ANGLETERRE

The gigantic growth of poverty and wealth throughout Europe is accompanied by a deluge of crime, and the consequences of this state of affairs are giving rise to alarm.[1]

---

[1] It is estimated that *unpunished* theft in England accounts for 700,000 pounds sterling each year.

And yet the Warrant Act is a law concerning suspects which gives local authorities the power to deprive of his freedom any individual reputed to be a thief or found loitering near any river, canal, navigable water, dock or basin, or any quay, port or warehouse adjoining thereto, or any street, thoroughfare or avenue giving access thereto, or any public place or its environs with the intention of committing a felony.

And the commissioners report that, in virtue of this act, a great many mayors make a general sweep of all the suspicious individuals of their towns, put them under lock and key on the eve of fairs, holidays or racing days, and they release them when the holiday is past.

And when asked what law authorizes them to act in this manner, they reply: "I take it upon myself."

(Moreau-Christophe)

Governments are realizing at last that, up until the present time, prisons have been schools where crime festered. Numerous investigations have been undertaken in recent years, and experiments are under way in various countries to find solutions to this ever-growing problem. That is all very well, but it is not enough. Soon people will come to realize that, in order to stop the march of crime, it is not enough to set up penitentiaries where an attempt is made to reform the criminal through education and strict discipline. They will realize that society can be bettered in this way only in so far as other institutions are made to complement the penal system.

Indeed, far from gradually diminishing in intensity, those things which turn people to crime increase day by day; how then can learning a trade be expected to prevent offenders from repeating their crimes? What sort of salutory terror can silence and cells inspire? The new convert, unable to earn a living at his trade and repeatedly exposed to criminal example, will inevitably revert to crime. In the present state of things, what European country has sufficient resources to maintain the penitentiaries which the increasing number of criminals will soon require? Is it not clear that if governments persist in maintaining their systems based on privilege, on creating obstacles to commerce, on taxing workers and on spending huge sums unproductively, they will have to resort to mass deportation, erect scaffolds everywhere and arm half the population to shoot down the other half when it asks for bread.

Large scale poverty as seen in Ireland and England inevitably leads to revolts and revolutions; but hunger is not the only motive for attacks on property. Since in our societies all passions can be satisfied through money, since there are no obstacles nor any resistance that money cannot overcome, since it takes the place of talent, honour, integrity, and finally, since money opens all doors, people balk at nothing in order to procure it. No one is satisfied with his lot, everyone strives to rise above it, and this universal ambition is responsible for countless shameful deeds.

As for murders, poisonings, infanticides, it is an established fact that the knife or the poison in the hands of husband or wife is put there by the indissolubility of the marriage tie. It is a fact that the barbaric and fanatical prejudice brought to bear against the unwed mother sometimes drives her to crime. Finally, since women are excluded from almost all the professions, when their children have no father to earn their bread, they find themselves faced with infanticide, prostitution or theft.

Legislators, statesmen and you to whom God has entrusted the destinies of nations, before you think of reforming the guilty, make it your first concern to eliminate the causes of crime so that there may be no guilty. A mother does not punish her child for having fallen into the fire; her tender concern anticipates the danger and she puts a railing around the hearth, and with maternal vigilance avoids all danger.

I had heard contradictory reports of English prisons, and my interest in the social aspects of prisons in general was heightened by the desire to see if my doubts concerning England's progress in that area were justified; but, as in London a foreigner who is not privileged to be a duke, a marquis or a baron, nor to lodge in one of the great houses of the city encounters extreme difficulty in observing the most ordinary things, it was only after repeated interviews and requests that I obtained permission to visit Newgate, Coldbath Fields and the Penitentiary. In addition to these three prisons, there are eight others, but national vanity will not permit any foreign eyes to see them because, so I am told, of their mean appearance, their poor interior arrangement and finally, because of the abuses of all kinds and the confusion which reign in these sinks of English civilization.[1]

---

[1] The average population of Giltspur Street Compter is 150 inmates per day and 5,300 in a year.

There is another London prison (Mill Lane Tooley Street) which serves as a police station for individuals arrested in the Borough of Southwark. The prison is under the direction of the Lord Mayor and the council of Aldermen of the City of London, and under the supervision of the High Bailiff of Southwark: it is called Borough Compter. The average daily population is fifty; the average yearly population is 1,500. The mingling of inmates of all classes, the inadequate segregation of the sexes, the necessity for greasing palms, the

(*cont.*)

Newgate has a most forbidding appearance.[1] Ah, it is just so that one imagines the prisons of the barbaric ages to have looked. It is a large square building occupying one corner of the square; the stones are of enormous size and grey-black in colour, their chiselled surface reminiscent of a tiger's pelt; they give the edifice a grimmer tone than that of any other landmark in London, and the effect is terrifying. The scattered windows covered with iron bars are scarcely visible, lost in the thickness of the walls. The main entrance is a masterly example of design; the enormous quantities of iron which have gone into its construction must be prodigious; I wish I could give the reader an exact figure, so that he might share my stupefaction at the sight of that door! If visitors are filled with terror at the very sight of it, what must be the emotion of the unfortunate man whose crimes have brought him to prison, when that iron mass closes upon him, and he finds himself in the anteroom of this dreadful gaol! Newgate's greatest failing is lack of light, and it is probable that, under the influence of the thirst for revenge which haunted the wretches imprisoned by man's justice, that failing was long considered a merit which testified to the moral character of the architect. The anteroom is somewhat less dim than the rest of the prison; even so, in the

---

number and almost constant presence of visitors who are for the most part thieves or prostitutes, the drunkenness due to the ease with which the inmates can procure spirits, the profaning of the Sabbath, etc., are, according to the inspectors, the principal abuses of prison regimen, there and at Giltspur Street Compter. The inspectors are not guilty of exaggeration.

The average population of Clerkenwell Prison is 150 inmates per day, both men and women, and 6,000 for a year. The evils are the same there as at Giltspur Street and Borough Compter.

(Moreau-Christophe, *Rapport sur les prisons de l'Angleterre*)

---

[1] It appears that the sole purpose of constructing old Newgate was to prevent prisoners from escaping.... It is said that prisoners who had displayed courage and pluck during their trial, who seemed unmoved when the sentence was pronounced, were horror struck and wept when they entered this dark and lonely abode.

(John Howard, *The State of Prisons and Penitentiaries*)

darkness, one does not, at first, discern one's surroundings, and what dreadful surroundings they are! Why are such things there? To what purpose do they seek to play upon the fears of the prisoner? Is his terror and ignorance to be used to force a confession? Is he to think that he is destined for the tortures impressed on his memory by stories heard long ago; or is it a warning that he beware of the justice of men, which until recently resorted to such means to discover the truth? Is it not of utmost importance that the unfortunate man who has broken the law regain his trust in that same law, that he not doubt the justice of the magistrate who enforces it? Do you want him to persist in his revolt against society, or is it your intention to reform him? These surroundings would do very well in an historical museum along with Henry VIII or Charles IX; but in the nineteenth century they should not be found at the entrance to a prison; such is Newgate's arsenal! The walls are studded with hooks from which hang the instruments of torture in use since the prison was built. They are the annals of the prison, the trophies it displays. There are massive iron collars from which hang chains attached to wrist-irons, saws for sawing limbs, pincers for breaking bones, bludgeons for crushing, axes, swords; in short, a complete collection of instruments of torture used to put prisoners to the question.

I must admit that I felt very ill at ease in this first room, there is not enough air, light or room; the prisoner can hear the noise from the street, can see above the door little spangles of sunshine shimmering on the public square; what a dreadful contrast! What torture to think of one's lost freedom! But scarcely has one left the anteroom behind when nothing more is heard. The atmosphere is cold, damp and oppressive: it is as if one were in a cave; the corridors are generally quite narrow, as are the stairs leading to the upper levels. First I was shown the section reserved for women.

Over the past few years Newgate's role has undergone various changes; although still a prison, it now harbours only those awaiting judgement (condemned prisoners do not serve their sentence there), and in this respect corresponds to Paris's Conciergerie; moreover it is in Newgate that most of those condemned to death are executed.

The governor was kind enough to accompany me on my inspection; he told me that, thanks to the writings of philanthropists, the intervention of people devoted to mankind and their oft repeated appeals, Newgate had been improved as much as was possible. The best improvement according to Mr Cox, was the segregation of prisoners who, for such a long time, had all been thrown together.

Newgate prison is not well laid out and there is not enough room to permit the addition of more cells. In each room, the beds are like those on board a ship, they are boxes two feet wide and six feet long, stacked two or three high against the wall. There is a large table in the middle of the room, with wooden benches around it; it is there that prisoners eat, work, read and write. Upon careful examination one sees that all the rooms are well kept and very clean; but as the floors are in bad shape, the arrangement of the rooms faulty, and as they are dark and poorly ventilated, they have an unpleasant look about them.

Almost all the women I saw were wretched creatures from the lowest class: prostitutes, servants, peasant girls accused of theft; four of them had been charged with crimes punishable by death and classified by English jurists under the name of felony.

Most of the women's faces expressed stupidity; however, I noticed several whose thin, tight-set lips, sharp noses and pointed chins, and most particularly, whose deep set and wild eyes were indicative of their extraordinary wickedness of character. I saw only one who excited my sympathies.

She was confined, with six others, in a low-ceilinged room which was extremely dark and damp. When we came in, all of them stood up and made the customary curtsey with just the degree of obsequiousness that borders on servility. Only one abstained, she did not make the curtsey which I had found so painful and tiresome ever since I had entered the prison. Her independent spirit captured all my attention.

Imagine a twenty-four year old woman, small, well-favoured, tastefully dressed, standing with her head high, displaying to the visitor the most perfect profile, the most beautiful neck, the daintiest ear, the shiniest and most gracefully arranged blond hair. My readers, who have had occasion to notice the influence which beauty has on me, will easily understand what I felt at the sight of that pretty creature; my eyes filled with tears, and only the governor's presence prevented me from going up to her and taking her hand that she might know my concern for her plight, and that my sympathy might calm for a few moments the torments of her heart.

Ah, beauty alone is powerless without the lofty qualities of the heart! Had I met, in this sad place, the most beautiful of women without that inner life, she would have left me unmoved. But in the face of that young beauty, who bore the height of misfortune with courage and pride, there was such sublimity of expression that, heeding the promptings of my heart, I did not for a single moment believe that she could be depraved. Her heart was pure, I could see that in her eyes, in the way she carried her head, in her whole being. Violence of passion may have led her to commit a crime; but, made in the image of God, she was conscious of her own dignity, and had not debased herself.

I applied to the governor and the matron in order to discover on what charge the young woman had been sent to Newgate; what her social position was, how she conducted herself in prison, what education she had had, etc. In asking these questions my voice betrayed my concern for this unfortunate creature, and awakened the interest and sympathy of my interlocutors. "Oh! Madame," said the matron, "this poor woman is truly worthy of compassion; she is six months big with child and has three small children. Alas it was to get bread for her children that the unfortunate creature committed the theft that brought her here; she is married to a drunken seaman who left her without a shilling; abandoned with no money whatsoever, she sold, one by one, all her belongings; but then came the day when she had nothing left to sell, and her three children were crying for bread! So the poor mother, growing desperate and crazed by her plight and by her children's cries of hunger, took some things from the room she was living in and sold them. She has been here for two months awaiting trial."

Just as I thought! Such a creature could not be a prostitute or a professional thief. She was a *mother* who had felt the awful hunger gnawing at her children's bellies ... she had stolen. Yes, to be sure, it was wrong, but the poor woman had been carried away in a moment of despair. But which was the guiltier, she, or a society which, without any justice or any humanity exposes the poor to a horrible death, and thus drives them to madness and crime?

The matron told me all this in a low voice, so as not to be heard by the prisoners, and so that her words would not wound the mother whose cruel position she understood and whose distress excited her sympathy. But the room was very small, and the young woman was well aware that we were talking about her; nevertheless, for the fifteen minutes that she was the object of our attention, she never lost her proud bearing nor her composure, her face revealed no inner turmoil. Ah, it was because, in her own eyes, her maternal devotion atoned for her crime, and even increased her sense of her own worth. She understood her maternal duties and took pride in having fulfilled them at the expense of her honour and at the cost of the torments of prison! In certain women, mother-love is such a strong passion that no human law can stop it. I was struck with admiration for the courage that God had put in the heart of this mother, and it grieved me to think that her life was going to be blighted and ruined: that there would be judges incapable of *feeling*, of *understanding* the sacredness of a mother's duty! Judges who, with eyes only for property, forgetting that they themselves owed their lives to a mother's love, would sacrifice maternal devotion to respect for property; and unable to distinguish between the *heroic mother* and a *professional thief* would sentence her to the same punishment. I cursed the laws of man which make no distinction between crime and virtue! I cursed Property which must be defended from the hungry by means of imprisonment and suffering! And it seemed to me that the luxury enjoyed by owners of property was bought with the blood of the poor!...

While the matron was talking to the governor, I contemplated the young mother, hoping that she would finally turn toward me:

she stood calm and motionless. I wept, and a sigh escaped me. The poor woman heard it, and with a start, turned her head to look at me, and our eyes met. Oh, how can I describe the tenderness and pride I saw in those eyes! How to describe all that I could read in them!...Poor victim of our social conditions! I seemed to see a halo around her head! Her eyes misted with tears, her efforts to control herself, her trembling lips were so eloquent that I could almost hear her saying to me: 'Oh, you too are a mother! You understand my anguish! You would have stolen as I did; your children's hunger would have given you too the courage to do it! You know what it cost me to go through with it. Thank you! thank you, sister, you understand me!..."

Oh, because of that woman, Newgate is forever in my memory!

The men's part of the prison is larger, but perhaps even darker than that of the women. All the faces I saw there were hideous.

Children are separated into two categories: those locked up for a first offence, and repeaters; they all display such incredible impertinence that to understand it, one must first realize the facility with which children become accustomed to risk anything, fear nothing and endure everything. On an average, forty children a month arrive in the prison. They are taught to read, write and count.[1]

I saw, in one of the courtyards, eight of the unfortunate soldiers of Canadian freedom who had been captured by the troops of the English aristocracy: five of them were wounded. For two years they had been waiting for their fate to be decided. One of them spoke French; he told me that they were forbidden any communication with the outside, that they could receive neither letters, newspapers nor visits, and that for two years they had had no news of their families. The English government had the power, by law, to have them condemned to death. But the

---

[1] One can be convicted of a felony at the age of seven. Consequently one can be hanged at that age. Blackstone reports that in his days the jury sentenced to death children of eight years old and that they were executed. I have seen children of that age sentenced to be transported!...

(Moreau-Christophe)

government's cause is no longer that of the people; and it was no doubt feared that the blood of these victims would spatter the aristocracy, and the government, afraid of the Canadians' patriotism, was prudently letting them die in prison.

I noted that the prisoners were treated with much kindness, and even a certain respect. I mention this fact because I see it as a sign of great progress. The English are finally beginning to realize that war prisoners must be regarded as hostages and not as criminals. Would to Heaven that they had thought so during the war with France! They would not then have treated our unfortunate prisoners so infamously and with a degree of cruelty which covered the government of Pitt and the Tories with eternal shame! I have heard truly frightful things on this subject...[1]

I was told of two murderers, one vicious, the other remorseful. The latter's room was on the ground floor; I went there. I saw a short young man of about twenty, very thin and pale. He was sitting in the darkest corner, apparently wishing to escape notice, and he was crying. I did not like the look of him: he had shifty eyes and seemed to beg for pity. In a fit of jealousy he had murdered his father's serving girl who was his mistress.

From the precautions taken before I was allowed in the other murderer's room, there was every reason to believe that he had the fierceness of a hyena and that he was in the habit of pouncing upon visitors in order to devour them. First, the governor tried to dissuade me from seeing him. Then, giving in to my entreaties, he sent two of his officers[1] into the prisoner's room and provided

---

[1] Hunger knew no limits: corpses were kept for five or six days without being reported, for the sake of obtaining their rations: the others called that living off the dead. Lord Cordower, Colonel of the Carmarthen Regiment, on duty at Porchester Prison, rode his horse inside one day and tied it to a post, in ten minutes the flesh had been stripped from the bones and devoured. Lord Carmarthen came for his horse and upon inquiry was informed of what had happened: he refused to believe it, and said he would not believe until he saw the remains of his horse. No sooner said than done: he was taken to where the hide and the entrails had been left, and a starving wretch devoured, in his presence, the last piece of raw flesh. An enormous butcher's dog, or rather all the dogs who happened to enter the prison met with the same fate.
(Pillet)

[1] In England all men appointed to any kind of office are called officers.

two more to accompany me. These elaborate precautions spurred my imagination, and as I climbed the dark, narrow staircase, I imagined the horrible face that I was about to see; the ghosts of Lacenaire, of Shylock, incredible vampires flitted across my mind. What was my surprise upon entering! I saw, seated at a table, a soldier of twenty-two or twenty-four, reading the Bible, with the most pleasant physiognomy imaginable. He had a small round face, full red lips, a small aquiline nose, dark blue eyes full of merriment and mischieviousness, a high forehead, a fine head of naturally curly brown hair and a peaches and cream complexion. And this was the monster everyone was afraid to approach! As soon as he saw me he blushed as might a young girl, and his first impulse was to button up his coat, straighten his collar and prepare to pass muster; then he gave me a timid look, and I saw in his eyes, more than on his lips, a smile that seemed to say: "Madame, please excuse my attire, I was not expecting your visit, and you have caught me unawares." Hapless young man! There was such childlike simplicity in his embarrassment, and it stood in such painful contrast to his cruel situation! Oh how I was drawn to that unfortunate young man, and what would I not have given to be able to speak to him! I refrained from asking any questions in front of him for fear of embarrassing him, and my eyes conveyed to him the pain and compassion I felt for his plight.

As soon as I had left, I asked what signs of fierceness the soldier had given to justify such close surveillance. "Ah, he is a thorough scoundrel!" I was told by one of the prison officers, "not only does he not repent his crime, but he says to all who will listen that if he had it to do over again, he would; he laughs, sings all day, never tires of mocking the people who come to visit him; in a word, we have never had such a shameless murderer." I must confess that all these dreadful accusations served very little to tell why the young soldier was supposed to be so very ferocious.

Just as I was leaving with my curiosity unsatisfied, I met at the bottom of the stairs Dr Elliotson, whom I had met several times at the home of a doctor friend of mine. Dr Elliotson is a devotee of the theories of Gall and Spurzheim; he can always be found in prisons and insane asylums studying convex protuberances and divining concave ones; Dr Elliotson speaks French perfectly, and I told him briefly of my astonishment at everything concerning the young murderer.

"What can you expect," said the doctor with a slightly contemptuous smile, "the governor of Newgate is an excellent fellow, full of kindness; the officers too treat the prisoners with kindness, but they do not have the knowledge, that divine light, without which they will never be able to understand why one man *steals* and another *kills.*"

I asked the divinely enlightened doctor, who could so unfailingly discover the cause of human actions, why the young soldier I had just seen had murdered an officer of his regiment.

"He killed him because he has two pronounced protuberances, that of *pride*, and that of *revenge.*"

"Very well, but have you spoken with him, doctor, and do you know what reasons made him act as he did?"

"Well of course. I have been studying him for two months. He is a charming lad, gay, amiable and good-hearted."

"But in that case ..."

"Here is his story. The boy is twenty-three years old. He had been in the ✱✱✱Regiment in Cornwall for a short time when a new officer arrived. Apparently the officer had a high-pitched, nasal voice, and a peculiar way of talking; the poor boy, who had just left home for the first time, was not yet acquainted with the strictness of English discipline; he thought he could have a laugh with a friend at the officer's comical voice. One day, on parade, the unfortunate lad favoured his comrade with one of those clever, well-timed quips which make one laugh in spite of oneself; the officer, enraged, threw himself upon the two mischievous boys, struck them viciously in the face, tore their rifles away from them and had them locked up. The other soldier swallowed his humiliation, but our soldier's protuberances of *revenge* and *pride* were too strongly pronounced for him to do the same; he resolved to kill the man who had publicly struck him. After his release he kept close watch on the officer, and twenty two days later he aimed a rifle at him point blank and shot him dead. In the proper place that young man would have been superb, sublime! But one thing is certain, he was not intended to serve in the English army, where in the name of discipline soldiers are flogged like mules."

Poor child! It was simply because he had a sense of his human dignity, because he revolted against a despicable act, because he had the courage to obey the voice of his conscience which told him to punish the author of that act, that the unfortunate was going to the gallows! But God is great, and from the blood of martyrs new ones are born; the young soldier would not die in vain; with each new day there will be others who, preferring death to slavery, will die for the redemption of their brothers! Thus the time will come when English soldiers will no longer tolerate being led by gentlemen officers who actually pay for the right to lash them into submission. If the English people ever have the courage to be free, they will not allow their army to be made up of slaves.

I must confess that I felt a deep satisfaction. Such instances of pride are rare, it is true, but they suffice to prove that the English people, although staggering, more than any other people, without exception, under a heavy and oppressive yoke imposed upon them by their aristocracy, yet retain the divine stamp. The sacred fire is not dead in their hearts; if they are today weighed down by an overwhelming burden, the day will come when they will stand erect and restore, for all men and women, the equality of rights that God bestowed on us in giving us life. Then the aristocracy will pay a heavy price for its long oppression, its violence and its hypocrisy!

I had spent more than an hour in Newgate, and the farther I penetrated into that frightful dungeon where misfortune is mistaken for vice, hunger for thievery and pride, the noble voice of a pure conscience for murder, the greater became the oppression which had seized me upon my entering the arsenal of instruments of torture; it had reached the point where I could scarcely breathe. And yet, there was still the chapel to visit, as well as the courtyard where the toilette of those condemned to die takes place, and also the window through which they leave the prison for the gallows which puts an end to their sad and dismal lives, lives of anxiety, vice, crime, misfortune and misery. As for the infamy of such a death, the lower sorts are insensitive to it, and the nobler rise above it.

The chapel is very well laid out: there is an upper gallery reserved for women; the men's section is below. The gallery is curtained off so that the two sexes cannot see each other.

The pew[1] for the prisoners sentenced to death is on the ground floor, against the wall, near the middle of the chapel. Oh, there, on the part of the Anglican Church, is a ceremony inhuman to the utmost degree, an absurd imitation of Catholicism! What is the good of torturing a poor wretch in such a way, of making him live with death for a whole day and night? Of what moral benefit can it possibly be to society? The Catholic priest finds, in the faith of the condemned man, the power to reconcile him with death, to make him even accept it with joy by absolving him of all sin; in that light his presence is easily understood; but what can be the use of a Protestant preacher's ministerings to a man who believes in sin but not that another man has the power to absolve him of it?

At three o'clock in the afternoon, on the eve of the day set for the execution, the condemned man is brought to the chapel where he must undergo the ordeal of the pew. The pew is round and resembles a pulpit, though of smaller dimensions; it contains a bench and a praying stool; it is all draped with a black cloth for the ceremony, and when the condemned man enters, he too is clothed with a black shroud; he sits on the bench, and in front of him, on the praying stool, there is an open book; the chapel is sombre and only lit by a sepulchral lamp, all prisoners are present and must repeat after the chaplain the prayers for the dead.

The condemned man in the pew looks as if he is in a half opened tomb; above all the black drapery only his head is visible. Oh what a ghastly sight; it is as if his head were already separated from his body. What depths of terror are revealed by his pallor, his tense face, distraught eyes, hair in wild disarray and the

---

[1] Pews, in Anglican churches, are separate benches partitioned off like little pulpits.

convulsive trembling beneath the shroud! What a terrible thing to witness! It is the agony of a human creature buried alive, the death rattle from out of the tomb. The lugubrious and hellish ceremony produces such an impression on the onlookers that, unable to bear the sight, many prisoners faint, and the chapel resounds with cries of terror. The condemned man rarely lasts to the end of the ordeal; he often has to be supported or carried senseless from the pew. When he regains his senses, he is told that, as a special favour, on this last night, he may have a lamp in order to read his Bible. How absurd, and what cruel mockery! As if, at such a moment, the poor wretch were capable of reading or understanding what he reads. Those exceptional beings who can look with detachment upon their death, whatever guise it may take, must be very rare indeed. How then can one expect the condemned man to maintain sufficient presence of mind to meditate on the Bible's lofty thought, when, with every quarter hour, the clock of St Paul's tolls passing time, counting out to him the minutes he has left to live, and constantly recalls to his distraught mind the preparations for his execution. If, at dawn, the poor wretch, overcome by lassitude and suffering, is fortunate enough to be able to close his eyes, he is awakened at five o'clock by the clop of horses' hoofs and the rumble of wheels as the heavy machine of death is drawn from the courtyard next to his cell for his execution. Oh what a ghastly awakening! Thenceforth he hears not a single sound but what announces the hour of his death. At six o'clock, they come to take him to the so-called "courtyard of last moments" where the toilette takes place. He is stripped of his clothes, dressed in grey trousers, a long grey shirt of coarse linen; then his hair is cropped. During the entire operation, a minister stands by and exhorts him to resignation and speaks to him of the joys of the after-life. When the toilette is over, he is taken to the sheriff, who binds the arms of the condemned man himself. When all these preparations are finished, the sheriff, his assistant, the chaplain and the condemned man set out, and the lugubrious procession steps out the window which opens directly onto the platform of the enormous machine. There, the executioner and his assistants seize the condemned man, set him on the trap door, place the rope around his neck, thrust a hood down over his head, and place a handkerchief in his hand. When the condemned man signals by dropping the handkerchief, the trap door is withdrawn from beneath his feet, and then, as the English say, he is "launched into eternity".

Newgate, which is a prison intended to house only prisoners under accusation, has regulations less severe than in other prisons. Strict silence is not imposed; officers and matrons maintain discipline among the prisoners, prevent quarrels, tolerate a few words exchanged in passing, but put a stop to any attempt at conversation. The canteen has been eliminated, but any prisoner may pay to have his meals prepared by the resident cook.

Prisoners are not given any work to do, they are exposed to the corrupting influences of idleness. If it is intended as punishment, and it is indeed a harsh one, how can English jurists reconcile a punishment imposed before sentencing with the principle universally recognized on the Continent, that the accused is presumed innocent until tried and found guilty, and that until such time society has only the right to secure his person?

One of the most salutary improvements introduced at Newgate is the quality and number of officers and matrons charged with the surveillance of prisoners. When one thinks about what is needed to inspire respect in a shameless and thoroughly vicious population, to elicit obedience while rarely resorting to punishment, and when one thinks about the degree of self-control, firmness and self-possession needed to fulfil these functions well, one cannot but be pleasantly surprised by the fortunate choice of staff at Newgate; never does an employee speak unnecessarily to a prisoner, never does he resort to brutality nor to abusive language; officers and matrons exhort, command, are listened to in silence and obeyed to the letter, or punishment quickly follows.

I cannot leave Newgate without speaking about the worthy Mrs Fry: her love of humanity has brought about significant improvements in the prison; the most valuable of all is without a doubt to have found work for the women, she has also distributed a great number of Bibles among them.

PRISONS

It is well known that English sects consider it their religious duty to overwhelm the world with Bibles; each one is so sure of having understood the true meaning of that many-sided book, that there is not a single sect but that believes it is spreading its own doctrine when it distributes the Bible; but, if one is neither fanatical nor blind, one wonders if reading the Bible unfailingly leads to the betterment of the human race and if so far the results justify such expectations; one wonders if the various thoughts and precepts contained therein form a harmonious whole which ordinary minds can grasp, and if the examples both good and bad which it presents can produce only good effects.

The various books which make up the Bible are certainly too deep to be understood without extensive study, even by scholars, and the clergy's sermons are a far from perfect supplement to the understanding of the average reader; furthermore, religious doctrines nowadays have very little influence in Central Europe; they only affect outward appearances, men's actions are no longer motivated by religion. Everyone wants to rise above his station, to make a fortune, and in order to do so, he relies on the infallibility of his reason. What power can religion have over men's minds when they are so disposed? Will it incline the poor to resign themselves to their suffering if they are persuaded that they can get rich through their own efforts? Will it inspire the rich with humility if they are convinced that their fortune is due to nothing but their own merit? Will they not then believe themselves superior to their poverty-stricken fellow men? As long as men bestow blame or praise according to the outcome of their actions, how could they be inclined to abdicate their sense of self-importance and consider themselves blind instruments of God?

Be the event fortunate or unfortunate, the Moslem exclaims, "God is Great!" because, not being presumptuous enough to look beyond the immediate effect of his action, he has not the overweening pride to consider himself the author of an event which he could not predict with certainty, and good or bad, he accepts his lot, assuredly with joy or sorrow, but without vainglory or lamentation.

If, like the Moslems, each one of us, trusting in Providence, were content with the living our work provided us without striving after wealth; if, like them, we had no other goal but the performance of the duties prescribed by religious law, and found evil only in the violation of that law, then I would believe in the influence of religion to reform criminals; but considering that in our society the provisions of civil law are often in conflict with the precepts of the Gospel, and that the law in England sets aside any spirit of justice, institutes rights of inheritance by primogeniture, creates a maze of sinecures and every sort of privilege and make the poor bear three-quarters of the taxes, then I do not think that any amount of Christian teaching is capable of reforming men who have committed crimes against a society which has put itself outside Christian law. Among European peoples, religion nowadays is merely an appurtenance, the social order functions without it; it is influenced only by civil laws, and religious law commands obedience only in so far as there is no advantage in not observing it.

In support of this opinion, I shall quote the remarks of those who have written about prisons; they all draw attention to the fact that religious teaching is entirely unsuccessful, that it is wearisome, drives the prisoners to distraction and sets them against religion and its ministers; that monks, Quakers, priests, missionaries and chaplains reap no fruit from their preaching other than the sarcasm and contempt of their listeners.[1]

---

[1] The Bishop of London has stated that the Anglican clergy would never improve the morals of the masses by preaching to them; and in my opinion, what he said is very true. He has stated moreover that in order to raise the morals of the people one would have to speak with each one individually.
(Moreau-Christophe)

I do not know what role our clergy might have in the reform of prisoners; I only know that in our prison system in France, they have no role at all. In Paris the recent experience of a young abbot, whose zeal at least I applaud, have borne me out, although the newspapers claimed the opposite. The prisoners of Bicêtre and Sainte Pélagie to whom he distributed religious books sold them in order to gamble or to obtain brandy. My pen recoils from describing the godless scenes caused each evening in the prisoners cells by all sorts of persons who make it their business to go and preach in the prisons of Paris. Nevertheless, even if one concedes that so-called religious ideas have power only in so far as

PRISONS

What magical words could those salaried preachers borrow from the Bible to reconcile to his fate the hapless prisoner lying in the filth of his cell, without air, without light, without pure water, with no clothes to cover himself, not even a bit of fire to warm his shivering body and benumbed limbs, nor even sometimes a bit of black bread to allay his hunger. Will not the wretch exclaim, like Job: "There is no God!"

Resignation indeed! Is the man who has not found in his heart the strength to withstand physical and moral suffering likely to be induced by biblical prose meekly to accept his fate? Ah I can understand the influence of words of friendship, the power of sympathetic tears to calm the greatest suffering, but the speeches of paid sermonizers to alleviate the anguish of the soul have always seemed to me the height of absurdity.

---

they blind our reason, the good that they can do is too great for us to neglect them; so one must not err in the precautions to be taken. Experience and reason speak out against those who imagine that one has only to plunge right in preaching religious dogma to a pack of scoundrels in order to make honest men out of them. More than for any others, the way for religious ideas must be paved by those things to which heart and habit are the most susceptible. And he who has looked at prisons with an observing eye is thoroughly convinced that the things without which nothing can be hoped for if prisoners are to be prevented from exercising an evil influence upon one another are first of all to house them more decently, to separate them more than is now done, to provide each one of them with separate sleeping quarters, to have them perform some sort of work every day, to raise them from the profound ignorance into which most of them are plunged, to assure that their treatment, although severe, is just and humane, in short, to put them in a situation where they are not forced to become depraved, and where they find it to their own interest to mend their ways. This is the way to open the hearts of criminals to morality. I repeat: only after these precautions are taken will religion enter their hearts. If you want religious instruction to lead criminals to repentance and to make them virtuous, then begin by recognizing and abolishing everything that stands in the way. Until that it is done, you are crying out to wretches in an abyss to climb out, and you, yourselves, keep pushing them down ever farther. If I have dwelt on this point at some length, it is only because at the first meeting of the Royal Society for the Improvement of Prisons, it was announced that religious instruction for the prisoners would be their primary concern. The resolution came as no surprise; it stems from the fact that those who made it are not sufficiently familiar with prisons nor with all the prisoners' circumstances.

(Villermé, *Des Prisons telles qu'elles sont et telles qu'elles devraient être*)

What can Mrs Fry say to the unfortunate girls whom lack of occupation or work, seduction, prejudice, and the thousands and thousands of vices that infest the whole society have reduced to prostituting themselves, to bartering their bodies for a piece of bread! Does she find in the Bible consolation for such misfortune? No indeed! The prostitute, angered by grief, can see only the literal meaning. "An eye for an eye, a tooth for a tooth", she echoes, according to the terrible code of Moses. Will not the poor, rejected by the rich and seeing themselves doomed to poverty, to contempt, in order to feed the luxury and pride of those who call themselves masters, also cry out in indignation: "An eye for an eye, a tooth for a tooth"? And will not those born with some pride in their hearts and aware of their own worth, who cannot bring themselves to submit to the yoke of privilege, to the tyranny of prejudice, to the power of money, and who have revolted against an oppressive social organization, also repeat after the Bible: "An eye for an eye, a tooth for a tooth"?[1]

What sort of instruction then is appropriate for prisoners, I may be asked. First of all, training in several trades, so that if work is lacking in one branch of industry, they may find it in

---

[1] Moreover, the books given to prisoners are not of the sort likely to reach the intended moral goal. "Since we persist," say the contributors to a famous review (*Edinburgh Review*, Vol. XXXVI, p. 363) "in trying to convert our prisons into schools, let us stop supplying them with such intolerably stupid books: indeed, all prison books seem to be written from the premise that a thief or a criminal of any kind has less common sense than a five year old child. Generally it is the story of a poor worker who has only black bread and water to feed himself and his six children. And yet he is happy and content: never any complaining, never any grumbling, everyone envies his gaiety. However, even in his wildest dreams, the possibility of having bacon to eat has never occured to him, and mutton is practically unheard of. Does he not have black bread and water? What more is needed for his felicity? What greater blessing could move him to gratitude? Invariably, the local squire or the parish priest happens to pass the poor man's workshop and finds him praying for the King or for the Church and for all those in authority; invariably they wind up offering him a shilling, a sum that the honest worker never fails to refuse, stating that he has no need of it. Such are the moral books which charitable ladies and nice people go about distributing right and left in our prisons with untiring energy. It would be a heaven sent blessing if there were to be born among us some genius with the talent to write for the people!..."

another; then they should be taught order, thrift, love of work, sobriety; they must be taught that they must expect no improvement in their condition except through the practice of these virtues; and that the most patent absurdity for one or several individuals is to attack society. In a word, since it is society's laws that they have transgressed, they must be given hope of sharing in society's benefits in reward for their efforts; at the same time, it should be made clear to them that if they reverted to vice and crime they would inevitably end their days in a prison, penal colony or on the gallows. I do not believe that the joys of heaven or the torments of hell can have as much influence on them.

I was still painfully affected by the memory of my long visit to Newgate when I went to Coldbath Fields. From a great distance, one can see the high walls that surround it; the entrance, though severe and simple in style, is in no way frightening; the building is forty years old and well kept. The prison, built according to the ideas of the philanthropist Howard, is spacious and airy, and there is plenty of light and water and a two-acre garden. But the vanity of the architect has prevailed over the plans of the philanthropist: Howard wished to make this prison the counterpart, but improved, of the penitentiaries of Pennsylvania; the builder took no heed of this desire and has shown ignorance, lack of taste and, I would go so far as to say, complete want of intelligence. On a magnificent site he could think of nothing better than to erect great thick walls; the yards are not spacious enough; the main buildings have stairs that are too narrow, and they are poorly laid out and do not provide as many separate cells as they ought. Nevertheless, incomplete as it is, the prison is a veritable pastoral retreat compared to the grim and dreadful Newgate! Coldbath Fields is both house of detention and house of correction. The governor of the prison, Mr Chesterton, is a very distinguished man; he speaks Spanish and French with equal facility; he has widely travelled and has gathered a wealth of knowledge in the countries he has visited. Everything about him denotes a man heartily devoted to the well-being of his fellow men, each observation he makes, every word he says indicates how deeply his soul is penetrated with that universal charity preached by Jesus; his philanthropy is set off by his gentle, kind and extremely polished manners.

Mr Chesterton was kind enough to accompany me about the place and show me every detail. One can see that it has become his creation, that he considers the unfortunate prisoners as his own family; he knows almost all of them by name. Given such a governor (he has held the post for ten years), one can imagine what the officers are like. If, remembering what most of our prison guards in France are like, I was amazed by the excellent behaviour of Newgate's warders, I was full of admiration for those of Coldbath Fields! These men, almost all of them chosen by the governor, have a gentle physiognomy quite in harmony with the sound of their voice and their obliging courtesy. What a beneficial influence regular intercourse with such guards must have on the prisoners! How can one doubt the influence of pleasant and humane manners in reconciling with society men whose hearts are embittered?

In Coldbath, Mr Chesterton has carried the separation of prisoners as far as possible. Habitual offenders are divided into five categories; those sentenced for the sixth time are sent to Millbank or to Botany Bay; other prisoners are classified according to the nature of their crimes.

The governor insists on the scrupulous enforcement of the rules of the prison entrusted to his care. These rules, I must say, seemed very harsh to me! They impose perpetual silence and idleness, and solitary confinement for the slightest offence.

Under no circumstances may the prisoner speak to his comrades, nor address any request to the officers. If visitors ask him a question, he must not answer; only if he feels ill may he ask to see a doctor. Taken immediately to the infirmary, he is examined, put in a good bed, and all care that his condition requires is lavished upon him with kindness and affection.

A prisoner who breaks silence is severely punished.[1]

---

[1] It is difficult to believe that this rule of silence can be enforced, and yet it is, and scrupulously. It is so painful that several prisoners say that they would prefer death.

(Villermé)

We visited the men's side first, where I saw the same faces as in Newgate, but what a metamorphosis they had undergone! These men, whose faces before sentencing betrayed insolence and the ugly mark of crime, now had their heads bowed and their eyes downcast, and everything about them was indicative of total submission. Subjected to strict discipline, not a single one of them would attempt, nor even dare think of not observing it. They were neat and clean, recently shaved (they are shaved twice a week), their hair was combed, and their hands and faces were clean.[1]

They wear duck trousers in summer and heavy woollen ones in winter, jackets of the same cloth, woollen caps, coloured shirts, woollen socks (they change their shirts and socks every Sunday), shoes, vests, ties, handkerchiefs. The clothes are all clean and very well cared for.

I also visited the children's section; their number is appalling: of 1,120 prisoners incarcerated in Coldbath when I visited it, there were 300 children from nine to seventeen years old! What drove these children to crime? Poverty, want of a trade and the examples of corruption which surround these poor children. Nothing could be more painful than the sight of those little creatures, with their fair hair, pale faces, thin bodies, who are destined very likely for transportation or the gallows! The worst offenders among the children are sentenced to so many hours each day on the tread-wheel; the others do nothing. Thus these children, who have been driven to vagabondage, thievery and crime for lack of trade and out of idleness, will leave the so-called "house of correction" after two, three, four or five years of imprisonment, without having a trade which might enable them to earn their living.

In all of this I can see nothing but the infliction of punishment, but no sign of "correction"; instead of correcting, such institutions are in actual fact hotbeds of corruption: the child who is delinquent but not vicious sees no example anywhere which

---

[1] In London, coal smoke makes everything so grimy that soap must be given to prisoners so that they may scrub their hands and faces.

might inspire in him a love of good, he becomes accustomed to idleness, indolence and all kinds of vice.

I could not refrain from expressing to Mr Chesterton my astonishment that the children were thus left in idleness instead of being engaged in some productive work. "In England", he replied, "the working class is so numerous that the government would not care to reduce their employment by having prisoners work." "But Sir, is England so rich that she can make of her prisons spacious recluses whose inhabitants are comfortably lodged, well dressed, well nourished, without doing anything? If such is her intention, within twenty years half the population, weary of struggling against poverty, will seek refuge in the prisons!"[1]

At Coldbath, there are 520 cells: they are assigned to children if possible, in order to keep them completely apart, at least at night. All the cells are kept extraordinarily clean: the trestle bed has a good mattress, a pillow and two blankets; a board affixed to the wall serves as a table. All the cells are airy, but through the fault of the architect some of them are dark. All the walls and stairways are whitewashed twice a year. There are no bad odours to besiege you as in French prisons. Children and women have great difficulty observing the rule of silence, consequently I saw a number of poor children being punished by solitary confinement.[2]

---

[1] A poor chimney sweep of sixteen, dressed in rags, barefooted, his legs red and chapped by the cold, was put in prison for a mere misdemeanour. The hot bath he was given upon his arrival in prison came as a delight to him, but the thing that surprised him most was being told to put on socks and shoes. "Am I going to wear this and that, and that too?" he would say with each article of clothing he was given. His joy reached its height when he found himself in his cell; he kept delightedly turning his blanket over and over in his hands, and could scarcely believe in so much good fortune; and it was in a faltering voice that he asked if he were really going to sleep in a bed. The next day, upon being asked by the governor what he thought of his situation: "What do I think?" he exclaimed, "I'll be damned if I ever work for a living!" The child kept his word: later on he was transported.

(Report of the Commissioners)

[2] Punishments: Lashes   9
                  Shackles   4

While I was in the last yard, the schoolmaster in charge of the children's instruction arrived to teach his class. I greeted the venerable old man with the utmost respect. He has been teaching for fifteen years. Oh what devotion one must have to resign oneself to live in this way, among children doomed to ignominy, vice and suffering! One can see in the man's face the goodness of his heart; he is soft-spoken, and speaks to the children with kindness and with a solicitude which reassures them and banishes all fear from their hearts.

After visiting several sections where I noticed everywhere the same cleanliness, the same orderliness and the same facial expressions, I came to the yard of those imprisoned for the fifth time.

I expected to find more of those horrible faces in which the mark of crime is forever engraved, faces furrowed by unbridled passions, and betraying the dreadful features of cunning, boldness and a permanent criminal bent. Imagine my surprise at seeing on the prisoners' faces an expression of ennui — ennui of the profoundest sort! Not one of them cast a glance in our direction, our presence there was a matter of complete indifference to them, they seemed sunk in an apathetic torpor. At the sight of these men who were living like automatons, whose passions seemed to have been annihilated, whose soul was absent, but whose faces nevertheless still carried the imprint of their crimes, the stamp of society's reprobation together with profound despair, the observer is struck with terror as at a vision from hell.

There were far more prisoners in this section than in the others; they were older; they appeared to me to be in poorer health, more dejected, less careful of their person. Struck by this difference, I was curious as to its cause and applied to the governor. "These prisoners", he replied, "give us much more trouble than the others, not that they are guilty of any act of

---

Solitary confinement	3,232
Other punishments	8,760

(Moreau-Christophe, "Table of the punishments at Coldbath Fields in a year's time.")

insubordination, but their excessive listlessness, the enormous difficulty one has in getting them to comb their hair, wash themselves or brush their clothes, all this requires a great deal of surveillance. There are some who refuse to take exercise, others will occasionally go so far as to refuse to eat, consequently they are almost always ill; this section keeps the infirmary full."

"And to what do you attribute this behaviour, apparently in such contradiction with the violent disposition that one might expect them to have?"

"To the chronic malady of boredom; habitual offenders can rarely accustom themselves to prison life."

That is understandable, the monotony of their idle, silent existence necessarily leads to total apathy, and thereafter, life becomes an overwhelming burden. Such men feel alive only through excess; they take pleasure in risking their lives, they like the excitement of debauchery, and cannot accustom themselves to a vegetal existence. The life of the mind has never exerted any power over them and their faculties have remained fallow. A life of safety and inactivity is the greatest torment for them! They bitterly miss their adventurous life filled with danger and privations, and the time when their intelligence, imagination, courage and skill were in constant use. Alas the unfortunate truth is these men have a need for struggle, a struggle to the death against poverty, against obstacles of every kind and against society; and those who once found a savage joy in defying prison, penitentiary and the gallows cannot now bear the dreary lack of activity, the sepulchral silence of Coldbath; it is a torture beyond their strength and worse than any other.

Moreover, the number of habitual offenders demonstrates that it is not through punishment that men are reformed. They must be taught, because only the practice of orderliness and industriousness has the power to reform the habits of vice and crime.

But whatever the penitentiary system adopted by a nation, when the repetition of offences has proved the individual to be incorrigible or the means of reform to be ineffectual, it seems to me absurd to put the habitual offender back into that social milieu for which we have not been able to prepare him; if the penitentiary system has not been able to reform the criminal, society must transport him, send him to the mines or make it impossible for him to do further harm. In all the prisons of England there are a great number of habitual offenders.[1]

The men in this section are noteworthy for their taciturnity; it is almost useless to impose silence as a punishment; they often refuse even to answer questions addressed to them by the officers.

Coldbath's infirmary is a haven of peace and comfort. As a rule there are very few patients. I saw, in two large rooms, from twelve to fifteen men, more listless than ill; some were having tea, others stretched out at their ease, reading; there were men strolling about, while others quietly conversed among themselves — they did not look unhappy, and one might have taken them for free men. The well-being prevailing in the infirmary shows clearly that the governor sees in each ailing prisoner nothing other than a man who is ill, an unfortunate brother whom it is his duty to care for.

I saw there a man of twenty-six, condemned to death for having killed one of his friends in a quarrel; the murderer comes from one of the best families of the aristocracy and has an income of £6,000; if he had sprung from the lower classes, without a penny to his name, his neck would already have felt the kiss of the hangman's rope, but thanks to his family's influence and even more to the sacrifice of a part of his fortune, his sentence has been commuted to six years in Coldbath. Here again, the strange fascination that rank holds for the English can be felt: the young man, though in excellent health, spends all his time in the infirmary; in fine weather, he strolls about the garden and occupies his time by learning French, as he intends to come and

---

[1] Out of the 109,495 individuals in various English prisons during the year 1837, 24,876 were habitual offenders and of these, 12,920 were imprisoned for the second time, 5,190 for the third time, 2,312 for the fourth time, 4,454 for the fifth time or more. Habitual offenders for which there are no figures must be much more numerous.

(Moreau-Christophe)

live in France as soon as he gets out of prison.

With this sole exception, quite understandable among a people who worship gold and still believe in the value of aristocratic distinctions, there are no special privileges whatsoever at Coldbath. Canteen privileges have been totally eliminated for everyone, and the food is the same for all without exception. I saw the prisoners at their dinner: each section has its own refectory. The handsome deal tables, rubbed to a high lustre, are carefully washed and scrubbed; their brilliant surfaces are not marred by the slighest speck. The little bowls out of which prisoners eat are made of pewter, they are scoured, polished and glittering like silver. The food is wholesome and plentiful, but tiresomely monotonous: in the morning, a large bowl of gruel, for dinner, soup with vegetables, and meat twice a week, in the evening, they are given gruel again; the bread is excellent. At dinner each prisoner receives a loaf done to a turn, with a fine golden crust, giving off the most appetizing smell. I tasted one of the loaves; it is white like the fine bread of Paris and better than any I tasted in London; I can assure you that the most prosperous farmers in Ireland have never eaten bread so good, even on their wedding day. The bread at Newgate is not quite so fine.

After dinner, each one went back to work, those on duty began cleaning the refectory and the yards, others went to the classroom, many of them were busy making tow from old ropes, while those sentenced to the tread-wheel climbed into the instrument of their torture.[1]

Seeing the immobility of the prisoner suspended in the tread-wheel, his slow tread which seems to require no effort, the visitor more often than not passes by the wheel without suspecting that the man who makes it go round is undergoing the most excruciating torture, and I would never have believed it possible to devise such a refinement of cruelty as this infernal machine

---

[1] It is estimated that the construction of a tread-wheel costs fifteen to twenty pounds sterling per person. It is said that the treadwheel at Coldbath Fields prison cost more than 12,000 pounds (3,000,000 francs).

For an instrument of torture, this is a bit on the expensive side!

(Moreau-Christophe)

represents, if the governor had not explained its effects to me. The torture is precisely in the excessive slowness with which the enormous drum turns; it revolves only twenty-eight to thirty turns a minute because the steps are far apart, causing the condemned man's treading to be extremely slow, laborious and painful; he must take great strides in order to reach the step, constantly lifting one leg high in the air and transferring his entire weight on to it as the step comes toward him; during the whole horrible process the rest of his body is completely motionless; the vertiginous slowness of the motion benumbs his limbs, brings on giddiness and stomach cramps; sometimes he faints, falls off the machine, and breaks a limb or kills himself. The torture irritates the entire nervous system of the prisoner, often cripples him, causes hernia and chronic ailments. I have seen men and children just off the tread-wheel at Coldbath; not one of them had the slightest trace of perspiration on his brow, on the contrary, they all seemed to be cold rather than hot; they were pale, some were blue in the face; their muscles were strained, their eyes lifeless, and everything about them proclaimed the highest degree of physical suffering; several were stretching their limbs, others were yawning: it has been observed that women, young people and especially children suffer a great deal more from this torture than grown men and old people; which would indicate that rather than requiring strength, it affects the nervous system.

Are such means really likely to reform the unfortunate young man who has been brought to the point of transgressing society's laws? Does anyone suppose that by irritating his already too susceptible nervous system, by ruining his health, in other words by crippling him for the rest of his life, by weakening his body and his mind, one is going to lead him back to the right path? Truly, it is inconceivable why a nation, known for its good judgement, tolerates such an inhuman form of torture as a punishment, and idleness and the silence of the tomb as a means of correction!

Exaggerated forms of punishment always do more harm than good, and even the most judiciously administered among them can produce only temporary results if they are not accompanied by instruction. True, attention and obedience are forthcoming from those being subjected to punishment, but it would be an error to suppose that pain remembered can have any corrective influence: experience has shown the opposite to be true. Once returned to society, criminals increase their subterfuges in direct proportion to the degree of surveillance to which they are subjected; the memory of punishment, far from reforming them, almost always makes them vicious. Prolonged physical pain brings death to him who endures it, or else it causes untold physical harm and affects his mental faculties; a moderate punishment inspires respect for authority and puts a stop to any thought of resistance; but the harmful effects of torture fill man's heart with perpetual anger, and then crime becomes not only a means of satisfying his needs and his vices, but of getting revenge!

At Coldbath, my attention was caught by two prisoners being held for trial. One of them, as I learned from Mr Chesterton, is a Jew, and the greatest scoundrel in England. He had been imprisoned for the eighth or tenth time (for various types of forgery). I made a point of seeing the face of this greatest scoundrel in England.... His window looked out on a little passage, and I paused to examine him. He was seated at a table on which there were papers covered with numbers. He must have been totally absorbed in his figuring because he did not seem to notice my shadow falling across his cell. Oh it was truly a face worthy of Rembrandt! I have never seen a face more surreptitiously evil, more blatantly hypocritical! Although he was at least sixty, his fiery looking grey eyes indicated the resourcefulness, the tenacity of will and the avarice ... of the Jew!

The other criminal's ignoble face betrayed the revolting crime he had committed. Four months after his marriage to a seventeen year old girl, a rich and beautiful heiress, he had forced himself with unbridled brutality upon his wife's sister, a child of twelve, who died as a result of the attack. The man was a satyr; he had the satyr's grotesque form: an enormous paunch, herculean shoulders, the face of a swine and little short legs; his lusting eyes, his enormous protruding lips, his warty nose, everything about him proclaimed the satyr as painters have always depicted him.

What sort of mother could be such a poor judge of character, so lacking in woman's intuition that she could have given her daughter to such a vampire!

At Coldbath prisoners being held for trial have no communication with those already convicted.

Next we went on to the women's section, separated from the men's section by a garden. There too all is cleanliness and order, there is the same silence and the same severity in enforcing regulations. The women have more to occupy them than the men; they make the linens needed for the whole establishment, keep them clean and mended; they also make their own clothes which consist of coarse white linen skirts for summer and woollen ones for winter, long high-necked camisoles of the same material, and coarse white linen bonnets. They are much cleaner than the men; they have two chemises, two petticoats, two handkerchiefs, two bonnets, two pairs of stockings for the week, and a fresh skirt and bodice every other week; their shoes are so well blacked that they appear to be new; their cells are also better furnished than the men's; they have sheets on their beds, a towel, a basin, a glass and so forth.

Their food is like the men's; in addition, the women who do the washing and ironing have meat every day, as well as beer and tea.

There is a superb laundry room, a large drying room and a fine linen room.

There is a great deal more activity among the women than among the men; they wash and iron; some hang out the clothes, others do the mending, still others do the cooking, and a great number of them are constantly scrubbing the floors of the prison from one end to the other, together with rooms, cells, corridors, staircases, even the paving in the yards is scrubbed. One could safely wear white satin shoes and a muslin dress anywhere in that vast collection of buildings; they would remain spotless, for there is not a single drop of water, not a speck of dust to be found. It is truly amazing.

In spite of all this activity, the women are no livelier than the men; they are sad, their eyes are lifeless, and their faces impassive; it is as if they neither saw nor heard. I listened at the door of several workshops before going in; everywhere a deathlike silence reigned. Any whom their work obliges to speak with the matron do so in a low voice, and she replies in the same manner, as in a sickroom.

All these women, with rare exceptions, are prostitutes accustomed to that life of debauchery, drunkenness and insolence which they flaunt in the streets of London; under prison discipline they nonetheless become sober, humble, subdued and on the whole hard-working. As at Newgate, they all made the servile curtsey which is required of all women in this sort of establishment. A hypocritical demonstration of this sort seems immoral to me; it must humiliate them and can have no salutary effect. Among all the 208 prisoners, I did not see a single pretty one; only three were even presentable; all the rest were hideous, although they had a general air of good health and a freshness of complexion rarely seen among women in London.

I noticed fewer Bibles in the women's quarters than in the men's.

In the infirmary, I saw an infant of seventeen months, remarkable for her beauty. The hapless child had been born in prison. In the same room, there was a woman nursing her newborn child. I also saw, in the last yard, a three year old girl, a thin, sickly little creature with an intelligent look about her; she was clinging to the iron gate which closes the yard. As soon as she saw the governor, her face lit up; she slipped her tiny little arm through the bars and held out her sweet little hand to Mr Chesterton and said to him in a voice which expressed at one and the same time impatience and cajolery: "Sir, I should like to go to the garden; there is nothing to do here: I haven't been out for three whole days." Mr Chesterton took her by the hand, had the door opened, and as soon as she was free, she ran after him, weeping like a child convulsed.

The poor little thing was at Coldbath with her mother, who usually worked in the garden and took the child with her, but the mother had made the double mistake of breaking silence and of asking one of her companions for what reason she was in prison. Such questions are punishable by fifteen days in solitary confinement, and the poor child was serving the sentence along with her mother.

The number of children found in women's prisons clearly indicates the total lack of institutions for children. Education starts in the cradle, and one may imagine the influence prison life must have on impressionable young creatures; prison will always be, in spite of all efforts to the contrary, a school for subterfuge, deceit and vice of all sorts. It would seem that in England children of thieves are fated to follow the profession of their parents!

Mr Chesterton showed me around the garden, which is very well tended. Working in the garden is a reward granted for good conduct. I saw a workshop whose iron roof was a fine piece of work executed by the prisoners. It is there that the workers of various trades make everything that is needed in the prison. Tailors, shoemakers, locksmiths, carpenters, masons are all engaged in the upkeep of the establishment, and in this manner it is kept in such good repair and so admirably clean, but they produce nothing to be sold outside.[1]

In taking my leave, I said to Mr Chesterton: "Sir, I believe that it would be impossible to find a prison in England better administered than yours, but I do find fault with the idleness in which you keep your prisoners, it is in my opinion a deplorable system, which must inevitably nurture the seeds of corruption in the hearts of prisoners." "Madame," answered the governor, "not everyone is of your opinion. Last year, when Marshal Soult honoured me with a visit to Coldbath, what he most admired is precisely that which you condemn." "Very good, very good," he said to me, "I can see that you are on the right path here; you do not penalize workers with families to support by depriving them of their livelihood in order to provide work for convicts, as we are stupid enough to do in France, to the detriment of honest workers who are the victims of unfair competition on the part of prisoners."

---

[1] Nowhere in English prisons are there workshops organized like those of French prisons; private industry would feel itself threatened.

(Moreau-Christophe)

Did not Marshal Soult know that in France the wages of prisoners are lower than those of workers only because the former are fed by the State and subjected to a monopoly? The difficulty mentioned by Marshal Soult could be avoided if, instead of giving the work to contractors, one followed the example of penitentiaries in the United States, which have shops outside the prison, to sell the things made by the prisoners. These penitentiaries open an account for each prisoner, charge him for the cost of his food in prison and for his raw materials, which are supplied to him, and credit the account with the proceeds of the sale of the things he has made; the balance is given to him only when he gets out, and if at the end of his term the expenses of his stay in prison are not offset by his work, he stays until he has settled his account. In this way the prisoner works under the same conditions as the worker, cannot compete with him in such a way as to give him just cause for complaint. But the way things are done in our country, the expense of the prisoners' upkeep is borne by the State; and it is still unusual for prisoners to leave prison at the end of their term with a nest-egg proportionate to the length of their stay in prison, but on the other hand, the contractors make a fortune at the expense of the State and the labourer's toil.

This system is not only onerous to the State, it is also fundamentally immoral! What! you punish the prisoner for having violated the laws of property, and you yourselves violate them at his expense by forcing him to work for a fifth or a quarter of what his wages ought to be! Do not treat him unfairly lest he imagine that everything is subject to the rule of force or deceit, and lest in his conscience he take pride in his crimes! In the American system, competition among prisoners is stimulated by the most powerful motives, and in general they become excellent workers. If one supposes that food, clothing, heating and lighting for prisoners cost as much as these same expenses at the Hôtel des Invalides (one and a half francs per day), a number of prisoners having served from eight to ten years would then return to society with sufficient capital to enable them to work, for their own benefit, at the trade they had learned in prison. I do not believe many of them would be tempted to return to crime.

Why did Marshal Soult, so keenly aware in England of the threat which the work of prisoners represents for free workers, countenance when he was Minister of War the practice of hiring out to contractors the work of convicts in military prisons? Could it be that the Marshal only pays lip-service to reform? In any event, coming from the Marshal, such an opinion did not surprise me. Did he not refuse to allow our soldiers to be used for public works? Do not expect a soldier of the Empire to entertain any notion of social science. All he knows is military glory, which then was everything and now is nothing!

The impression that Coldbath had made upon me had entirely faded away when I went to Millbank to the Penitentiary, a model prison,[1] where the system of separated cells is in effect with no worthwhile results whatsoever.[2] If Coldbath seemed like a pastoral retreat to me in comparison to Newgate, the Penitentiary was a sumptuous palace compared to Coldbath. This time I was not received by a governor, but by two gentlemen, one a Member of the House of Lords, the other a Member of the House of Commons, and both members of the commission on prisons. These gentlemen, scrupulously polite, stiff and taciturn, were, from the beginning to the end of the visit, English in every sense of the word. They knew perfectly well, I presume, what

---

[1] The prison cost the enormous sum of 788,000 pounds sterling (19,700,000 francs of our money).

(*Leçons du Dr Julius* Vol. II, p. 47)

[2] But prisoners of a single category meet twice a day in the yard assigned to them for exercise: all is done in silence. The prisoners march and countermarch one behind the other under the watchful eye of a guard.

As we have seen, they also meet in chapel.

They meet likewise at school, at the water pump, in the passage ways, and where they wash up and so forth.

These meetings, although momentary and subject to the strict rules of discipline, nevertheless result in dangerous relations developing among prisoners, if not while they are serving their sentence, at least after they are freed. Therefore, I do not doubt that the negligible results obtained up to the present time at this institution must, in part, be attributed to the flaws this penitentiary shares with ordinary prisons.

(Moreau-Christophe).

conclusions were to be drawn from the figures which the staff submitted to them for inspection, but one thing I am sure of: they do not know the slightest thing about the prisoners; after I had discovered that this was the case, I dared ask no further questions. How different from Mr Chesterton who makes, as it were, a special study of each of his prisoners!

I arrived at an upstairs gallery, it was long and wide and contained forty-two cells; the gallery is lighted by large windows which are almost always left open to admit air, light and sunshine. The floor, like that in the cells, is made up of narrow boards of deal resembling the tables at Coldbath; it is as clean and as well polished as a fresh sheet of drawing paper. Each cell has two doors: the outer one, made of wood, is always open; the inner one, of iron bars, is always closed. In the back of the cell there is a small window giving light and creating a draught with the gallery window directly in front of it. The prisoners' furniture was not limited to the bare minimum, one might even say that the cells were well furnished; there were neatly made beds, clean white sheets, a small wardrobe, a table and a shelf on which toilet articles were arranged; all these things, in keeping with the premises, were spotless, shining as if like new.

I cannot say anything about the prisoners because the two gentlemen deemed it improper for a woman to visit the men's section. I was not surprised: they do not allow women to visit men's prisons, they also exclude them from the galleries of Parliament; all this reflects the same way of thinking. When it comes to ridiculous susceptibility and stilted formality, the English aristocracy is not to be outdone. Here, women prisoners were even better dressed than at Coldbath: they were sewing, with chairs to sit on and footstools in front of them. As in the other prisons, each time we stopped at their doors, they would get up and make their eternal curtsey.

I noticed over and over again on each table, one, two and sometimes three Bibles; I had seen them at Newgate and at Coldbath in the hands of criminals and of all habitual offenders. I could not restrain my indignation. "Ah," I exclaimed, "prisons in England are the Golgotha of pious books!" True, the existence of a numerous society whose aim is to distribute Bibles to all and sundry is the most monstrous stupidity. If one examines at random ten, a hundred or a thousand of the people who have read it, one will be convinced that the greater part of the Scriptures is unintelligible to the ordinary reader. However, the Biblical Society's subscribers believed it when they were told they would be doing a good work in giving their money to sponsor an indiscriminate distribution of the Bible. If they had understood that holy book, they would have realized that preliminary instruction was essential so that reading it might improve the reader without danger of corrupting him. Indeed, one might be tempted to believe that criminals find in the Bible reasons to continue in a life of crime! It has been established that those avid "readers of the Bible" are habitual offenders caught over and over again for new crimes against society. From a religious point of view, can it not be considered a profanation to entrust a horde of bandits with God's revelations to the chosen ones? It is unquestionably an abominable sacrilege from which no good can come.

Prisoners in this establishment enjoy all the comfort compatible with their situation: abundant and healthful food and little work.[1] The extreme cleanliness which reigns everywhere is the final element which makes their life as comfortable as possible from the material point of view.

The expressions on all the women's faces were like those at Coldbath: lack of suffering and a profound ennui.

---

[1] The expenses for each one (prisoners at Millbank) amounted to approximately twenty six and half pounds or 665 francs in our money.... In 1837, the proceeds from work in all the prisons in England amounted to only 6,601 pounds, and the expenses of maintenance and guards' wages for the same prisons, the enormous sum of 243,989 pounds. The income of the same prisons, including the proceeds mentioned above from the work of prisoners was 21,711 pounds, consequently, the total expenses of prisons in England, during the year 1837 amounted to 222,277 pounds not including expenses connected with the buildings. The cost per day of each prisoner usually varies according to the diet adopted in each prison, between one and two shillings *per capita* and *per diem* (between one franc and twenty centimes and two francs and fifty centimes). Millbank Penitentiary is not included in these figures.

(Moreau-Christophe)

The prison is very large: it can hold 1,200 prisoners; there were 800 at the time of my visit.

Nothing seems to have been spared in the construction in order to prevent the escape of prisoners and to ensure their comfort. However, it is inconceivable that, for an establishment destined to receive so many people, they should have chosen so unhealthy a site; it is located on the banks of the Thames, in marshland, and is surrounded by factories which perpetually belch forth billows of coal-smoke and emit noxious fumes.

X

St Giles Parish
(The Irish Quarter)

I have seen the Indian in his forests and the Negro in his chains and I believed as I contemplated their pitiful state that theirs was the ultimate in human misery; I was unaware then of poor Ireland's lot.

Ireland's destitution is unique; it conforms to no pattern and has no counterpart anywhere. Seeing it, one realizes that it is theoretically impossible to assign any limits to the misfortune of populations.

Whenever I see a nation which has had the misfortune to fall under the yoke and to submit to it, I do not inquire as to the vices it may have; I ask what vices it does not have and what virtues it might have.

De Beaumont, L'IRLANDE, SOCIALE, POLITIQUE ET RELIGIEUSE

More than two hundred thousand Irish proletarians are living in various parts of the British metropolis: they are the porters, the men who are given the most arduous tasks because they work for modest wages. These people are poor, of course, but they have work and they give no inkling of the poverty of the Irish, that ragged poverty which wrests potato peelings from the dogs in the street! Irish poverty, as Mr De Beaumont depicts it, is shown to exist in the midst of one of the richest districts in London. It is there that one must go to realize in all its horror the poverty which occurs in a rich and fertile country when it is governed by, and for, the aristocracy.

Oxford Street, a fine, long street thronged with carriages, a street of broad sidewalks and smart shops, runs almost perpendicularly into Tottenham Court Road. Where the two streets meet, there is a small alley invariably blocked by an enormous coal wagon, so that there is scarcely enough room to squeeze by. The little alley is called Bainbridge Street and gives access to the Irish quarter.

Before I left Paris, a Spaniard brought to my attention three London districts as being instructive to visit: the Irish quarter, the Jewish quarter and the area where stolen scarves are sold.

In England, patriotism is merely a spirit of rivalry. It consists, not in loving one's neighbour, but in insisting that England surpasses all other nations. Their absurd vanity, which I shall frequently have occasion to point out, explains why everyone conspires to conceal the country's ills. A strange sort of patriotism which dissimulates evils that can only be cured by exposure, by drawing the attention of every man with a voice to speak, a pen to write, so that the mighty may blush for shame! Vainly did I ask to be shown the Irish quarter; everyone I approached seemed unaware of its existence. Finally I did meet a Frenchman who offered to take me to the three districts I wished to observe.

The visitor cannot venture into Bainbridge Street, that dark and narrow alley, without a feeling of trepidation. Scarcely has he gone ten paces when he is overcome by a foul stench. The alley, entirely taken up by the great coal warehouse, is impassable. On the right we found another alley, this one not even paved and full of nauseating, stagnant pools of greasy, soapy water and other filth.... Oh how difficult it was to overcome my loathing and gather up sufficient courage to proceed through the mire and nastiness! In St Giles one feels asphyxiated by the stench; there is no air to breathe nor daylight to find one's way. The wretched inhabitants must wash their own rags, and they hang them out to dry on poles that stretch from one side of the alley to the other, so that fresh air and sunlight are completely blocked out. Foul odours rise from the mire at your feet, and dirty water drips upon your head from the paupers' rags above. The ravings of a demented imagination could not equal the dreadful reality of such horrors! When I reached the end of the street, which is not very long, I felt my resolve beginning to abandon me; my strength is not equal to my courage; my stomach was churning and my temples throbbed. I was about to give up the idea of venturing any farther into the Irish quarter, when suddenly I remembered that these were human beings, my fellow men, all about me, and that for hundreds of years they had suffered in silence the agony to which, in the space of ten short minutes, my frailty had succumbed! I overcame my distress, the promptings of my heart came to my rescue; and I once again felt up to the task I had set myself, to examine these evils one by one. Oh what ineffable compassion then filled my heart, and what dark terror!

Imagine men, women, children, all barefooted, ploughing through the nasty, filthy mire. Some were leaning against the wall for lack of a place to sit, others were squatting on the ground, there were children lying about in the mud like pigs. No, unless one has seen it with his own eyes, it is impossible to imagine such squalid indigence, such utter debasement, nor a more total degradation of the human creature!

With my own eyes I saw children without a stitch of clothing, young girls, nursing mothers with no shoes on their feet, wearing only a tattered shift which barely covered their naked bodies ... old people huddling for warmth in rotten straw, young men dressed in tatters. Inside and out the decrepit hovels are like the rags of the people who live in them. Neither the windows nor the doors of most of these lodgings can be closed off; floors are mostly bare earth; each one has its old, crudely made oak table, a stool, a wooden bench, a few tin bowls; everyone sleeps in the one room, father, mother, sons, daughters and friends, like so many animals. Such is the comfort of the Irish quarter! It is a dreadful thing to see! And yet it is nothing compared to the expressions on the faces! They all are dismayingly thin, debilitated, sickly; their faces, necks and hands are covered with sores; their skin is so dirty, their hair so filthy and dishevelled that they look like woolly-headed Negroes; their hollow eyes express intense stupor; if you look with authority at these wretches, the assume an obsequious and wheedling look. I recognized the same faces, the same kind of expressions I had seen in prisons. Ah what a happy day it must be for them when they are sent to Coldbath, at least in prison they have white linen, decent clothes, a clean bed and pure air. How do these people earn their living? By prostitution and theft. At the tender age of nine or ten boys go out to steal. At eleven or twelve girls are sold to brothels. All of them, men and women alike, live off of thievery; and old people beg. If I had seen this district before visiting Newgate, I would not have been surprised to learn that fifty to sixty children and as many prostitutes are sent there every month. Theft is the logical consequence of poverty carried to its ultimate limits.

"Ah dear God!" I exclaimed, "how can such evils be remedied?" And as I was thinking about the doctrines of all those British economists, their pronouncements appeared to me written in blood!...

"If the people suffer, they must understand that they themselves are the cause of their suffering. They, and they alone, can remedy them, society can do nothing. When the worker's wages are insufficient to support his family, it is an unmistakable sign that the country needs no new citizens, the king no new subjects." These are the words of Malthus! And he is not alone in thinking thus. Ricardo and the whole English school of economists profess the same principles. Lord Brougham, one of the most relentless of these modern cannibals, has uttered the following words in the House of Lords with the sang-froid of a mathematician: "Since it is not possible to bring subsistence to the level of the needs of the population, it is necessary to bring the population down to the level of subsistence."

Therefore in England, moralists and statesmen, whose words are listened to, can find no other way to save the people from poverty than to prescribe fasting, to forbid marriage and to throw new born children in the sewer. According to them, only the well-to-do should be allowed to marry, and there should be no hospitals for foundlings ...

I came away with a feeling of horror!

"Oh merciful God!" I exclaimed, "what ostentation and what hypocrisy in the ways of this nation, what duplicity in their words!"

"There is less duplicity than you think," said my companion. "Their seemingly austere, disinterested and humanitarian actions and words deceive only foreigners, for whom they are intended, few people here are taken in by them."

"Then it is your opinion that they are false and hypocritical only to impress others? That may very well be. But since I have not been initiated to the great mysteries of their politics, I cannot guess why they make such a display of religion, philanthropy and generosity."

"It is simply to spare themselves the trouble of being fair and humane."

"After what I have seen, I am quite disposed to believe you. However I must also admit that I am almost taken in by their parliamentary oratory, and that, coupled with their contradictory actions, makes it difficult for me to believe they are inspired by the same principle! Take for instance the millions of enslaved Irish and the millions of workers in England and Scotland who receive wages quite insufficient to cover their needs in payment for labours that exceed their strength and shorten their lives; how can this horrible oppression be reconciled with the abolition of the slave trade and the emancipation of the Negro?"

"My dear Lady, any tradesman in the city could answer your question. You know that the products from their colonies and their factories, products which they are clever enough to foist upon the entire world, enable them to squeeze money out of other nations. It is quite obvious that in order to ensure, on European markets, an advantageous price for the products of India and their western colonies, they must arrest the development of subtropical agriculture. To achieve this, there is no other way but to outlaw slave trade among all nations and to run down any ship engaged in it. India has a vast population and the English colonies in America are well-supplied with workers".

"I can easily understand these motives, but I cannot account for the emancipation of their Negroes."

"So, you believe that they freed their slaves in the same manner Christian nations freed their serfs, making them tenant farmers? Oh no! The Jamaican Negroes are, without a doubt, less fortunate than the English factory workers or the Irish peasants because the fruit of their work has more value, but they are not more free. They have been turned into real English proletarians. They are forbidden to own any land, they are required to pay a high rent for the cabin they live in, they have to maintain the roads through statute labour or by taxation, and the theft of a banana is deemed, by the white parish police, just as in England the theft of a few potatoes is judged by the justices of the peace, to be punishable by flogging. Trust the British imagination to create statute labour and taxes, which demand no less work from the Negro than his master used to demand of him before emancipation. Making punishment less arbitrary is certainly an improvement over the slave's fate, but this improvement, which will spur an increase in population, is well calculated to further the interests of property owners."

"It is clear that emancipation of this sort is one of those acts of generosity which benefits its authors, but the government has set aside the sum of six to seven hundred million pounds to that effect."

"Well! that is another secret.... In proposing this type of emancipation, the ministers were sure of the support of English business, because the inhabitants of the colonies, being indebted to the merchants of the mother country for sums equivalent to two-thirds of their property, could only get out from under their obligations by means of the compensation paid them for emancipation. Since only simultaneous emancipation could guarantee that English creditors be paid, the ministers would not have succeeded in getting through the much more economical system. This consisted of gradually paying for Negroes with the work of Negroes already paid for, even though this system would have had the distinct advantage of ensuring the emancipated slaves' moral education and apprenticeship."

In other words, that great humanitarian act, which has been so vaunted for the last thirty years, is nothing but a carefully thought-out commercial scheme, and the whole Continent has been taken in for thirty years. The charlatanism of the honourable gentlemen who make up the British Parliament made people believe in the philanthropy and generosity of a society of *merchants*! Faced with such duplicity, one would be tempted to think that Europe and the entire human race suffer, as do individuals, from attacks of atony, unconsciousness and madness. However, this varnish of hypocrisy gilding their actions is not only intended to impress strangers, they also expect to make the proletarians, whom they thoroughly fleece, whom they squeeze dry in every possible way, whose bread they begrudge, believe themselves to be free. They expect and what a cruel irony it is, that these slaves, bent under their burden, respect and honour their masters. That is why they toss them glittering words like liberty, philanthropy and religion. But the pinnacles of society are not taken in by these pompous protestations of disinterestedness, even though it is in their interest not to appear sceptical about them. Their opinions on any subject, the associations to which they belong, even their least actions, are all determined by their own self-interest; it prompts them to smile at a friend in the street, to vote for war or for peace, for the subjection of the Indians or the emancipation of the Negroes.

There are hundreds of societies in London whose pretentious titles are nothing but so many advertisements directed at such and such a clientele; many of them purport to have a philanthropic purpose. One of them claims to be the champion of all God's creatures and has as its aim to prevent the beating of horses, asses, dogs and other animals. People who are deceived by the title, by the prospectus, might believe in the universal goodwill of the society's members; to be concerned with the well-being of horses, asses and dogs! What might they not do for their own kind!... One more example of charlatanism. The society is made up of horsemen, horse dealers, hunters, carriage owners, enthusiasts;

their aim was to organize a system of surveillance over the servants to whom these animals are entrusted because "He who would travel far must spare his mount."

XI

The Jewish Quarter

Jerusalem sinned grievously,
therefore she became filthy;
all who honoured her despise her,
for they have seen her nakedness;
yea, she herself groans,
and turns her face away.
Her uncleannes was in her skirts;
she took no thought of her doom;
therefore her fall is terrible;
she has no comforter.
All her people groan
as they search for bread;
they trade their treasures for food
to revive their strength.
Is it nothing to you, all you who pass by?
Look and see
if there is any sorrow like my sorrow.

LAMENTATIONS OF JEREMIAH CH. I

Eighteen hundred years have elapsed since Titus captured Jerusalem and the Jews were dispersed; and yet the Jews, with their religious beliefs, their laws and customs, have preserved themselves in the midst of other nations. The Romans and those who destroyed them have come and gone, and these people are still with us! When we compare Moses with all other law-givers, the prodigious longevity of his institutions strikes us with wonder; his revelations have marked the world for all time! Eighteen centuries of fanatical persecutions have changed nothing; the people of Israel have not faltered, they have remained Jewish in the midst of their tribulations and misfortunes as they were in the days of their glory!

Eminently industrious, thrifty, never losing hope, living within nations but beyond the protection of their laws, subject to all sorts of exactions, obtaining justice only as a favour and not as a right, continually obliged to pay for the permission to exist, the Jew has been unable to engage in agriculture and everywhere he has turned to commerce.

Treated everywhere as PARIAHS, everywhere rejected from society, they have formed their own society, and because of their situation, they have had the invaluable advantage of being able to choose their means of existence completely unhindered by any prejudice or other considerations; at the same time, the persecutions to which they were subjected have made them prone to help one another, while their trust in Providence and the waiting for the coming of a *Messiah* gave a divine ideality to an existence steeped in abjection!... and made them endure suffering with a truly religious resignation.

Rich Jews are very charitable towards their coreligionists and live with each other in a more brotherly fashion than is the rule with the various Christian sects.[1]

---

[1] The widow of Nathan Rothschild is admirably charitable toward her coreligionists. She has established in London a school where 500 children from the ages of six to twelve receive the education appropriate to their circumstances; she provides clothing for them and pays for their apprenticeship to masters under whom they are to learn their trade; she also provides layettes and assistance to expectant mothers, and supplies the needs of old people who are helpless or sick. Furthermore, the numerous members of the Rothschild family are distinguished by their generosity and the judiciousness of their charity.

THE JEWISH QUARTER

In London there is a large Jewish population; they are found in all parts of the city; but they are so concentrated in the parish of St Giles that the streets in which they live are referred to by the name of the Jewish quarter.

If, before visiting the Irish quarter, I had gone to the Jewish quarter, the degradation of the people of Moses would have struck me as extreme, but compared to the Irish I had seen, the Jews in London enjoy a prosperous existence.

Jews, in general, are better at buying and selling than the merchants of any nation; but the price they ask for or set is always in proportion, not to the value of the things, but to their knowledge of the people they are dealing with: that is what often gives them the reputation for sharp practice. To tell the truth, there are few merchants who do not do the same whenever they can, unless it is to their advantage to attract customers with the low price of the merchandise. All Jews are very industrious, very clever and always busy. The Jews of St Giles are shoemakers or old-clothes dealers.

The streets of Monmouth, St Giles, etc., are filled with shops where worn out shoes, old rags and old clothes are displayed; the other shops are taken up by dealers in odds and ends, ironmongers and so forth. Oh the sight of the thousands of old worn out shoes, the rags and the rubbish, and all of it making up such an important branch of commerce gives a truer idea of the destitution of the monster city than all the findings and reports that could be published. It makes one shudder! One wonders with dismay who could buy such rags! Who? Have you forgotten that the people of Ireland go naked. That they have never had a pair of shoes, never had a shirt to wear! Heavens! what poverty! How can one bear to think about it...

The ground floor of all the old hovels in this quarter is given over to shops, so that the poor shopkeepers live in the kitchen located in the cellar; to reach it, a steep stairway, or rather a ladder, leads down from the street at so precipitous an angle that I have never seen its like on board the meanest merchant ship. When one walks along the narrow sidewalks of the streets, the sight of these steep ladders makes one giddy. The cellars are all nothing but *kennels* where the hapless people of Israel are crowded pell-mell. In each one can be seen six, seven or eight dirty urchins, thin, gaunt, lying on the bare floor among the old shoes, the filthy rags, and crawling up and down the ladder like the slugs one sees crawling on cellar stairs. What miracle keeps these children from breaking their necks going up and down the stairs a hundred times a day? It is a mystery. Poor creatures! There are thousands of human beings in these cellars, English subjects who speak English and to whom no one pays any attention: one merely says with disdain: "They are Jews ..."

Ah, how convenient it is for egoism in England when it can hide its cruelty under religious prejudice!

However, although this quarter is very dirty, very poor, so distressing to look at, it is nothing compared to Petticoat Lane, the real Jewish quarter, where old clothes are sold.

I remember that while trying to find our way to Petticoat Lane, we inquired of a policeman who said in alarm: "You mustn't go there ...; policemen never set foot in it, and if you were to be attacked, there would be no one to come to your rescue." I shall never forget the worried look on the good policeman's face when he saw that we were determined to pursue our plan and go to Petticoat Lane.

We passed through four or five streets entirely unpaved and full of filth; most of them are so narrow that a carriage cannot get by. But this quarter looks quite different from the Irish quarter: the latter is deserted, depressing and silent; in the former, the crowd is so dense that one cannot move about. There is no air; one cannot breathe; all those shopkeepers are milling about; everyone, men, women, children, have the same expression, one of active cupidity. They all speak at once; this one to praise the merchandise he is trying to sell, that one to denigrate what he is trying to buy; it is all shouting, quarrelling, name-calling, a deafening hubbub.

We saw great heaps of old worn-out clothes! These rags give off such a strong odour that it turned our stomachs we came away from the filthy place with a feeling of nausea.

However, visiting this quarter was less painful to me than

visiting the Irish quarter. The material distress of the Jews is extreme, but it is not as painful to see as that of the Irish; one can tell that the dirty rags which cover them in no way affect their state of mind. The Jew loves money *for its own sake*, not for ostentatious display, it matters little to him if he is ill-dressed, ill-housed, ill-fed, as long as he has a nice little "nest-egg" hidden away or safe from bankruptcy or revolution, that is sufficient for his inner satisfaction. He is happy, not to be thought rich, but to know that he really is so, and that is why the Jews, miserable as they may seem, are courageous, busy and content.

Not far from the market, there is a street where the Jewish prostitutes live; its aspect is so disgusting and so hideous that I must admit, at the risk of being taxed with faint-heartedness, that I did not feel equal to visiting it. I caught sight of five or six women at their windows who were in a state of almost complete undress ... oh, it was really too loathsome!

There are no policemen to make the rounds of this quarter: the poor pariahs are left to their own devices. Theft and murder are not uncommon.

XII

Stolen Scarves

In a country where the desire to make money is uppermost in every mind, where the government itself takes advantage of the ignorance of other governments to get them to sign commercial agreements unfavourable to them and uses violence against the weak in order to extort ruinous concessions from them, it is understandable that scruples must very rarely interfere with a profit to be had without danger, and that even Dr Cumming's "scriptural education" must be quite powerless to overcome the lure of profit. In England money dominates everything: consciences are for sale and the idea of buying cheap and selling dear is common to everyone, therefore the exploitation of ignorance, carelessness, passions, vice, crime, is distasteful to few people. Honest merchants, in consort with the Exchequer, promote drunkenness so as to sell their gin; luxurious gambling houses pay for the sufferance they enjoy, send out their invitations and throw open their rooms to players for rouge et noir, roulette, etc. There are speculators who buy young girls from their parents in order to traffic in their charms; others offer sumptuously appointed retreats for upper class prostitution.

Since, as is well known, there is no Public Prosecutor in England, in a country where impunity can almost always be purchased either by buying off the plaintiff, or with the bail that is put up, or by bribery, it is not at all surprising that buyers can always be found for the fruits of crime, and that the receiving of stolen goods, like similar occupations, enjoys semi-official status.

In London, there is no pawn office similar to the *mont-de-piété*, so pawnbroking is one of the most lucrative businesses; the police exert no control over it; the pawnbroker is not concerned with the nature of your right of ownership of the object that you bring him; he assesses its value, and if within the year you have paid neither principal nor interest, the pledge belongs to him and you cannot claim any further compensation. Stolen jewelry, and many other things as well, are brought to these shops. Finally a great number of individuals, men, women and children, dandies and ragamuffins, go about filching scarves; the harvest is so bountiful that so-called honest merchants specialize in reselling stolen scarves.

Not far from Newgate is a little alley too narrow for carriages, which runs into Holborn Hill and is called Field Lane. It contains nothing but dealers in second-hand scarves. I do not suppose it is necessary to warn the curious traveller, tempted to follow in my footsteps, to leave watch, purse and scarf at home before venturing into Field Lane; for he must assume that the "gentlemen" who frequent the place are light-fingered. This den of thieves is especially interesting to visit at night, it is thronged then, and that is understandable, because buyers and sellers alike are anxious to preserve their anonymity, for, after his purse, nothing is more precious to any businessman than his mask — the reputation he has managed to acquire.

The shops, or rather stalls, display the scarves to passers-by in the street; they hang from a rod, so that buyers may recognize the scarves that were stolen from them. The men and women who offer the scarves for sale, and whose physiognomy is in perfect harmony with the nature of their trade, stand at the doors of their shops and, in a most alarming manner, fight over the customers, who come under cover of night to buy for next to nothing the scarves stolen during the day. There is a great deal of coming and going in the alley. There are prostitutes, children, footpads of all ages, of all shapes, who come to sell scarves. They are taken to the back rooms to discuss the price; as the scarves come in they have their identifying marks removed and are then washed by a servant whose sole and constant occupation it is. Under the pretext of looking for two scarves that had been stolen from us, and of which we were very fond, we visited four or five shops, where we were shown all the scarves that had been brought in in the last five days. There were more than 1,000 of them; and since there are more than twenty shops in the alley, one must conclude that four or five thousand scarves are brought each week to this bazaar of stolen goods. I saw superb scarves at the price of two or three shillings. The trade in Field Lane is as brisk as any in the city, and apparently fortunes are made there.

Forgery, which casts credit in a bad light, theft accompanied by violence, murder, arson and other crimes which imperil safety are the only ones the police try to solve; as for the perpetrators of frauds and swindle, they are hardly ever arrested except when caught in the act.

The administration would have too much to do if it made a point of solving ordinary thefts; it is aware that the law is powerless to put a stop to the numerous thefts due to social conditions, and it turns a blind eye to the concealment of stolen goods so as not to encounter too many culprits; if England did as we do in France, there would not be enough prisons to hold the thieves and receivers of stolen goods, nor enough ships to transport them to Australia.

XIII

Ascot Heath Races

h e usual size of horses is about four feet nine or ten inches. Their legs are slender but the development of their hocks and the pronounced shape of their joints are indicative of great strength and explain the speed which they display; they are slight and tapered of body, their muscles and even their veins can be clearly seen through the thinness of their hide with its extremely short and smooth coat. Race horses are fed rather sparingly. Their stomachs, and consequently their bony structure, particularly that of the trunk, are not very developed. The movement imparted to the muscles by the stresses of racing give to their muscular parts a relief that is accentuated by a complete absence of fat.

In order to bring overly heavy jockeys down to the proper weight, a substantial but not copious nourishment is accompanied by frequent purging, exercise under heavy wraps to promote perspiration, and a number of other such precautions.

Baron d'Haussez, LA GRANDE BRETAGNE

In France, and in any country with some pretentions to courtesy, the most revered being in creation is woman; in England it is the horse. In these happy isles the horse is king! Not only does he take precedence over woman, but over man as well.

The best known races are Newmarket, Epsom and Ascot Heath; I am familiar only with the last two.

In England races are great events which assume in the eyes of the beholder the character of a solemn rite. The Ascot races are held during the last three days in May; for the people of London and its environs they are what the august ceremonies of Rome's Holy Week are for Catholics, or what the last three days of carnival are for Parisians.

The great holiday exercises a universal appeal for the English of whatever sex, age or station. Everyone goes to some expense in order to cut a decent figure during the three days; ladies of the upper aristocracy send off to Paris for the latest and most elegant gowns; lords, financiers, the wealthy, the fashionable, dandies all, order luxurious carriages, buy new horses and dress their servants in new livery. The city's merchants close up shop, hire a carriage and forsake business for the races. Courtesans, decked out in their finest array, queen it in fine coupés drawn by four horses preceded by two jockeys, and the jockeys are distinguished by the colour of their jackets: red, yellow, green, blue, etc., but each wears the costume which is *de rigueur*: white buckskin breeches, top-boots, little hunting caps; even the lowest of prostitutes, though she be obliged to pawn her only chemise, manages to buy new shoes, gloves, a frock and bonnet for the great day. Frugal women who have deprived themselves all winter of the bare necessities, will, in order to go to the races, spend all their meagre savings with a lavishness bordering on extravagance.

Frivolous ladies in Paris may imagine that the Ascot races are outings no different from our own Longchamp, where the ground is sprinkled with water so that the dust will not spoil the ladies' finery, and that English ladies, comfortably seated on chairs, have nothing more tiring to do than to allow themselves to be admired. No, in England that is not how it happens.

Ascot is thirty miles from London, and, as the first race begins usually at noon, devotees must leave London at four, five or six o'clock in the morning in order to arrive in time. There is only one route to Ascot, and from four o'clock in the morning till noon or one o'clock, more than 3,000 vehicles of every sort throng the one road. For the most part the road is quite wide; however in spots it is extremely narrow; there are several bridges and a number of toll-gates; on these occasions everyone goes in single file. The road is sandy, and as it had rained the day before I attended the races, the road was badly rutted in spots. After we passed through Windsor, the wheels sank into quick sand having the consistency of ashes; yet extraordinary as it may seem, in spite of the hazards of the road and the jumble of vehicles, there was never the slightest hint of disorder, nor did I hear of a single spill.

The English, one must admit, have a special instinct for driving horses; moreover they are trained to observe order in the streets, roads and in crowds, and they do so with the rigorous discipline of a Prussian regiment on parade. The respect for order, which is found in no other nation, also has something to do with the nature of their government; in England there is a hierarchy in everything, even down to the vehicles on the public roads. Carriages painted with a coat of arms take precedence over all others, middle-class carriages with four horses have precedence over those with only two, the latter over cabriolets and tilburys, hired landaus over coaches, coaches over omnibuses, omnibuses over cabs, and so on and so forth down to the trap, and even it has the right of way over the cart. There you have the secret of all this admirable orderliness. Everyone has his place! Now the reader is no doubt curious to know what the occupants of 3,000 vehicles, all these people of every class, were saying and doing. We French would expect them to be gay, to talk, to sing, to provoke one another with remarks of varying degrees of wit, as happens at the St Cloud fairs: not so. The ladies of the upper aristocracy, magnificently dressed, were lolling deep in their carriages and seemed perfectly indifferent to what was going on about them; some of them were reading novels. The young dandies were smoking cigars; the financiers were drinking champagne at little tables set up in their carriages; the middle classes, crowded into and on top of coaches and other public conveyances, were travelling side by side without uttering a word; the lower classes, stuffed willy-nilly in great covered charabancs, were playing cards and drinking beer; and finally the small landowners and farmers in their tilburys, cabriolets, carts, etc., were concentrating on their driving; so it was that in the midst of that crowd of people, horses and vehicles, silence reigned.

From time to time, however, one would hear the voices of coachmen hurling coarse insults at one another, each accusing the other of their mutual carelessness, or berating one another for their insolence in trying to get ahead of the other; but their words, uttered without feeling, without anger, did not presage any serious dispute; their meaning was contradicted by the phlegmatic and monotonous inflection with which they were spoken. I was dumfounded! I could not help but reflect that, if similar races were being held in France, three companies of mounted gendarmes would not suffice to maintain order among the 3,000 vehicles. What quarrels, what disputes, what battles among coachmen; how many horses would be lamed and how many carriages turned over! What singing, what laughing, what shouting would be heard from my boisterous compatriots if forty or fifty thousand of them were to travel the road from Paris to Pontoise between four o'clock in the morning and noon! Yes, but their excitability, the ease with which they are moved to enthusiasm, can transform Parisians into heroes. Any people who have brought about a revolution in three days would not stand for having their bread measured out to them! While English workers endure poverty and suffer from hunger, the English aristocracy peacefully enjoy their country houses, their fine carriages and their race-horses...

The English climate makes any outing, if not impossible, at least very difficult. In the morning, when we left, the fog was thick, damp and cold; toward eleven o'clock the sun came out; it soon became bright enough to blind those travellers perched on top of the coaches (where the majority were, and I among them), and to dry out the ground: then there arose from the dirt road, trampled by so many thousands of horses, an endless cloud of dust so thick that it was impossible to see anything ten feet away. Upon leaving Windsor Park, we were completely swallowed up in the cloud of dust. I had never before seen anything like it.

We arrived at Ascot at half past noon; there were already an enormous number of carriages; they were all drawn up in a horseshoe around the place where the horses were to race, and in the arrangement of the carriages the same hierarchy was scrupulously observed. Policemen had been posted at intervals of ten feet, and they were seeing to it that the horses were unharnessed as soon as the carriages arrived and that each vehicle was put in its proper place according to its class and in such a way as to take up the least possible room.

The spot where the races and the festivity are held is quite spacious, it is on high ground and affords a magnificent panorama.

The area set aside for the horses, the heroes of the event, was surrounded by ropes supported on posts set at intervals; but between races the public was free to walk about in the list. There must have been fifty or sixty thousand people gathered there, perhaps even more, for they were spread out over such a large area that it was difficult to assess their number.

The spectacle of the crowd was quite different from that presented by Parisian crowds on the Champs-Elysées or the Champ de Mars; silence reigned; no music, no dancing, no entertainments, no acrobat with his bass drum, no monsters nor living curiosities displaying themselves to savants for the sum of four pence; no cake shops or toy vendors, no children with paper whistles; in short none of those things to be seen at our fairs. But on the other hand, I saw in one spot on the vast grounds twenty-five or thirty tents on which was painted in large red letters: ROULETTE PLAYED HERE.[1] Moreover, every twenty feet there were roving bankers with little folding tables just one

---

[1] Roulette bankers also indicate on their tents the name of the London club for which they are agents, so that players will, as necessary, accept their paper as money.

foot square, on which there were three thimbles and a pea; a crowd was invariably gathered around these little tables, and the stakes were high. I saw a young countryman lose as much as six pounds on a single bet. Games of chance are strictly forbidden by law, and yet they flourish openly through the connivance and corruption of the agents responsible for enforcing the law. I truly wonder if it would not be better to sell poison to the people, to treat them like Chinamen, than to instil in them a passion which gives them an aversion for work and predisposes them to all sorts of acts hostile to society.

In the present state of societies, gambling, confined to the wealthy classes, is nevertheless a necessary instrument for the redistribution of wealth which social forces tend constantly to accumulate. Not only do I consider the financial ruin of men of independent means, living in idleness and luxury, to be advantageous to society; I can not so much as imagine a single instance when the accumulation of wealth in the hands of one individual would be useful to society. For large undertakings men can always combine their capital as well as their forces, and accumulated wealth which dispenses a man from the necessity to work corrupts him and is the greatest of society's calamities.

They are off! six neck and neck: exclamations are heard on every side. Oh, what a speedy racer! prodigious rapidity indeed! astonishing! wonderful! astonishing! wonderful! wonderful!

I fully expect to find myself at odds with the opinion of most people, but at the risk of appearing to be a barbarian in the eyes of connoisseurs, unworthy of setting foot in a stable, I must admit that English horses are not the least bit to my liking.

The horse without doubt is one of the beautiful animals in creation, but domestication does alter the beauty of its forms, and the English have, more than any other people, bred out nature's graceful lines. Please take note, gentlemen, that I am speaking as an artist, as a passionate lover of beauty, without taking into account those qualities which you require. When one sees an English race horse with its long, narrow, thin, gaunt body, its disproportionately long legs, its outstretched neck with the head always thrust forward, its nostrils flared like those of a large

ASCOT HEATH RACES

hunting dog; when one sees their unvaryingly sad, dismal and stupid expressions, if one has any sense of harmony, any feeling for form, one really cannot help but say: "There goes an ugly animal indeed!"

Arabian horses, Andalusian horses, Chilean horses are divine creatures! They combine everything: elegance and grace, strength and agility, suppleness and vigour of movement, beauty of coat and purity of line, liveliness of expression and fiery eye. At the sight of one of these horses, whether in repose, at a trot or galloping at full speed, everyone is moved to cry: "Oh, what a superb animal!"

But, you will object, the purpose of the English horse is not to appear beautiful, graceful, pleasing to the eye; it is bred for the harness or for racing: it is made for running. Poor beast! they have ignored God's design; you are their creation. How the wretches have treated you! They have robbed you of your mane and your tail; they have deformed you, destroyed several of your faculties in order to exaggerate others; you are now nothing more than a stunted thing; your origins are lost: poor beast! how they have debased you! They have reduced you to nothing but a machine for locomotion, or a roulette wheel whose speed determines the loser or the winner. Poor beast! wicked men!

Jockeys are people of importance. Their talent, as much as the horses' legs, determines the outcome of the race. It is interesting to see how carefully and warily the punters examine the horses and jockeys; for, in this under-handed game, trickery is common, and grooms and jockeys are past-masters at it.[1] The punters inspect the horses' feet, mouth, belly and ears; then they proceed to the jockeys whom they question, analysing their replies.

The horses are designated by the colour of the jackets worn by the jockeys who are riding them; when I saw vast sums being bet on the red jacket or the black, I was reminded of gambling

---

[1] They use various means, I was assured, to prevent a horse from running with its accustomed superiority; they weaken it by administering drugs, bind one of the legs tightly with a silk cord hidden by the hair, or the jockey may ride the horse in such a way as to fall behind.

houses, but their games of chance struck me as less immoral, for they do not endanger the lives of horses and men. It seems to me that race horses could advantageously be replaced with velocipedes which would serve the same purpose for the gamblers without subjecting the rider to danger.

There were five races with eight, six, four and two horses; and the enjoyment is of very short duration: a few minutes at most for each race.

And now, let us turn our attention back to the crowd. At first the fashionable set headed for the pavilion where the Queen and the Grand Duke of Russia were; then after walking about for a few moments, they went to the tents to play roulette, and the common people played at three dice with the strolling bankers.

But whatever the pleasure afforded by roulette, three dice and the horses, the crowd's greatest pleasure was in eating and drinking.

All those fine ladies in silken gowns of pink, blue, yellow, green, etc.,[1] eating enormous pieces of ham, cold beef, pies and other such dishes off their laps, along with generous libations of port, sherry and champagne were for me a spectacle as curious as it was novel. The races lasted about three hours, and I saw barouches where the eating and drinking went on for three hours!

I kept waiting for the moment of gaiety ... but it never came. I saw women taken ill; others asleep; men with loosened tongues, and others, even more disgustingly overcome with drink, no longer able to stand upright; but it was all lifeless, dull and revolting. So much for the wealthy class: as for the people, they gathered in tents set up expressly for the three days. Poor people! They are not a pretty sight in their rags. The tents were very small, airless, dim and ill-lit; the men sat at crude wooden tables eating bacon and black bread (made with bran), drinking beer or gin and smoking abominable tobacco! There was dancing in some of the tents; the women who were dancing were prostitutes

---

[1] In general, English ladies are very fond of gaudy colours; at large gatherings one is particularly aware of how prevalent is their taste for them.

of low degree; in England there is no amusement for the wives and daughters of workers.

At the Ascot races I noticed an enormous number of gipsies telling fortunes with great success, particularly among the common people. Gipsies are found in every country on the surface of our ancient globe, living off begging, thievery and cunning; and their existence is more inexplicable than that of the Jews, since the latter work, whereas the gipsies refuse to subject themselves to any sort of work and flourish everywhere. Their wandering nation has preserved intact, even more so than the Jews, its primitive character. I saw whole families there, with their dark and swarthy skin, straight and oily black hair, white teeth, and eyes full of melancholy fire. They wore the costume of their ancestors, whose language they also spoke among themselves. I am told that the language is the same spoken by all tribes of gipsies in Europe, Asia and Africa. One of the women came up to me to tell my fortune; she was a pretty girl of seventeen, another Esmeralda, with the slender foot of a Peruvian lady, a supple and delicate figure, small hands and a voluptuous voice. The women are reputed to be chaste: an Englishman told me that he had offered one of the girls forty pounds sterling to spend the night with her; she refused. The gipsy children were almost naked.

Finally, toward six o'clock, the carriages began to set out. I thought the confusion would be frightful! Not at all. Everything proceeded with the same order as in the morning; the policemen had the horses harnessed to the first ranking carriages; the coachmen judged too drunk to drive were removed from their seats and replaced. Those people who were drunk were put inside the carriages, those who were only half-drunk were put on top, but between two people, so that they would not fall off, and all went their way in a cloud of dust so thick one could not see one's neighbour.

We arrived in London at one o'clock in the morning, having left more than a third of the carriages behind us. It was extremely cold, the fog was thick and the dampness penetrating: we were chilled to the bone.

It was truly a pity to see all those ladies, who that morning were so neatly, so elegantly turned out, coming home covered with dust, dirty and completely unrecognizable.

In England, a celebration of this sort is called a "pleasure" trip.

XIV

Bethlehem

The soul, dreams, madness, tell me, great philosopher, how do you explain them?

CHINESE SAYINGS, ASIATIC RESEARCHES

The organic disturbance which gives rise to madness is the result of physical or psychological causes. Heat or cold at high degrees of intensity is capable, it is said, of upsetting certain systems in the brain. Excessive drinking, an overdose of mercury, accidents, sickness can also induce derangement; but in general it is due to psychological causes. As long as man continues to put all his trust in the power of his reason, in the affection of his loved ones, and to disregard the subordination of all things to the universal order, frustration will continue to destroy man's vainglorious intelligence, which seeks to dethrone Providence, and man's heart, which shuts out God!

It would be interesting to see statistics concerning the number of insane in each country, in proportion to the population; it would surely show that the more a people is inclined, by its religion and its philosophy, to resignation, the fewer madmen there are in its midst; whereas those peoples who by reason govern their religious beliefs and their conduct in life are those among whom one finds the greatest number of insane. "God is

Great!" cries the Islamite in the wake of an event; and there are very few madmen among those peoples who do not recognize the authority of human reason.

It is generally accepted that England is the country with the greatest number of insane; it is also the home of the greatest excesses of every type and it is the country where free inquiry gives rise to the greatest number of religious and philosophical sects. Innumerable are the private establishments to be found in London in which madmen are kept and cared for in return for a fee. All of these establishments are, in general, well run. I will confine my remarks to the best known public hospital, Bethlehem.

I visited it in the company of Mr Holm, one of the most famous phrenologists of England; and Mrs Wheeler, the only woman socialist I have encountered in London. Both of them take great interest in the phenomena of madness, and through them I was able to obtain precise information about all the more unusual cases.

Henry VIII was the first king to found a London hospital for the insane, in the priory of St Mary of Bethlehem, in Moorfield, and in 1675 a vast hospital, a faithful reproduction of the façade of the Tuileries, was built on the same site. Demolished in 1812, it was replaced by the present hospital, built in 1814 in the extremely salubrious Georgefield area. The building's handsome façade offers a central portico embellished with six doric columns. The building and its grounds cover approximately twelve acres.

The entrance to the hospital presents a cheerful aspect: its handsome gate, the large lawn, the beds of flowers have all been devised to deceive the deranged wretch at his arrival; he thinks he is entering one of the palatial country houses of the rich; he proceeds without misgivings and of his own accord goes to be shut up in the sad abode of madness.

There are two statues in the vestibule, *Raving Madness* and *Melancholy*, by Caius Cibber. The two statues, which adorned the entrance to the previous building are so forcefully executed that it was deemed necessary to remove them from public view. The sight of them produced a most painful impression upon visitors, friends or family of the insane, to the house, and on several occasions the statues excited calm and peaceful madmen to violence, with unfortunate consequences. To prevent further incidents, they have been covered over with a drapery which entirely hides them from view, and only those visitors judged capable of withstanding the effects of gazing upon them are allowed to see them.

Bethlehem is enormous. It can contain 700 patients; at the time it harboured only 422, of whom 177 were women. The entire building is kept scrupulously clean. The patients are well-nourished; some doctors think they are even too well-fed. The administration gives scant attention to clothing the madmen: they wear the clothes they brought with them and which are often reduced to rags without anyone's appearing to think of mending them.

The yards where the madmen take exercise are like those of a prison; neither tree nor greenery to please the eye nor to suggest sweet thoughts of country tranquillity; most of the yards are devoid of any sort of shelter from the sun or rain. The poor lunatic, whose heart is embittered and whose brain seethes with baneful schemes is reminded, by all he sees around him, of his captivity, which he considers a monstrous injustice. Oh what lack of foresight in the design of the place—or what cruelty.

Among the madwomen there were thirty or so who had committed crimes. They were lodged in a separate building. I confess that I could not discern even the slightest difference between these madwomen and the criminals I had seen at Newgate, Coldbath Fields or the Penitentiary. They had the same wild and haggard eyes, exhibited the same mournful silence, the same feverish preoccupation and bore upon their faces the same stamp of stupidity. Several had murdered, others had stolen. From there we went to the men's hall.

There I was to have one of those bizarre, extraordinary encounters which, I believe, happen only to me. One of the gentlemen in our company spoke French quite well; he said to me, before we had reached the first yard: "We have one of your compatriots here; his madness is unusual, he thinks he is God."

Not so unusual, I thought; after all, what hospital could possibly be big enough to hold all those who believe, as he does, that they are infallible! "During the five months he has been at Bethlehem," my Cicerone continued, "he has been frequently observed to pass abruptly from a state of excitement bordering on rage to one of lucidity; at such times he thinks quite clearly. He used to be a seaman, has seen the world, speaks all the languages and seems to have been a man of excellent capacities." "What is his name?" I asked. "Chabrié". "Chabrié!!...." I cannot describe the effect produced upon me by that name; I could not ascertain exactly what I felt. Joy? Pain? Surprise? Anxiety? Nonetheless I did not hesitate before entering the yard where I was to see Chabrié again!... I was impatient for the meeting; it was as if God had inspired me with the idea of coming to London in order to save the unfortunate Chabrié![1]

Once inside the long corridor leading to the main yard, I looked eagerly this way and that among the unfortunate inmates milling about in the corridor, searching for the man who had loved me with such purity and such devotion. My agitation betrayed my inner turmoil, and the hospital's officer pointed out a man sitting alone on a bench, saying: "There he is, there is Chabrié." It was not the captain of the *Mexicain*.... It occurred to me that the French name had been improperly pronounced; I asked the officer to write it out for me, and I saw that the name I had been given was pronounced the same, but spelled with an *r* at the end.

Nevertheless, it was with an intense feeling of concern that I examined this other Chabrier; his features, his face, his dress, his actions were in sharp contrast with the expressions of those around him. The man looked at me with his large, bright, dark

---

[1] This passage is incomprehensible to anyone who has not read my *Pérégrinations*. After I wrote it, Monsieur Chabrié left once again for Peru on board the *Amérique* which was his ship, and the unfortunate man perished. At least it is supposed, in the absence of any news, that he sank in the open sea, but it is not known for certain. That explains why, upon discovering a French seaman bearing the same name, in Bethlehem Hospital, I could for a fleeting moment entertain the belief that it was in truth the unfortunate Chabrié, captain of the *Mexicain*.

eyes; his handsome Latin face lit up with a smile of joy, of happiness, and he brightened like a sombre valley struck by the rays of the sun. He approached me and bowed with the courtesy and naturalness which characterize the well-mannered man. He said in French: "Oh! Mademoiselle, how pleased I am to encounter at last a compatriot! a woman! We speak the same language and I can convey to you my suffering! I can tell you of all the pain which afflicts me in this asylum of misery, where I am shut up by the most odious of injustices."

He followed me into the yard where the lunatics were gathered; I had eyes for no one but him. He spoke for more than half an hour, so sensibly, so reasonably, with such penetrating observations, such profound reflexions, that I truly believed he was not mad. I was obliged to take leave of him in order to continue my inspection of the hospital, but I promised to see him again on my return.

Just as I had done on the women's side, I saw stamped on the faces of most of the criminally insane the same expression as on the faces of the criminals at Newgate; there are three or four exceptions who deserve special mention.

There was James Hadfield, the madman who had tried to kill George IV by throwing a rock at his head; he has been there for twenty-two years. I do not know if he ever was really what is meant by the word mad, but his actions and his speech today betray no trace of madness. He lives in a small room and he is not averse to passing the time of day with visitors. We had rather a long visit with him; his conversation and his habits denote a sentimental and loving heart, a pressing need for affection, he has had in succession two dogs, three cats, several birds and finally a squirrel. He was extremely fond of his animals and was grieved at their deaths; he mounted them himself and keeps them in his room. These remains of his beloved animals all have epitaphs in verse which express his sorrow. Above the verses for his squirrel there is a coloured image of the friend he lost. I might add that he does a brisk little trade with his feelings, handing out the epitaphs to visitors who in return give him a few shillings. Besides James Hadfield, a kindly, amiable and talkative old man, there are the two "Queen's lovers". One is a young man of twenty-two who laughs and runs away when asked if he is still in love with his "betrothed". The other is a man of thirty, with the head and neck of a bull; as he is violent, we saw him only through the bars of his room.

While I was inspecting Bethlehem, poor Chabrier had worked himself up into a state of excitement. He was waiting for me behind the bars of the door to the corridor; his movements, his agitation were indicative of keen impatience; his eyes were bright, his voice full of emotion; he was trembling in every limb. "Oh! my dear sister," he said to me in a voice which might have been that of an angel addressing his brethen, "it is God who has brought you here to this place of desolation, not to save me, for I must perish here, but to save the idea which I have come to bring to the world! Listen! You know that I am the representative of your God, I am the Messiah foretold by Jesus Christ. I have come to complete the task he set. I am here to bring an end to all forms of slavery, to free woman from enslavement to man, the poor from enslavement to the rich, the soul from enslavement to sin."

Chabrier's speech did not, to my mind, denote madness; Jesus, Saint-Simon, Fourier had all spoken in this way. "Here", he said to me, "I bear on my breast the sign of my mission." Whereupon, unbuttoning his coat, he drew forth a large cross which he had fashioned of straw from his bed and wool unravelled from his blanket. I was still uncertain as to his condition when suddenly, casting a dreadful look at Mrs Wheeler, he said, with the voice and appearance of madness: "That woman is English; she embodies matter, corruption, sin: out, ungodly woman! You are the one; you have murdered me! Arrest that woman! Sister, she is the one who has murdered your God! You are under arrest!" he cried, throwing himself upon her, "You are under arrest in the name of the new law!"

Mrs Wheeler was greatly frightened and fled. I too was somewhat less than reassured.

"My dear sister," he said to me, "I am going to bestow upon you the sign of redemption because I deem you worthy of it!"

BETHLEHEM (BEDLAM)

The poor man had around his neck a dozen crosses made of straw, wound about with black crêpe and a red ribbon. They bore the words: "Mourning and blood". He took off one of them and gave it to me saying: "Take this cross, wear it upon your breast and spread the new law abroad in the world." He knelt on one knee and took my hand in a crushing grip, repeating all the while: "Dry your tears, sister, soon the reign of God will supplant the reign of the devil!"

The guards were extremely worried; they wanted to pry open his hand by force to make him let me go, but I would not have them provoke him; I sensed that he would do me no harm. I politely asked him to let go of my hand; he obeyed without resisting and prostrated himself at my feet, kissed the hem of my dress, saying over and over in a voice choked by tears and sobs: "Oh woman, woman is the image of the Virgin on earth and men do not know her! They humiliate her ... they drag her through the dirt."

I made my escape. I too was weeping. The poor man! How he must suffer when he comes back to his senses. When I passed by again at the end of the corridor, I peered in past the dividing bar to see what he was doing. He was still in the same spot, kneeling, hands clasped, bowed down, gazing at his large cross lying in front of him on the floor. Ah, in that attitude, he was truly beautiful. I might have been looking upon a new St John.

Is that man really mad? Everything he said to me is indicative of a man whose head is filled with social, political and religious ideas and whose heart is overflowing with love of his fellow creature. His soul rebels at the sight of baseness, corruption, hypocrisy, and he cannot contain his holy indignation. I saw that he was very impassioned, but I could not discern the mark of insanity. The spark of genius shown in his words. There was hatred, of course, for his persecutors, but his discourse was logical, and I had no difficulty in following the order of ideas which inspired it.

What an extraordinary thing! With four hundred madmen shut up in Bethlehem, one Frenchman has been admitted, as a special favour, and that Frenchman thinks he is the Messiah, calls himself God's representative and speaks in the name of the new law![1]

The things I related above were told to me by persons whose trustworthiness is not to be doubted. Monsieur Chabrier was too absolute in his opinions and his zeal too tempestuous, but his ideas are, at bottom, incontrovertible. The decline of the Bible was announced by Christ. If it had not even then outlived its usefulness as a social and moral code, how then explain the success of Christianity and, six centuries later, the success of Mohammedism?

Monsieur Chabrier is from Marseille. The director of Bethlehem told me that he had written to the mayor of Marseille and to Madame Chabrier. Why no one has come to claim the unfortunate man is inexplicable. There he is, alone in London, abandoned and at the mercy of strangers. Could Monsieur Chabrier's family have some reason or other which might excuse such cruel behaviour?...

---

[1] I was told at Bethlehem that, before coming there, Mr Chabrier used to write constantly and that he treated the most serious questions; but it was particularly on religious doctrines that he emitted significant philosophical and social ideas. His arrest as a madman was brought on by a great scandal.

He was living in a small hotel in the city.

One Sunday, as everyone was absorbed in reading the Holy Bible, Monsieur Chabrier was strolling in the parlour; all at once he stopped in front of the lady of the house and interrupted her devout reading to inquire what she ordinarily did with her old brooms when they became too worn out to be of further use. The English woman, astonished at such a question, replied that she used them to kindle the fire. "And why do you not save them?" "Why, because they would clutter the house to no purpose." "Then, woman, do with the old law as you do with old brooms: throw it into the fire and henceforth let there be no place in your mind for ideas which, albeit good in their day, today have outlived their usefulness." Whereupon he seized the Bible the woman was holding and threw it into the fire.

The episode caused a great scandal: there was very nearly a riot in the neighbourhood. The fanatical were all for laying hands upon the heathen; but the "madman" overawed the crowd, both through the power of his gaze and the strength of his arm; no one dared to touch a hair on his head.

XV

English Drama

Rest assured, it is not dramatic talent that our age lacks, it is a public of common moral beliefs upon which one can securely build.

Hippolyte Fortoll, REVUE DE PARIS

The greatest drama for man is man himself! And knowledge of man can be arrived at only through knowledge of one's self. When we have arrived at such self-knowledge, which instantaneously reveals to us the motives of our actions, then we see not only our passions but also the most hidden tendencies of our hearts, the aspirations whose existence we recognize in our souls, reflected both in historical narrations and in the events which happen around us; then everything is of interest to us, everything takes life and breathes with our own breath.

"Bread and circuses!..." All mankind repeats the Romans' cry. Great inspiration, strong emotion, the process of thought correspond respectively to the soul, the heart and the mind, which, like the body, are in need of sustenance. We all seek to be moved and to move others. Emotion spurs thought, and thought has no power except through the emotion it inspires. All that can inspire feeling and thought is therefore reproduced by art; that is why dramatic representations have been common to all peoples, whatever the level of civilization they may have attained. The man incapable of comprehending the sermon from the pulpit or the speech from the rostrum will be deeply moved by misfortune's thoughts, grief's tears and passion's cries. How indeed can the written word or its translation upon the canvas compare with the spoken word!... Does the human voice even require the meaning of words to make itself understood? Does it not assign to them whatever value it desires? And is not gesture, like speech, an inspired language which we no more learn than we do the expressions reflected in our features? If painting reproduces forms and colours, the countryside and its animals, men and their habitations, if it renders the physiognomy proper to each individual and the impression with which he is affected; if music excites every passion, delights, enraptures, lifts us toward God, plunges us to earth and resounds to the very heavens; if it is beyond doubt that the signs created by the mind to represent thought make up the most powerful of languages, then that art which makes use of all these means together must act with irresistible force!

There is nothing new under the sun. In the art of drama, the plot is borrowed from history, adventure and contemporary deeds. As the past recedes, details fade; the principal actors of the events, the immediate causes of great changes, alone remain. Awe-inspiring in the midst of the ruins, they subsist, like the arches, columns, remains of temples and theatres bearing the names of Caesar, Augustus, Titus or Trajan. Thus historical figures are endowed by time with the capacity to personify passions larger than life, and to show us souls in control of their passions, because the passing of time effaces whatever is vulgar in passions or base in the soul.

In England, in the sixteenth century, there appeared William Shakespeare. He was great among dramatists. Around him Marlowe, Massinger, Johnson and Shirley fed upon his genius and drew life from his greatness. The generation which had admired him was long dead when his works crossed the Channel, and an astonished Europe placed him among the select geniuses of that great period of renewal. The motivating thought hummed simultaneously in several minds. Hamlet's "To be or not to Be?", Montaigne's "Que Sais-je?" characterize the period of doubt when the ancient philosophies confronted Christian dogma; when pagan gods played their parts in poetry, drama and painting along with the saints of legend; when the Sibyls were represented alongside the prophets, Mercury in the company of cardinals, the Angel Gabriel with Cupid, and the Virgin with Minerva or Venus.

Shakespeare offers striking proof that genius is independent of merely "bookish" learning; and that he is gifted with genius which knows how to read the great book of nature. Shakespeare's knowledge went no further than his own language. His country's chronicles and Plutarch translated by B. Johnson furnished him with characters for his tragedies, costumes, and the stamp of the times; his observations provided him with "types", but nature and his heart were the inexhaustible sources his intelligence drew upon for the psychological development of his characters; and when he introduces comic figures on the stage, the spectator immediately recognizes them as true to life. Essentially a painter of the soul, he is not much concerned with nicety of form; carried away by his verve he amasses a profusion of sketchily-drawn details and accessories. One may suppose that had he lived in a more recent age, the construction of his plays would have been less irregular, the plots would have unfolded systematically, entrances and exits would always have been motivated; but freedom of action is too vital to his genius for anyone to suppose that he could have born the yoke of the three unities and endowed his characters with a pure and poetic language if Queen Elizabeth's court had imposed its shackles upon him.

Until the time of Charles II, Shakespeare's shadow lies across the English stage; the plays that are performed abound in comic figures; they are loaded down with incidents and characters together with frequent changes of scene; the language is full of puns and obscenities; in short it is the prolongation of Shakespeare's manner, all that can be copied from genius: the form, the accessories, but without the psychological truth, without the life-giving verisimilitude.

Under Charles II, comedies of adventure appeared; the licentiousness of the court was reflected on the stage; there are scenes and dialogues in the plays of the period which shock all notions of dramatic propriety because of their extreme cynicism. It is remarkable that, in spite of present-day hypocrisy, in spite of the fact that prudishness in language is pushed to the point of absurdity, modern comedies are hardly less indecent than those presented under the Stuarts, unless they be translations or imitations from other literatures; one has only to read the plays of Sheridan: *A Trip to Scarborough*, *The School for Scandal*, *The Belle's Stratagem*,[1] etc. One is forced to conclude that in England the contradiction between drama and society is only an apparent one, and that the public would not tolerate such loose representations if the manners they depict did not exist somewhere.

It was also at this time that French plays began to invade the English stage; first the masterpieces, then any that had been more or less successful. The egotism of English writers is so prodigious that not one has ever confessed that the play he had written was a translation. Addison himself, in his critical analysis of the tragedy entitled *The Distressed Mother*, which he praises with exquisite feeling for the art, does not see fit to inform his readers that it is translated *word for word* from Racine's *Andromaque*.

In the reign of Queen Anne the example set by the Continent and the influence of classical studies introduced to the English stage drama constructed according to Aristotelian rules; Addison's *Cato* was the model for this academic type of drama which was only partly successful; it was in opposition to the taste that habit had created, for, whereas the English in their novels treat every impulse of the human heart with painstaking accuracy, they require dramas with two or three plots and quantities of characters; their writers have often included two French plays in a single one of their bizarre dramatic constructions.

---

[1]The author is perhaps thinking of Farquahar's *The Beaux Stratagem* (Translators).

The theatre has on the whole had a great deal of influence on modern nations, principally in the great cities of Southern Europe. In France especially, it has had a profound effect on manners; French drama does not confine itself to reproducing manners, it judges them, and its censure has been a powerful impetus to reform. Its lessons are without a doubt the cause of that charming Parisian urbanity, unexampled in any other peoples.

In France, there has always been a quantity of intermediate levels of existence between the poor and the rich. The castes have never been so separated that the manners of one were unknown to the other. In England the change from opulence to poverty is abrupt. The landed aristocracy and the mercantile elite each form an isolated society, separated by an iron wall from the ninety-five per cent of the population living in poverty. The theatre-going public is thus less numerous than on the Continent, and much less homogeneous. What goes on in West End drawing-rooms or lordly manors interests the spectator in the upper gallery only in so far as it satisfies his curiosity; it no more resembles manners within his family than would a picture of French life, and the dramatic interest is therefore nonexistent; that is why the theatre has had no influence on the people's way of life.

In France, starting with Corneille, there is an uninterrupted succession of dramatists. Since Shakespeare, England has not produced a single one worthy of being presented to literary Europe. It has never had a Molière to portray the avarice, jealousy and despotism of a Géronte, nor to ridicule the Tartuffes which the English soil produces in such abundance. If one examines the dramatic career of English writers after Shakespeare, one sees them striving to excite the highest possible degree of curiosity and, in order to do so, resorting to every possible device, every conceivable piece of stage machinery; some of the plays are as crowded with events as a tale from the *Thousand and one Nights*; but rarely does one encounter, along with a portrayal of the manners of the period, any dramatic interest. The dialogue in these plays is rapid and spasmodic; puns and witticisms are introduced through questions and answers;

otherwise there are no conversations which depict the characters or manners of the times. In English plays, everything is in motion; they are nothing but more or less scandalous adventures acted out, and Sheridan is no more an exception than Vanburgh or Falquier.[1]

The common people in England have always been in such an abject state that the portrayal of their manners would have shocked the theatre-going public. That public is currently composed principally of those who have grown rich in commerce and who are no less disdainful of the common people than are the aristocracy. As for the spectators in the upper gallery, artisans and seamen for the most part, they make up too small a minority in the hall for their wishes to have any impact on the theatre.

The working class in England, like the slaves in the nations of antiquity, is beyond the pale of social life; yet in the Greek and Latin dramas which have come down to us we see slaves play more important roles than do common people in English plays. In this country, relations between masters and servants are so different from what they are in France that it would not be possible to put on the English stage the valets, soubrettes and villagers of French comedies. In England one does not speak to servants and subordinates except to give them orders; certainly no thought is given to their joys or to their sorrows; one is infinitely more solicitous of one's horse or dog, and the impious pride of the aristocracy with regard to their helots has filtered down to the newly rich plebeian. As for dramas with subjects and characters drawn from the common people, I do not think that any exist, aside from French translations; the English public, never having seen the originals, obviously could not be expected to take more than a passing interest in such plays, just as they might take a passing interest in Chinese drama.

In such a state of affairs, no theatre has any regular following, because the plays do not reflect the manners of any segment of the public. There have been attempts to portray middle-class households on the stage, but they are as monotonous as the brick

---

[1]The author is referring to Vanbrugh and, apparently Farquhar (Translators).

houses which harbour them, and the boredom to which such portrayals have subjected the public has demonstrated that there is nothing less dramatic than the stilted life of that part of the population.

In France charlatans are fair game for the theatre, whatever their position in society may be; religious frauds and prudes are no more respected than those with noisy pretensions to wit, patriotism, service to mankind or honesty. On the French stage one sees by turns *precieuses ridicules* and Philinte, nuns and monks, sorcerers, soothsayers and mountebanks of every kind. Ministerial intrigue is exposed and election manipulations, as well as Stock Exchange swindles. But in England, no one would tolerate seeing on the stage the Tartuffes of the Anglican religion, nor the sainted bishops with incomes of forty, fifty or eighty thousand pounds; not even the ones who we know have come seeking the protection of French tolerance for their sodomitical and gomorrhean morals. It is even forbidden to laugh or poke fun at Methodists and street preachers; the dramatist must also steer clear of parliamentary privilege; he must refrain from showing the election mysteries and from representing the Honourable Members of Parliament who, in order to be elected, pose as champions of the public's money and then, once elected, dip their hands in the purse, obtain sinecures or make a deal with government ministers. It would not even be wise to base a play on certain goings-on familiar to the respectable gentlemen of the Stock Exchange, nor on the shady dealings in government ministries; all those high-born vultures would sue the unfortunate author, and he would end his days in prison, unable to pay the damages.

All this explains why English plays are without exception extremely monotonous or grotesquely absurd; *censorship* is to blame, not the authors.

Shakespeare's dramas have had their day; they no longer touch the public; and as for those plays whose sole interest is in the curiosity they arouse and that idle attention one pays a procession of unfamiliar things of no great concern, one cannot, without the risk of boredom, see them more than once: for the public to flock to the theatre, the plays would have to present an ever changing spectacle, like passers-by under the windows of the aristocratic ladies of Piccadilly or Bond Street. Today, it would require nothing less than a social revolution to permit a rebirth of the drama, for how could anyone's interest be captured with those pasteboard figures from the West End, with John Bull of the City, or with the other types which luxury and comfort have turned to dolts? Neither the excesses of the manor house nor those of the tavern are dramatic, and "criminal conversations" no longer arouse any curiosity, unless royalty or high government figures are involved. Not until the people are emancipated can there be a return of the splendid characters and varied scenes which prodigal nature, when unfettered, supplies in such abundance.

Now that peace has given free rein to the English propensity towards locomotion, they have swarmed over the Continent in every direction, and there has been an enormous increase of theatrical importation into England; there has even been some attempt at imitating French vaudeville. But God, who has so generously endowed the Anglo-Saxon isle with fanatics, wranglers, great criminals, novelists, blue-eyed lasses and green meadows, has steadfastly withheld all cuisiniers, coiffeurs, milliners, singers and vaudevillists. To excel in these fundamental professions requires imagination, gaiety and taste; three things that have little currency in London; they are of no use in obtaining a seat in Parliament or a bishopric, nor are they quoted on the Stock Exchange. Nevertheless the continental public, the europeanized public from beyond the Channel, was calling for vaudevilles! And theatre managers, pained at the sight of an empty hall night after night, whereas the plain and poorly lighted French theatre was always full, put in their order for gay, witty, sparkling and frothy vaudevilles in the French manner. The gentlemen of the pen were fully aware of the import of the mission entrusted to them; as they saw it, the literary reputation of the nation was at stake in the struggle with the little French theatre, and they vowed to haunt the fashionable gatherings of the West End in order to collect the *bons mots* imported by recent arrivals from the Continent; some even came to Paris for the express purpose of studying the "physiology of the vaudevillist". Upon their return to England, the sight of their metamorphosis caused untold astonishment! They had completely abandoned the national diet: roastbeef, plum pudding, porter, even turtle soup! That same turtle soup for which any John Bull from the City would sell his soul! Henceforth they fed on nothing but *salades d'anchois, écrevisses, charlottes russes, beignets aux pêches* and *meringues*. They sought inspiration in champagne, sauternes and quantities of black coffee.

This regimen from the Parisian Parnassus had been prescribed by the great master vaudevillists Désangiers, Scribe and Mélesville, but it did not at all agree with bards from climes so far removed from the sun; it did not put a sparkle in their eyes, it did not sharpen their wit, but they nevertheless kept at it with typical British tenacity; within six months they had wasted away; their eyes, sunken in their sockets, were like the last flicker of a candle about to go out; they spent sleepless nights tossing and turning on a feverish bed. Alack! these happy omens were followed by nothing other than complete disappointment; not one of them gave birth to a really gay or witty vaudeville as they are conceived on the banks of the Seine. Unable to succeed even after having followed all the proper steps, they resolved to tread incognito the path so many had taken before them. They set themselves to translating the authors from the Gymnase, the Variétés and the Vaudeville and threw out all of the regimen except the sauternes and the champagne.

These gentlemen saw no point in exposing the sterility of their minds to the public; they almost invariably changed the titles of the French plays they translated, and with brazen impudence offered them as the children of their own genius. They continue to ply their trade, and not content with making money, they are ever on the alert to pilfer someone else's fame.

The principal dramatic authors who write for the theatre are: Knowles, Jerrold, Planche, Buckstone, Serle, Bernard, Dance, Peak, Poole, Fitzball.

Excepting Knowles and Jerrold, who sometimes write original plays, all the others do nothing but translate, mutilate, travesty and rearrange after their own fashion.

I obtained some plays by Mr Buckstone, and had no difficulty recognizing that those whose titles follow were nothing more than literal translations or travesties of French plays, and in none of them is the plagiarism ever disguised by the presence of original thought.

English titles	French titles
Victorine or I'll sleep on It	*Victorine ou la Nuit Porte Conseil*
The Rake and his Pupil	*Faublas*
The Happiest Day of My Life	*Le Plus Beau Jour de ma Vie*
Husband at Sight	*Mariage Impossible*
The Christening	*Le Parrain*
The Irish Lion	*Le Traiteur de J. J. Rousseau*
Two Queens	*Les Deux Reines*
Our Maryanne	*Les Cauchoises*
Love and Murder	*Procès Criminel*
New Farce	*Cabinet Particulier*
Henriette	*Henriette*
The Pet of the Petticoats	*Vert-Vert*

Since international law in Europe protects only material property, products of the mind go undefended; extradition is demanded for the thief who has stolen a pair of scissors, but he who has plundered the thought of others carries his head high, wears a medal of distinction on his breast, is showered with applause and acquires great wealth; whereas the real author frequently dies of hunger in a garret. These literary Bedouins ransack almost every play published in Paris; they are so ravenous that they would likely even negotiate with those poor writers of ours whose plays languish in the censor's files or in the bottom drawers of selection committees, and in lieu of money would offer them calico or cotton bonnets in exchange for their dramatic ideas.

I have just said that these gentlemen are ravenous, I ought to have said they are desperate; for even with a hotchpotch made up of French plays, they can no longer succeed in rousing the public's jaded taste.

Their zeal at first reaped rather handsome rewards; but the fashionable public, a public which is as familiar with the repertory of Parisian theatres as any dandy on the Chaussée d'Antin, no sooner perceived that the plays it was being offered as new were composed of the shreds of French plays it had already seen, or that it claimed to have seen in Paris, and that those plays presented as translations resembled their French originals as a sign painter's work resembles a Teniers or a Rembrandt, than they concluded they had been duped; the fashionable cosmopolitans cried out in protest, deserted the importers of drama and flocked to the little French theatre.

As for John Bull, our ways are foreign to him; and too, French plays do not offer the interwoven adventures whose inextricable labyrinth holds his attention on those occasions when, after dinner, the wines of Portugal or Madeira have brought him out of his habitual apathy; our plays are devoid of situations which play upon one's nerves, the torture, for instance, of an English soldier or sailor subjected to two or three hundred lashes. John Bull, with no stomach for the claret[1] he was being served, soon returned to his fortified wines.

Roman society, sunk in luxury and sensual indulgence, blasé about every physical pleasure of which we are capable, could no longer be impressed by the representation of vices which had become common to all. Liberty and patriotism had succumbed; social life was lacking in any generous motives, in any really dramatic action. Adulation, baseness and tyranny would no more have been permitted on the Roman stage than parliamentary venality and religious hypocrisy on the English stage; the life of slaves, like that of the English working class, was too abject to be dramatized, and neither the Greek theatre nor the plays of Terence and Plautus were still capable of exciting any interest; in its state of universal degradation Roman society turned for

---

[1] Bordeaux wine

emotional excitement to danger, pain and death! It flocked to the circuses to watch gladiators in combat and men fighting for their lives against wild animals!

The dominant class in England is no less blasé than Roman society under the emperors; the means of stirring society from its torpor is merely less developed than it was in Rome. For the English to be moved to some emotion, the sight of men in danger is required. There was for a while a craze for lions, hyenas and tigers; but when it was seen that Van-Amburg and Carter were in no danger, there was no further interest in them; soon nothing will do but the spectacle of men pitted against animals. Once launched along this path, English society will follow it to the end, unless a popular regeneration prevents it.

In France too, wild beasts on the stage have drawn large crowds, but such exhibitions cannot be expected to last, even if no accident brings about their suppression. The fondness for theatre is deeply rooted; in addition the spirit of equality which prevails allows subjects for drama to be drawn from all ranks of society; dramatic representations can thus take infinitely varied forms, and weariness will be forestalled.

London has between fifteen and twenty theatres; originally they were classed according to the type of spectacle they offered the public; nowadays there is a general overlapping of types: only the Italian opera has remained faithful to its intended purpose. Each theatre owes its existence to its having been granted a licence which determines how many months it may be open to the public, and the type of plays it is permitted to perform.

The theatre begins between six and seven o'clock, the opera at eight; and all performances end at about midnight. All the halls are lighted by gas and are excessively hot in the summer; in the winter they are very cold as they are not heated. The smell given off by the gas causes giddiness and can make one ill; also no matter which way one looks, one is blinded by the unsteady light from the candelabras affixed to the first three tiers of boxes. These are not the only nuisances: at half past nine in every theatre admission is half price; it is then that throngs of prostitutes and men of every station crowd into the theatres; the women go wherever they please, will even sit next to you if there is a seat, nearly asphyxiating you with the smell of gin they exhale with every breath. They keep going into and coming out of the boxes, for the performance is in no way the object of their attention; they are there to ply their trade, and one is constantly exposed to draughts sweeping through the doors they leave open behind them. The corridors are full of raucous laughter and ribaldry, one is revolted by the confusion of hoarse and shrilling voices, it is as if one were surrounded by the dregs of so-called civilization. The very air is somehow poisoned and oppressive to breathe; the lobby is the scene of unbridled licentiousness, and prostitutes openly ply their trade; there are such scandalous goings-on that the pen balks at recording them.... In all the theatres the lobby is luxuriously appointed, the seats are elegant, the mirrored hall sparkles with myriad lights, there is a restaurant with all manner of refreshments and, in winter, a roaring fire, but in all the theatres the lobbies have been taken over by the prostitutes whose shameless solicitations prevent women with any degree of modesty from frequenting the place, as well as those men who have not entirely renounced all delicacy of feeling.[1]

Covent Garden and Drury Lane are designated as national theatres. They enjoy the privilege of being open all year, a privilege which, originally granted for the purpose of encouraging the art of the drama, assured their prosperity for quite some time; when new forms of theatre appeared, the weary public forsook the ancient gods and went to worship before the altars of Baal; music and the dance enticed them away from the savage grandeur of Shakespeare. Covent Garden and Drury Lane turned to those charming means of expression in an attempt to prevent the defection of the public, but to no avail. With no

---

[1] During my stay in London in 1835, the prostitutes at Drury Lane carried shamelessness to the point of undressing a young man in the midst of the lobby; they stole his clothes and left him completely naked. The unfortunate young man cried out for help, but, set upon by forty or fifty viragos, to no avail. No one came to his aid. When the hall was emptied, he was found cowering in a corner afraid to show himself.

orchestra and no specially trained players, they could not compete with their rivals.

Such paucity of means of execution explains, as much as a lack of feeling for the art, the transformation undergone by the plays they borrow from us; in order to be able to make some use of them, they mutilate them in the most dreadful way; they substitute gigs[1] and other English dance tunes for the charming music of our comic operas, eliminate dramatic seriousness by imparting to the plot an absurdly rapid pace, introduce English buffoons, deprive the action of its motivation, prevent love from voicing its feelings and turn the whole thing into a "musical farce", a type of play beneath our *théâtres de foire*. Our grand operas fare no better, and the comedies of our best authors could be found, in the repertory of Covent Garden and Drury Lane, travestied as ignoble antics. Such misdirected efforts were powerless to sustain Shakespearian tragedy.

The two so-called national theatres, deserted by the public, have more than once been obliged to suspend performances for four or even six months; both of them have finally fallen into the hands of speculators who care for nothing but making money and have no thought for the progress of dramatic art nor for the reasons behind the granting of the privilege. They have introduced by turns upon the stage, first lavish melodramas whose opulent decor and picturesque costumes took the place of originality, then ballets, buffoons, acrobats, talking dogs, extraordinary monkeys like Jocko, horses, and, as the grand finale, wild animals! Covent Garden and Drury Lane, where the Garricks, Kembles, Keans, Youngs, Siddonses, O'Neils for so long brought to life the words of Shakespeare, incarnated his characters and gave them such imposing greatness, are now nothing more than circuses!

As for Queen's Theatre, it is the home of second editions of the Italian operas sung the preceding winter in Paris. It is fortunate for our virtuosos that the English are by nature unmusical. The gentlemen of the *Théâtre-Italien* go to London for the summer to

---

[1]Gig, a type of English dance

earn a little money and recuperate from the fatigues of Paris; they neglect their voices, sing in pitch, because they could not possibly sing out of pitch; but the unresponsiveness of the audience deprives them of any enthusiasm; they remain cold and merely perform their task. The brilliant assemblage is unmoved, or at least its emotion is not manifested by voice, gesture or facial expression. It is the sort of calm which in London is known as "attention" and one is forced to conclude that this aristocratic elite is indeed attentive, or else composed of statues.

The English have the peculiar notion that nothing is beyond their capacities. Like Naples, Vienna and Paris, London would have its national opera.

The English Opera, built in luxurious style, is destined solely, so states the privilege, for the performance of English operas. It is easy enough to look down one's nose and utter pretentious claims, but alas! success or failure is beyond our powers to determine. What a lot of pretentions to beauty and talent for the few who have any mastery over them!

Three or four managers successively placed in charge of the new academy of music have, with truly English patience, awaited the musical work to be conceived by British minds; to date the soil has proved infertile. Nothing the English Opera has performed surpasses musical farces in merit, and as it has no singers capable of adding lustre to its rhapsodies, it has fallen into complete decay. The hall is quite attractive, and when it ceased to reverberate to the chords of the English lyre, it was in constant demand: Spanish dancers, magicians, French vaudevillists, German physicists and so forth, cropped up by turns to occupy it. What was to be done? The privilege stipulates that no play may be performed unless three musical pieces are sung. Fortunately for the subscribers the privilege is no more specific about the type of music than about the instruments or voices which are to execute it; and the new manager, whom I do not believe to be much of a connoisseur of music, certainly proved to be a very capable administrator when he found a way to satisfy the necessary conditions. Melodramas, comedies, vaudevilles, ballets, etc., he finds them all acceptable by introducing the three obligatory airs, placed without rhyme or reason and sung by any Tom, Dick or Harry. This master-stroke enticed the fickle public back to the English Opera; nevertheless, for half the year the hall is given over to concerts known as Musard's concerts: the reader will kindly excuse me if I cannot bring myself to describe them.

The Astley Theatre is without a doubt the most frequented. The English are very fond of horses and clowns, and in the London equivalent of the Franconi the two types of performers are indeed remarkable. However I find the horses at the Parisian Franconi cleverer and the riders more skilful and more graceful, but I must admit that the clowns are nowhere near as good as the English Jack-puddings. The Astley is always full: when I was there they were performing the eternal *Battle of Waterloo* in which we see French soldiers beaten and taken prisoner *single-handed* by one English sutler, and a *woman* at that. I report the episode because it gives some idea of the play, as well as the exaggerated partiality of the authors of the caricature. When it was announced that all was lost for the French, the voice of a man of the people was heard from the gallery shouting with a heavy English accent: "Vive l'empereur Napoléon!"

The Haymarket Theatre is licensed to remain open ten months out of the year and to present comedy, tragedy and short plays. In this respect it is on the same footing as the two national theatres. So far the Haymarket has not stooped to including buffoons among its players; it has not given roles to dogs, monkeys or wild animals; its stage has seen no monstrous alliances; quite the contrary, the management has constantly striven to uphold the art of drama. The last manager, Mr Webster, who is an excellent actor, tried to revive on his stage the plays of the immortal Shakespeare, but he was obliged to give up the attempt: the public deserted the theatre. This is the theatre where most of the vaudevilles translated from the French are performed.

The Olympic, Madame Vestris's Theatre, the Victoria, the Garrick-Surrey, the Adelphi etc., are all secondary theatres; their existence is precarious, subject to the caprices of fortune; the managers are in desperate financial straits as are the players, authors, designers and suppliers.

On the whole, the only presentations to find favour are the farces: extremely broad, extremely coarse, comic farces; buffoons are all the rage. In painting, Ostade's pictures and Brauwer's are preferred to those of the Italian school. In truth, everything that brings to mind that prim and proper society, so vice-ridden and so corrupt, wearies, disgusts or repels.

XVI

Tribulations of Life in London

> *Throughout history and throughout the world, it has always been easy to establish a false reputation, whereas to establish the truth about the simplest thing is almost impossible.*
>
> *Rousseau*

The English are so boastful, and they glorify England and its customs in so many parts of the world that it is now taken for granted that England offers the greatest degree of physical comfort! Thousands of respectable gentlemen categorically affirm this reputation in all the inns, cafes and cabarets of France, Germany, Switzerland and Italy. One would think they had left England to mortify their flesh, and not because they are more comfortable on the Continent. However, people who have lived in the country of John Bull take it all with a grain of salt ... but in the face of so many testimonials, woe to him who would dare say the contrary!

In considering the advantages and resources of a country, it would be well to examine those pertaining to intellectual needs, because they are the true measure of the progress of a nation.

In England there is no "free" education of any kind; he who has no money must forgo cultivating his mind or increasing his knowledge.

Access to libraries, museums, churches and scientific collections is practically impossible for the working class. The library of the British Museum is the only one I know where there is no entrance fee, although one must have references, guarantees, etc. In England any poor man is *ipso facto* considered a *thief*. There are no reading rooms in London; foreign newspapers and the latest books are found only in the clubs, where admission is restricted to members. Of course one may read English newspapers in cafes and inns, but one must order something.

There are numerous scientific institutions, however I know of no classes given gratis in any of the sciences. The word gratis has no meaning in England, or else it masks a scheme for doubling the price: clergymen, professors, Members of Parliament, all turn their profession to profit; nothing is free, there is a price for everything, gratis is unpardonable!

The proletariate is treated like a beast of burden. Little if any attention is given to his material existence. As for his intellectual needs, it has never occurred to anyone that he might have any. The working man has no other distraction than drinking. In respect to study and intellectual pleasures, there is no city in Europe which does not offer the people more resources than London and England.

If we turn our attention to the mundane aspects of living we see that, in this respect, England provides comfort only to those with well-lined purses. In cities on the Continent, there are facilities, available to those with the slenderest means, which help to satisfy all the little requirements of social life. In London, nowhere does one find those hundreds of little things which make life more pleasant for everyone, lighten domestic toil and, by providing the poorest with some of the comforts of the rich, mitigate the horrors of destitution.

Suppose you are in a hurry to send a letter and to receive an answer, there are no errand boys at the corner always ready to serve you for a few pennies; suppose you are, after a long trip, covered with mud, there are no street bootblacks; suppose you are detained on business at the end of town, you will not find any restaurant there in which to dine, no cafe where you might take some refreshment. If the doctor prescribes baths, the patient cannot take them at home, there are no portable baths in London. In the churches one must listen to a long two hour sermon seated on bare wooden benches. In the boxes at the Italian Opera there are only little wooden chairs, so narrow and so uncomfortable that it would be sheer torture to sit on them for five hours in a row. Suppose you wish to invite the friend you have just met to dinner, the restaurants have only ordinary fare to offer you; if you appear surprised, the owner says: "My dear Sir, whenever anything out of the ordinary is wanted, it must be ordered the day before." And the same holds true for everything else: in London, one is never prepared as in Paris, it always takes at least twenty four hours to get ready.

And now if I go looking for comfortably appointed houses, oh! I shall be even more disappointed. In England, when all the floors are covered with rugs from the entrance to the last little bedroom, when there is a tray big enough to cover the drawing-room table set for tea, when the fireplaces have handsome fenders, brightly polished shovels and tongs, then it is understood that one need not be ashamed of the house, since it offers all the requisite comforts for well-to-do gentlemen.[1] The drawing-room chairs are hard, heavy and awkward in design, they are uncomfortable to sit upon, as are those in the dining-room; all well and good for those two rooms perhaps, but let us now go upstairs to the bedrooms.

Of all peoples, the French have of course the most exquisite feeling for the comforts of life, they make their bedroom the most attractive room in the house. Ah how well they understand the sensuousness of solitude, of a peaceful retreat, of the *bueno retiro*. The objects around us have such power over us that they can

---

[1] I am referring only to the moderately well-off because wealthy aristocrats and financiers combine great luxury with all the refinements of a sybaritic life.

completely change the direction of our thoughts. Family portraits, paintings, all sorts of pretty little things each evoking fond memories, inspire in us a host of ideas and reflections. Who could not, after having lived for some years, write volumes under such inspiration? Besides, I am convinced that a beautiful room decorated in this fashion and elegantly furnished disposes the person who lives in it to more affection, gratitude, and even neatness. Among the English, things are backwards: their drawing-rooms are luxuriously and symmetrically decorated, while their women sleep in veritable kennels.

An enormous bed occupies the centre of the room, a big chest of drawers stands in a corner; the table in another corner, and the wash stand is in front of the window looking out on a very small courtyard (in London, all bedrooms are in the back of the houses, and the courtyards are so small that the rooms lack air and light), five or six chairs, here and there, are loaded with boxes of all sorts, shoes and so forth. Dresses, coats, shawls, hats hang on the four walls, from nails serving as coat-hangers; there you have, in general, the English woman's bedroom. It is difficult to imagine the utter disorder of their bedrooms, a French woman cannot enter one without a feeling of disgust. I have travelled a great deal and I can say that I have never felt so ill at ease as in an English bedroom.

An English bed sums up perfectly the appearance and the reality of things in England, it could not have a finer appearance! But the softness of the feathers is such that when one lies down, it is as if one were stretched out on a sack of potatoes! Finally, a word about that much vaunted English cleanliness!... Cleanliness too plays a part in the comfort of life. In England, one encounters at every turn that same system of keeping up what shows: the outside of the front door, the staircase, the hearth and its implements, the knives, the dish covers, all the things that show could not be neater or cleaner.

The distribution of rooms in English houses is most inconvenient in spite of their reputation to the contrary. In modest households where there is only one servant, it is impossible to get good service, the poor girl is worked to death, she spends half her time going up and down the stairs, because the kitchen is in the basement, the dining-room on the first floor, the drawing-room on the second, and the bedrooms on the third and fourth floors.

I shall stop here. I am afraid I would be accused of exaggeration if I were to enumerate all the tribulations that one encounters in London. In short, let me say that there is no mitigation to the misery of the poor, that the lower middle class lives in perpetual deprivation; even the rich cannot succeed in satisfying all their whims, and finally, the foreigner can find, in the British metropolis, neither French fried potatoes nor roasted chestnuts!

TENDENCY TOWARD ANGLOMANIA. Since 1830, a great change has taken place among the people of London. In spite of the efforts of the Tories to reawaken the old antagonism for the French, workers, sailors and the masses in general like the French very much and have a very high opinion of them.

During my last trip, on at least twenty occasions, I was greeted by coachmen, sailors, servants, in these words: "Bond jourre, Madame Franceze." The phrase, comically pronounced, was always accompanied by a friendly expression and a kindly smile which clearly said: "We are happy to see you." Each time they had the opportunity to show me some civility or to say a flattering word about my country, one could see that they did so with sincerity. The people are not the only ones becoming pro-French; a number of young people, and especially women, consider that nothing is good or beautiful unless it be French. These gallophils learn the French language, read French newspapers and books, dress in the French fashion, have everything sent from Paris, replace tea with coffee, roast-beef with lamb cutlets, beer with wine, feather beds with mattresses, and there are even some who carry this mania so far that they transform their bedroom into a French *boudoir*. Rational men in England are finally beginning to realize that, so far, the people have been the tool of the aristocracy, a pack of dogs to be unleashed upon its prey; they understand that it is in the interest of the English people to be united with a nation which stands for equality and tolerance. One no longer hears those fairy-tales zealously circulated among the people for such a long time in order to inspire prejudice and revive old hatreds against us.

The facility and low cost of communications bring 200,000 Englishmen annually to France: tradesmen, shopkeepers, workers; they all come to breathe the continental air for a few days; for a few brief moments they lay down the yoke of servility which the imperious English nobility impose on those they employ; in France, they encounter no one whose pride is insulting to them, and they are conscious of their inherent dignity. They find out for themselves that the French eat very good meat, are well-dressed, and that the women are not ugly and dirty as Goldsmith said in order to curry favour with his patrons, thus betraying with his lies both his poverty and his genius. Railways from Paris to Calais and from Dover to London would produce numerous advantageous results for the well-being of the two peoples and for their moral as well as their material progress! Railways! Railways! They are the instruments of union and brotherhood, bulwarks against which disgraceful tactics will be powerless! Let peoples mingle; let them impart their thoughts to one another; let them exchange talents as well as things, and quarrels between nations, which are always instigated by the mighty, will become impossible. The masses ask only to live in peace.

XVII

English Women

Is there a particle of justice to be seen in the fate meted out to women? Is not the young girl a piece of merchandise offered for sale to anyone wishing to settle on a price, thereby acquiring exclusive rights to the property? Is not her consent to the marriage bond absurd and forced upon her by the tyranny of the prejudices which have pursued her since birth? She is asked to believe that the chains she wears are garlands of flowers, but can she deceive herself as to her degradation, even in regions glutted with philosophy, such as England, where men have the right to put their womenfolk up for sale, with a rope around their necks and to hand them over like beasts of burden to anyone who will pay the price. Is the thinking of the public in this regard any more advanced today than it was in that ignorant age when a certain council of Macon, a true council of Vandals, entertained the question of whether or not women have a soul, and decided in the affirmative by only three votes. English legislation, so extolled by moralists, grants to men a number of rights which are equally degrading for the other sex: such is the husband's right to be awarded damages at the expense of his wife's avowed lover. Procedures are less crude in France, but slavery is, basically, always the same.

Fourier, THÉORIE DES QUATRE MOUVEMENTS

What a revolting contrast there is in England between women's abject servitude and the intellectual superiority of women writers. There are no sorrows, ills, disorders, injustices or misfortunes which result from society's prejudices, its organizations or its laws that have escaped their notice. The books of these English women are a shining phenomenon which lights up the intellectual world, especially if we consider the absurd education they had to settle for, and the stupefying influence of the milieu in which they grew up.

After spending only a few months in England, one is struck by the intelligence and sensitivity of the women; they are capable of sustained attention and have a good memory. With such aptitudes, nothing in the intellectual sphere is beyond their reach. Their demeanour is stately and noble, but alas! all these good, innate qualities are stifled by an education system based on false principles, and by the atmosphere of hypocrisy, prejudice and vice which permeates their lives.

English women's lives are unbelievably monotonous, sterile and drab. Time has no meaning for them—the days, months and years bring no change to this oppressive uniformity. As young women, they are brought up according to their parents' social position, but whatever the rank they are to occupy, their education always, with slight variations, reflects the same prejudices.

Although it has been fashionable for a long time to praise this country for its freedom, it is the home of the most dreadful tyranny, and woman is subjected by prejudice and by law to the most revolting inequalities! She can inherit only if she has no brother. She is deprived of civil and political rights, and the law has made her in every way a slave to her husband. She is trained to be hypocritical, and made to bear alone the heavy yoke of public opinion. Everything that her awakening senses perceive, everything that develops her faculties, everything that she has to endure, inevitably result in materializing her tastes, hardening her heart, and numbing her soul.

English novelists, disgusted by the scenes of family life, have dreamed up others which their imagination persuaded them were real. Consequently, true to life as they may be in depicting the fatuousness of the typical gentlemen, the bigotry and pretence of the middle class, the tyranny of fathers and husbands, the insulting pride of the high and the obsequiousness of the low, they are far removed from reality as they portray domestic bliss. Happiness without liberty! As if happiness had ever existed in a society of masters and slaves!

Here is what happens in well-to-do families.

Children are relegated to the third floor with their nurse, maid or governess. Their mother sends for them when she wants to see them, and only then do the children pay her a short and formal call.[1] The poor little girl, deprived of affection, becomes incapable of affection herself. She is totally unaware of the sweetness of intimacy, of trust, and of the demonstrativeness that any little girl is naturally inclined to show a mother who loves her. She barely knows her father and feels for him only respect tinged with fear. And from earliest childhood she is taught to demonstrate consideration and deference to her brother.

It seems to me that the system adopted for the education of children would stupefy the most intelligent of children.

Mr Jacotot says: "All is contained in everything." English education seems to demonstrate the opposite, that in everything there is nothing. All they care about is just stuffing young heads with words from all the European languages without worrying in the least about ideas. This absurd mania is as barbarous as it is stupid. The child is given a German nurse, a French governess, a Spanish maid, so that she will learn three or four languages by the

---

[1] Among the upper classes, young ladies remain in the company of their governess until they marry; when their mother wishes to see them, she sends the footman with a note inviting them to tea, and the young ladies dress for a visit to their mother's apartments as if they were calling on a stranger.

age of four or five. I saw some of these little creatures, and their fate was truly pitiful. They could not make themselves understood by the people around them. The charm of children's prattle was thus forbidden to them. They were obliged to make themselves understood by signs because they could not communicate verbally. Depending on their nature, this made them irritable or apathetic, some were wicked, noisy, obstinate, others were sullen and sad.

A child who is forced to load her memory down with words from three or four languages acquires only a confused idea of what the words mean. She retains the oral sign, but the idea that it represents escapes her. She has an overdeveloped memory for words, but the intelligence necessary to conceive thoughts is destroyed. A knowledge of foreign languages is no doubt necessary to a people whose greed overruns the whole earth, but any kind of teaching should be subordinate to the development of the mind. Then one must consider the usefulness of the language the child is being taught. The ability to speak fluently and elegantly in three or four languages is rare if not impossible. Since incorrect expressions and a foreign accent are grating in any country, and since women rarely have business relations with foreign nations, I believe that there are generally more useful things for them to learn.

Everything that is taught is taught in the same way as languages. A young girl must learn music whether or not she has any natural disposition for the art; she must draw, she must dance, and so on. The result of such an education is that young ladies know a little of everything and have not mastered anything they can use, not even for their own amusement. There are exceptions of course, but they are rare.

As for moral education, it comes from the Bible. The book contains good things, everyone agrees on that, but there are so many indecent stories, obscene images, so much lewdness that should be deleted before putting it in the hands of young people, if their imaginations are not to be sullied, and if they are not to find in it a justification for all that society condemns: theft, murder, prostitution, and so on. Whatever the clergy may say, "scriptural education" is the most antisocial education of all. Among the thousands of English contradictions, this is one of the most shocking. A young girl is expected to be pure, chaste, innocent, and she is made to read a book containing the stories of Lot, David, Absalom, Ruth, the Songs of Solomon, and so on. She reads Paul's sermons on fornication, her mind is filled with the scenes of rape, adultery, prostitution and debauchery which are depicted in the Bible, and with the language used in the Holy Book, and then she is told that she must not utter words like "chemise", "drawers", "breeches", "chicken thigh", "bitch", and so on.

Actually, young girls are taught the appearance of chastity and innocence, and the reality of vice, just as the working classes are taught the appearance of religion and the reality of idleness, with all the resultant disorders when they are made to observe the Sabbath. How ironic! there is no morality anywhere, no one believes in chastity, in integrity, in any of the meanings of the word "virtue". No one is taken in by appearances, and yet they continue to clothe national behaviour.

There are very few things young women can do for entertainment. The family atmosphere is cold, arid, deadly dull, so they plunge headlong into the reading of novels. Their reading gives rise to hopes that can never be realized; unfortunately England cannot supply lovers comparable to those in fiction. Our young ladies develop a romantic bent, they dream only of elopement. But, as might be expected in this century of comfort and luxury, their abductor must be the son of a nabob or lord, heir to a huge fortune, and they must be carried off in a superb carriage drawn by four horses. Wealthy young men, far from responding to such desires, have jaded senses and cold hearts, their calculating, practical minds are forever concerned with selfish ends. These young women would not be exposed to such disappointment if they had been given a taste for intellectual pleasures, if they could disdain wordly satisfactions, and if they had learned to live on modest means. If the Gospel had been explained to them, they would know that great wealth almost always corrupts, they would not wish to be loved by young men who spend their lives in gambling houses or getting drunk with prostitutes. Having waited in vain for the carriage and horses, when they get to be twenty-eight or thirty years old, these young women marry shopkeepers, modest employees, or the like. Many others remain single.

In actual fact, a married woman's fate is even sadder than the spinster's. At least the latter enjoys a certain amount of freedom, she can go about in the world, travel with relatives or friends, while a married woman can no longer go out without her husband's permission. An English husband is the lord and master of feudal times. He sincerely believes that he has the right to demand from his wife the passive obedience, the submission and respect of the slave. He shuts her up in his house, not because he is in love with her or jealous like the Turk, but because he considers her "his thing", like a piece of furniture for his personal use, which must be always at hand. It never enters his head that he should be faithful to her. For many people, the Bible sanctions this way of looking at things which gives free reign to passions. An English husband sleeps with his servant, throws her out when she is pregnant or has given birth, and does not feel any more guilty than Abraham sending Hagar and her son Ishmael into the desert.

In England, a woman is not, as in France, mistress of the house; indeed she is almost always a stranger there. Her husband keeps the money and the keys, he is the one responsible for expenses, he engages and dismisses servants, gives orders every morning for dinner, invites the guests. He alone decides the children's fate. In a word, he alone takes care of everything. Many women do not know exactly the type of business their husbands engage in, for what profession their children are being prepared, and generally they have no idea of the state of their fortune. An English woman never asks her husband what he does, whom he sees, how much he spends, where he spends his time. No woman dares ask such questions. The extreme dependency of English women and their respect for the wishes of their lord and master are as far removed from the familiarity and lively interest of French women toward their husbands as is present day French civilization from that of St Louis' time. An English woman has no control over her fortune; she is robbed of it without even her knowing it. It is usually through the newspapers that she learns her husband is bankrupt, ruined, or even that he has blown out his brains.

I have already pointed out that it is customary for the children to stay with their maid or governess in separate quarters, their mother never goes there. It is not she who teaches them to talk, she does not develop their minds nor form their character. When the maid or governess brings her children into the drawing-room, she inspects them to see that their hands and clothes are clean. Once the inspection is over, she kisses them, and that is all until the next day. When they are older, the children go to boarding school, and their mother rarely sees them. Once they are married their relationship ceases almost completely; they write to each other, and that is all.

A mother's or wife's coldness and indifference are not simply the result of the petrifying education she has received, they are also the natural consequence of the position an English woman occupies in the home. How could she be interested in a partnership in which her advice or wishes count for nothing? Are not slaves totally indifferent to their master's good or bad fortune?

I believe I can guess why these women are reputed to be homemakers: it is because of their sedentary life. Indeed, since they never go out, one might naturally suppose them to be busy at home. And yet, this is not what happens. English women not only do nothing at home, but they imagine that touching a needle would reduce them to the status of working women.[1] Time weighs heavily on them. They get up very late, breakfast slowly, read the newspapers, get dressed, then eat again at two o'clock. After that they read their novel or write letters twelve to sixteen pages in length. They dress for dinner. After dinner, around seven

---

[1] I am only speaking of well-to-do women. A poor woman and a shopkeeper are of course obliged to work. But many would rather be kept than stoop to working. In England, manual work is degrading.

or eight o'clock, they have a very leisurely tea. At ten o'clock, they have supper, and finally they sit all alone, by the fire.

Nothing is more revealing of the materialism of English society than the fact that men reduce their wives to such nonentities. Are not social responsibilities shared by women as well as by men? Why do men believe they can exclude women from them and condemn them to live like vegetables? One must admit, "scriptural education" produces marvelous results! These English households are the bitterest caricature of indissoluble marriage! Nothing better could be invented to show up the outrageousness of the institution. Judging from the number of admirable women to be found in England even in such circumstances, God must have endowed English women with a great deal more fortitude and intelligence than he gave their masters, otherwise the creatures would necessarily become totally stupid.

These are the reasons for getting married in England: for girls, the desire to escape paternal authority, to ease the yoke of prejudice which weighs so heavily on young girls and the hope of playing a larger role in the world — high-minded people have a need to take part in the world's events. As for men, it is simply the desire to get hold of a dowry, to use it to pay their debts, speculate or, if the dowry is very large, to squander the income in clubs, finishes or with their mistresses.

Women are the dupes in this bargain. Prejudice drives them to the altar where greed is waiting to despoil them. Men lead the same lives they did before marriage; the marriage bond which is so heavy for women does not impose any obligation on them. When the fancy takes them, they live with harlots, servants and actresses; most of them keep a mistress lavishly in a pretty little house in the suburbs. This is a universal practice among rich men, not only of the City, but also of the West End. They have a second home, a second family, and the little affection of which they are capable goes to these women of their choice, and to the children they have by them. They consider their legitimate spouses, whom they married solely for their money, to be shrewish and troublesome mates. The attention wives demand, the respect and consideration husbands are forced to show them in public are irksome duties which they escape by spending as little time as possible at home. What happens to a wife after she has turned her money over to her husband? She is nothing more than a baby-making machine, and the best twenty-five years of her life are spent turning out children.

Because of their isolation English women tend to be observant and contemplative, and many of them are drawn to writing. There are many more women authors in England than in France because French women lead more active lives and are less excluded from social events. A number of women writers have brought fame to England, and since the example of Lady Montagu, who wrote about her travels in such a pure and elegant style, a great many others have taken up the pen and demonstrated considerable ability. These ladies excel in the novel of manners. Everyone is familiar with the works of Lady Morgan; no one before her had described the Irish temperament so well or depicted Ireland so vividly. Lady Blessington's books are distinguished by her accurate observations and original ideas. And I could mention many other names. Recently, a young woman appeared on the scene: her debut could not have been more brilliant. Never before had a literary career started out with such promise and such glory, and Lady Lytton Bulwer won a place among the first. This superior woman is one of the many victims of the indissolubility of marriage. It is not surprising that her first book is one long cry of suffering. It is entitled *Scenes of Real Life*. There is a price to pay for talent; since Lady Bulwer's was beyond dispute, the public professed to be scandalized by such revelations. Poor women! They are only permitted to suffer ... even complaining is forbidden to them!

Lady Bulwer's husband, a well known novelist, had risen as far as Parliament and the Baronetcy when Lady Bulwer revealed the fine talent God had given her. From then on Sir Lytton Bulwer was devoured by envy and, blinded by her dazzling success, he has resorted to slander in order to tarnish her reputation. He had his wife surrounded by spies, and as her fame as an author grew, he attempted to sully her character as a wife! ... In truth, there is a rumour in London which explains both his consuming envy and his relentless hatred for his wife. It is said that Lady Bulwer is the author of all the novels published under the name of Sir Lytton Bulwer. The supposition is given credit by the fact that since their separation, Mr Lytton Bulwer has published nothing worthy of note, and in the House of Commons he has never risen above the mass of parliamentary mediocrity. Furthermore, the elegant simplicity, the lofty ideas, the action of the plot in *Scenes of Real Life* by Lady Bulwer, show her to be the author of *Rienzi* and *Pelham*, the two novels published under Mr Bulwer's name and which had the greatest success.[1]

It is easy to recover from the loss of a spouse, but to lose a source of wealth! To lose one's faithful Friday! To fall from the heights of Olympus! ...

Oh! Lady Bulwer, I sincerely hope your husband's hatred will remain forever powerless, so that, more fortunate than I, you will escape the assassin's bullet. But alas! I know the human heart well enough to predict that his hatred will be implacable, and that it will pursue you to your grave!

Women writers in England deal also with the most serious subjects. Miss Martineau has written remarkable works on economics. Mrs Trollope published a guide on her travels to North America which has had a great deal of success. Mrs Gore has written some very nice tales on Polish manners and history, Mrs Shilly[2] writes poetry full of music and feeling. Many of these ladies write for newspapers and magazines. But, to my great sorrow, I see no one who has yet taken up the cause of freedom for women — that freedom without which all others are very short lived, that freedom for which women writers especially should fight. French women are ahead of English women in this respect.

And yet, half a century ago, a woman's voice spoke out in England. A voice which derived an irrestible power, a splendid energy from the truth implanted in our souls by God, a voice

---

[1] I was told in London that *Rienzi* had fetched £60,000. The figure strikes me as a bit exaggerated.

[2] Perhaps the author means Mrs Shelley (Translators).

which was not afraid to attack every prejudice, one by one, and to show how iniquitous and false they are. Mary Wollstonecraft called her book *A Vindication of the Rights of Woman*. It was published in 1792.

The book was suppressed as soon as it was published, but that did not save its author from slander. Only the first volume was published, and it has become extremely rare. I could not find a copy to buy, and if a friend had not lent me one, I would have been unable to get it. The book has such a dreadful reputation that if you mention it even to so called "progressive" women, their horrified reply will be: "Oh that is a very wicked book!" Alas slander often triumphs over the best deserved renown and bequeaths its hatred from generation to generation, and it does not respect the dead: even fame is powerless to stop it.

Mary Wollstonecraft dedicated her book to Mr de Talleyrand-Perigord. Let us hear what this woman says, this English woman who is the first courageous enough to say that civil and political rights belong *equally to both sexes*, and who calls upon an opinion professed by Mr de Talleyrand in a parliamentary speech to show him that his duty as a statesman is to act in accordance with that opinion, to assure its triumph and to establish the total emancipation of women. Here are a few passages from the dedication:

"Contending for the rights of woman, my main argument is built on this simple principle, that if she be not prepared by education to become the companion of man, she will stop the progress of knowledge and virtue; for truth must be common to all, or it will be inefficacious with respect to its influence on general practice.... If children are to be educated to understand the true principle of patriotism, their mother must be a patriot; and the love of mankind, from which an orderly train of virtues spring, can only be produced by considering the moral and civil interest of mankind; but the education and situation of woman, at present, shuts her out from such investigations.

"Consider, I address you as a legislator, whether, when men contend for their freedom, and to be allowed to judge for themselves respecting their own happiness, it be not inconsistent and unjust to subjugate women, even though you firmly believe that you are acting in the manner best calculated to promote their happiness? Who made man the exclusive judge, if woman partake with him the gift of reason?

"In this style, argue tyrants of every denominations, from the weak king to the weak father of a family; they are all eager to crush reason; yet always assert that they usurp its throne only to be useful. Do you not act a similar part, when you *force* all women, by denying them civil and political rights, to remain immured in their families groping in the dark?...

"But, if women are to be excluded, without having a voice, from a participation of the natural rights of mankind, prove first, to ward off the charge of injustice and inconsistency, that they want reason, else this flaw in your NEW CONSTITUTION will ever show that man must, in some shape, act like a tyrant; and tyranny, in whatever part of society it rears its brazen front, will ever undermine morality. For, if women are not permitted to enjoy legitimate rights, they will render both men and themselves vicious, to obtain illicit privileges."

And now, here is how she addresses women:

"My own sex, I hope, will excuse me, if I treat them like rational creatures, instead of flattering their *fascinating* graces, and viewing them as if they were in a state of perpetual childhood, unable to stand alone. I earnestly wish to point out in what true dignity and human happiness consists. I wish to persuade women to endeavour to acquire strength, both of mind and body, and to convince them that the soft phrases, susceptibility of heart, delicacy of sentiment, and refinement of taste, are almost synonymous with epithets of weakness, and that those beings who are only the objects of pity and that kind of love, which has been termed its sister, will soon become objects of contempt.

"Dismissing, then, those pretty feminine phrases, which the men condescendingly use to soften our slavish dependence, and despising that weak elegancy of mind, exquisite sensibility, and sweet docility of manners, supposed to be the sexual characteristics of the weaker vessel, I wish to show that elegance is inferior to virtue, that the first object of laudable ambition is to obtain a character as a human being, regardless of the distinction of sex; and that secondary views should be brought to this simple touchstone."

Mary Wollstonecraft demands the freedom of women as a right, in the name of the principle upon which societies base the notion of justice and injustice; she demands freedom because without it there can be no moral obligations of any sort, just as she shows that without equality of obligations for both sexes, ethics have no foundation and cease to be true.

Mary Wollstonecraft says that she considers women from the lofty point of view of creatures who are, like men, placed on this earth to develop their intellectual faculties. Woman is neither inferior nor superior to man; as far as the mind and body are concerned, the two differ only to complement one another; and since the moral faculties of one are destined through union to complete those of the other, both must receive the same degree of development. Mary Wollstonecraft denounces those writers who consider woman as being subordinate by nature, and destined for man's pleasure. On this point she astutely criticizes Rousseau, according to whom woman must be weak and passive, man active and strong; woman was made to be subservient to man, and finally woman must make herself agreeable and obey her master, and such is the purpose of her existence. Mary Wollstonecraft shows that according to such principles, women are brought up to be cunning, devious and coquettish; while their minds are left uncultivated and their exacerbated sensitivity leaves them defenceless, they fall victim to every form of oppression. The author proves that the inevitable consequence of these principles is the subversion of morality. The pernicious bias of these books, she adds, in which authors insidiously debase women even as they worship their charms, cannot be too frequently pointed out nor too severely censured:

> ... Curs'd vassalage.
> First idoliz'd till love's hot fire be o'er
> Then slaves to those who courted us before.
>
> *Dryden*

Mary Wollstonecraft denounces with courage and energy all sorts of abuses.

"From this respect," she says,[1] "paid to property, flow, as from a poisoned fountain, most of the evils and vices which render this world such a dreary scene to the contemplative mind.

"... For all are aiming to procure respect on account of their property: and property, once gained, will procure the respect due only to talents and virtue. Men neglect the duties incumbent on man, yet are treated like demi-gods; religion is also separated from morality by a ceremonial veil, yet men wonder that the world is almost, literally speaking, a den of sharpers or oppressors."

Mary Wollstonecraft was already publishing in 1792 the same principles that Saint-Simon circulated later, and which spread so rapidly after the Revolution of 1830. Her criticism is admirable, she exposes the very real evils stemming from the present organization of the family. The strength of her logic cuts the ground from beneath her opponents. She boldly undermines the mass of prejudices shrouding the world. She wants, for both sexes, equality of political and civil rights, equal access to employment, professional education for all, and divorce by consent of both parties. She says: "Unless these conditions are met, any social organization which promises public happiness will bely its promises."

Mary Wollstonecraft's book is an undying work! It is undying because mankind's happiness depends on the triumph of the cause defended by *A Vindication of the Rights of Woman*. However, it has been in existence for half a century now, and no one has heard of it!...

---

[1] *A Vindication of the Rights of Woman*, p. 320

XVIII

Infant Schools

6. Only a small number of mothers are sufficiently educated to raise their children according to the most favourable precepts of education.

A smaller number yet have the necessary freedom to devote themselves to the study and the application of those precepts.

The wealthiest and most populous cities are indeed those which present the greatest number of difficulties and obstacles in this regard.

Nowhere in the infant school should the pedagogue or the doctor be in evidence; everywhere, on the contrary, there must be a healthy and philosophical instruction combined with the devotion and heroism characteristic of maternal love.

10. Great attention, no less enlightened than it is constant, is required for the physical development alone of small children; it is necessary, at their age, not only to maintain, but to create healthy organs: a great deal of fresh air and almost continuous exercise are necessary for the cultivation of a constitution which would perish from constraint or inactivity.

12. As for the development of the mind, it must take

INFANT SCHOOLS

place gradually, at play and without sustained effort, until the pupil's age permits greater attention.

M. Cochin, MANUEL DES SALLES D'ASILE

If the working class had any means of capturing the interest and respect of legislators, would not the legislature and that Church which costs so dear, set about perfecting the people's religious, moral and political instruction which, so far, has been the concern of private individuals.

BRITISH REVIEW

Great discoveries are always directly related to the needs of the time; this truth is revealed over and over again by history. The hand of God is seen in the establishment of infant schools, and I am convinced that, of all recent institutions, it is the richest in results, the one which best responds to the needs of Europe and of the whole world. With the system followed in infant schools, education which, as it were, starts with birth, is so superior to the education a child, whatever his social class may be, can receive in the home; and this first education has such an influence on those who receive it that working-class children who are sent as early as the age of two to infant schools will undoubtedly surpass the children of the rich who continue to be educated at home.

In infant schools the law of reciprocity and respect for what is intended for the use of all is inculcated in the child's heart; social distinctions disappear from his view; he recognizes only the superiority of the instructor. The necessity in which he finds himself of realizing what he knows, of teaching what he has learned, causes him to acquire great facility at expressing his thoughts; he becomes accustomed to association with others, to comparing things with their results, men with what they know, and acquires good sound judgement. Once in primary school, the child, if his education is continued following the same method, can have mastered, at the age of sixteen, reading, writing, arithmetic, drawing, descriptive geometry, and, moreover, the practice of most of the processes used in the mechanical arts or in agriculture, so that he need not be condemned, as his father was, to repeat the same task all his life long to earn his bread. The same method can be applied with equal success to any sort of learning, for we learn nothing so well as that which we are obliged to teach to others; brought up in this way, men would work in large associations because there they would find their work pleasurable and easy to perform.

If children were, at the age of two, sent to public institutions, the household's impecuniosity would be less of a burden; the wife, because of the nature of the education she had received, could, as well as the husband, provide for her needs by her labour; and such a situation would be a step toward phalansterian organization. In 1440, when the first attempts at printing were being made in Strasbourg, any prediction that 400 years later this revolutionary invention was to so predominate would have been met with incredulity.

When one observes the lot of children in all classes of society, one is astonished that infant schools were not invented long ago, and that more of them are not being established more rapidly in proportion to the needs of the population. The working class, obliged to work day in and day out to feed their families, cannot watch over their children; when the children are very young, they leave them shut up at home or pay someone to mind them, and older children are left to roam the streets. If, shut up alone in small damp rooms, with no fresh air or heat, the children survive diseases and accidents, they are etiolated, debilitated, often crippled for the rest of their lives. In the streets the dangers which threaten their lives are more numerous still; and, almost always, in the sink of iniquity which great cities conceal in their midst, children are perverted and trained to thievery before they can be trained to work.

Furthermore, if one thinks about the numerous contingencies which imperil the working man's means of subsistence, the decrease in wages and the lack of employment, the continual increase in the price of rent and food, illness and increases in the size of the family, one will be convinced that the working man would have to be possessed of a rare love of work, uncommon sobriety and thrift, much good fortune and fortitude in order never to be poverty stricken. However what becomes of the children of the working man in the midst of the dreadful tribulations which beset him?

In the evening, the father and mother come home from work, utterly exhausted, ill-tempered from the day's vexations and prey to worry. Oh the scenes that take place in such households are of a sort to stupefy the most promising child; he is often beaten because he has fallen down and torn his clothes, or let the dog eat his dinner; the poor child, constantly abused and ill-treated becomes secretive, mendacious, and nourishes a secret hatred toward father and mother. On the other hand, the penury of the parents, the taste for spending which they have acquired in order to forget the hardships they endure, extinguish in their heart any feeling of affection; they develop an aversion for their children who are the cause of continual privation, and they abandon them to a life of vagrancy or take the new-born child to the foundling hospital.

Open infant schools and, as if by magic, you will transform both the child and the worker's household. First there will be an alleviation of anxiety and distress; the child leaves home in the morning and finds a warm welcome in the infant school where, under the supervision of a kindly individual who is interested in his well-being, he spends the day among children his own age, in an uninterrupted succession of amusing activities: his attention is captured by demonstrations; then he sings in chorus, marches in procession, receives lessons from the more advanced, gives lessons to those who are less advanced, and derives a feeling of importance from being a member of the school. Every day he becomes more accustomed to associating with others, learns to use his mental faculties to play a greater role in the group, learns to know himself, and others as well, and learns to respect others so as to be able to command respect. He enjoys good health because the games develop his strength and agility; he learns to keep himself neat and clean and to be modest, and can give a reason for each of his actions.

When the child returns home at the end of the day, his parents are pleased to see him; he has done nothing to provoke their anger, nor taken up a minute of their time; pleased with his behaviour, they ask him questions during dinner, and each time they are more surprised at the soundness of the child's reasoning and at the progress he has made; when they see how good he has become, they will gradually reflect upon their own behaviour, they will be loath to incur the child's contempt; when they see that he is held in better regard than they, they too will work at reforming themselves to merit public esteem. They will see the advantages of education, will frequently go to the infant school to attend the children's exercises, and the parents will be improved by the charming spectacle of the infant school's moral development.

When one observes that part of the population which through the practice of a profession lives in easy circumstances, that class whose members are better educated and more capable than the idle rich, one will see that the children of that class have as great a need for infant school education as do working-class children.

The majority of moralists have declared in favour of public education because it has been demonstrated to them that education is more effective as practice than as precept, that the practical lessons the children give one another have more influence on the moral and intellectual development of the children than would the most capable teacher. If one thinks about the infallibility, the irresistible power that mutual education derives from having children divided into classes, from the intense spirit of emulation which is stimulated by the daily realization of the progress which has been made; if on the other hand, one considers how deep are first impressions and how numerous the sources of corruption which surround the child under the paternal roof, one cannot understand the aversion of the middle class, one cannot imagine why they do not accept the infant school education for their children, and thus deprive them of the social advantages which, ultimately fall to those of superior capacity.[1]

Of the various systems of education which have been more or less in fashion in modern times, the only truth which has gained an almost universal acceptance is the advantage that a public education has over a family one. The works of Xenophon, Plutarch and Montaigne are so full of acute observations that it seems inconceivable that they have not caused us to achieve long since the true, complete and only efficacious education, the one which follows nature's indications and starts at the cradle and continues to puberty. Rousseau's influence was only due to the truth of the ideas he borrowed from them; unfortunately he did not know what to do with them and did nothing to advance the most important of the social sciences: his bizarre system brings together society's falsest prejudices and the revelations of nature; fashion lent it credibility for a time, but now it is quite dead, and if I exhumed a few pages of it, it would only be to point out once again the absurdities it unleashed; since Rousseau the public has been assailed by numerous plans for education and new methods of teaching, welcomed or rejected, not on their merits, but according to who supports them. At the present time, the Catholic secondary schools and convents are engaged in a struggle with the institutions of government; those who are involved in social progress have no fixed opinion on this immense question; each one has developed his own little system. Ideas on education are still in a state of anarchy, and the mob, as is its wont, follows wherever it is led.

We live at a time when political thought is a universal preoccupation: philosophy, education, religion, even fashion,

---

[1] When infant schools were established in England, there was very strong opposition: and these are the objections raised by the opponents: "... But," they would say, "if the children of the masses are brought up with such care, from infancy, they will have too great an advantage over the children of the middle class who had not received similar care; the children of the poor will become too intelligent, too developed, they will inevitably surpass those of other classes, and a serious perturbation in society could result."

(*Report of the Committee of the Infant Schools Society*)

everything is coloured by it. Within families, there are as many ways of looking at things as there are individuals. What becomes of the children in this confusion of ideas, of desires, of whims and of passions? There is so little harmony today in the family that spouses appear to be dominated by the need to hold opposing opinions on everything: the father's assertions are inevitably contradicted by the mother; then there are the grandparents who din their old ideas into the children's ears; friends who see things from the point of view of their social position and who, convinced of being right, also impose their opinions; finally there are the nurses, maids, servants, whose ideas and actions leave their mark on the children. How could those young minds find their way in the bewildering chaos around them! Is it not evident that, in the midst of clashing contradictions, children with no solid ground to stand upon, with no landmarks to guide them, are unable to exercise their judgement without falling into inconsistencies, that of necessity they must be argumentative and headstrong, that their character must be embittered because they frequently must submit to the whims of others, that, in a word, they could not possibly have sound ideas about anything, since they receive no notion of truth? Since those around them express differing opinions about the same things, the children see nothing but individual whim, and they absorb self-interest at every pore.

One cannot expect a child brought up in such a way to become a good citizen; he will be the slave of his passions, of prejudice, of men and of all things; he will not rise above mediocrity, or he will descend to the level of scoundrels by giving free rein to his vices; for things to turn out differently he would have to be endowed with extraordinary faculties which would enable him to overcome the obstacles which stand in the way of the rational development of his mind.

If we now turn our attention to that part of the population whose wealth enables them to live a life of luxury, we will see that there is no child who suffers more, and whose spirit and constitution deteriorate more because of his family life than the child of the rich. Providence may save the child of the poor from the dangers of vagrancy, and from time to time we see men who do honour to mankind emerge from poverty; children from the middle class are almost never apart from their parents, who bestow upon them continual marks of affection, and the qualities of the heart can develop notwithstanding the shortcomings of their intellect and the defects in their characters. But among the rich things are done differently. There is every chance that the children will become depraved, and none at all for them to acquire any good qualities. They are brought up by nurses, tutors and servants. All these slaves endeavour to *please* the little ones whose tears can frequently result in their dismissal; they anticipate all their desires, give in to them on every point; they even put their wits to creating artificial needs for them, and the unfortunate little creatures, brought up in idleness, spoiled by adulation, puffed up with pride, fall prey to all the faults of tyrants, all the habits of despotism; they are demanding, irascible and incapable of denying themselves the least little whim. Their parents rarely see them, and according to their mood of the day, scold them, punish them for no reason or lavish undeserved rewards upon them. The servants, afraid of the children's tales, teach them to lie, and when the little despots are displeased, they discover calumny on their own, and the valets who have incurred their displeasure are accused of the very deeds they were at most pains to conceal. Everything is deleterious in the atmosphere surrounding the child of the rich! Hypocrisy is to be seen everywhere: it is the mask worn by the servants in the presence of his parents; it is the two faces which the parents themselves adopt alternately for the family or for strangers. He also hears two languages: the language of baseness and that of insolence. His nursemaid, in order to win his attention, tells him a thousand absurd tales. At home, everyone is at his feet; if he gets angry, or starts to cry, immediately everyone jumps up and attempts to soothe him; when he goes out, he is greeted with deference by all who know him; people pay court to him and they appear to be flattered at receiving him: how could the child fail to think himself an important personage, to adopt the unfeeling and haughty manners of his parents. Affection has found no place in his heart, vanity alone reigns there; his susceptible pride everyday demands more from those who approach him. Nature's imprint has been totally eradicated; one looks in vain for the child in this puppet decked out in rich clothes. He is the son of a lord, of a man who lives in a palace with numerous servants, who never goes out on foot, and to whom all the shopkeepers in the neighbourhood bow and scrape.

The health of the child has suffered equally, both from excessive eating and from the excessive precautions taken to protect him from the cold, heat, rain, draught and the least exertion. Under the influence of this regimen his constitution has deteriorated, and when it comes time for him to go to school, he is weak both physically and morally. Transported into this new world, he will find it difficult to adjust to the regulations of the school, to the egalitarian spirit of the other boys; he will complain to his parents who will reiterate their recommendations to the masters; the recommendations will not be entirely fruitless; the child will be indulged, excuses will always be found and he will never be obliged to do anything against his will; some poor and intelligent schoolboy for whom he buys sweets will do his composition for him. He will visit his parents on Sunday bringing good marks, he will often be first in his class and will receive the end of the year prizes. After seven or eight years he will leave school as stupid as when he entered, with new vices and having learned nothing.

It is no sophism to assert, as I do, that the rich child needs to be protected from the influence of the things and people around him as much as does the poor child from the influence of the streets and the brutality of his parents.

In infant schools, everyone receives the same education. The most insubordinate child, or the most capricious, follows where he is led, whatever may be the degree of his intelligence; he is on a par with the children in his group, and the lessons are the immediate result of the progress each has made. He gets nothing but sound ideas, learns to live with others, to perform with pleasure his share of tasks, to respect and to recognize as aristocracy only that of intelligence and talent; he accepts without resistance the guidance of poor children, if they are his instructors and surpass him in intelligence.

In the days of tyranny, the high valleys of the Vosges protected in their inaccessible retreats dauntless Protestants who had abandoned their fields to plundering in order to preserve their religious freedom; the area provided food only for goats and deer; they and their descendants lived the life of savages. In 1767, the Protestant pastor Oberlin arrived among those people: the man possessed that powerful energy which comes from a great love for his fellow men. Through his efforts he overcame the barrenness of the soil, founded schools, had trades taught, and poverty gave way to prosperity. As the parents, busy at their trade or in the fields, could not look after their children, Oberlin had the inspiration of gathering them together in spacious rooms, and he chose, as teachers, women whom he and his wife carefully trained: this was the origin of the infant schools. Oberlin's methods for the education of children were imitated and perfected in Switzerland. Robert Owen, convinced that education, in order to be effective, must start with the cradle, and that it must aim at preparing children to take their place in the society in which they are destined to live, founded, in 1816, his infant school in New Lanark, in Scotland; but it was only in 1827 and 1828, when that institution had already taken root in Germany, that France and England thought of adopting it.

In his infant school, Owen follows nature's indications, the instruction he gives is tailored to the degree of intelligence, and he makes use of Lancaster's method. Successive explanations of things, exercises in good judgement, a gradual apprenticeship in gymnastics and the methods used in various trades, simultaneously develop the intellectual faculties, a sensible love of one's fellow man, physical skills and strength. Owen rejects religious instruction, he bases his moral system on reciprocity: he was right in telling me that no infant school in London was run according to the ideas he had followed in establishing his own school.

When there was some talk in England of imitating Germany's example by establishing infant schools for children, Owen, when consulted by Lord Brougham, said that only abstract ideas which are not beyond the understanding of children, ideas susceptible to explanation through the perception of the senses, were admitted to his infant school, that he knew of no religious beliefs suited to a child's intelligence, that children, like all other living creatures, are motivated by pleasure and suffering, and are as capable as grown men of understanding that they can never, except to their own disadvantage, exempt themselves from observing the laws necessitated by reciprocity; that he considered the dogmas of original sin, hell and paradise, etc., to be of a nature to create false ideas as to what is just and unjust, to give rise to argumentativeness and to engender fierce prejudice against anyone of differing religious opinion. Lord Brougham opposed the introduction of this system on the grounds that religious beliefs still have a hold on men's minds. The infant schools known under the name of The National School and The British and Foreign School, which the learned Lord has favoured with his patronage, admit children of every persuasion, without attempting to inculcate the doctrine of any particular religion; nevertheless they allowed fanaticism to impose the reading of the Bible. Reading the Bible to children between the age of eighteen months and seven years! It is worthy of the converts of Otaheiti and New Zealand!

Schools and infant schools had been thriving for several years in Switzerland and in several German principalities before the English public became interested, for in matters intellectual, Germany is well ahead of England. Religious controversies have ceased long ago to arouse interest in Germany, and the life of the mind has forsaken the thousands of interpretations of the Bible to rise to hitherto unknown heights in the realm of thought. The establishment of infant schools, the method to be used for teaching children, accepted as being necessary, have provoked neither controversy nor theological dispute.

In the Austrian States, everyone is obliged to send his children to school: in stipulating this, the government is simply fulfilling the most important of its duties, for it is in society's interest that each one of its members receive an education in keeping with the social organization.

INFANT SCHOOLS

Struck by the importance of infant schools, I was most eager to visit the establishments where the children of the poor find refuge and education. There are, as yet, so few infant schools in London that I asked fifteen or twenty people if they would kindly direct me to one, but no one knew what I was talking about. Finally I applied directly to the founder of infant schools, the respectable Mr Owen, whom I had the pleasure of meeting during his stay in Paris in 1837. "Alas!" Owen said to me, "I know not of a single infant school in London which is in fact a true children's school. There are numerous schools supported by public charity, but none was established according to my principles." These words were doubly significant coming from Owen, and they frightened me. No infant schools in London, in the monster city! But where do the children go whose parents work by day? Where do these unfortunate little children go, barefooted, poorly clothed, where do they find refuge during the long days of cold, rain and fog? Who teaches them reading, arithmetic, drawing; who teaches them cleanliness, orderliness, sociableness? Who teaches them all the things children learn at play? No one; London does not as yet have anything that can truly be called infant schools, and the infant schools they do have, which are moreover insufficient in number, cannot by any means take their place. That explains why, between five and eight o'clock in summer, so many children are to be seen in the streets, especially in the populous parts of the city. At that hour, the day's tasks have been completed and the streets are less crowded with vehicles, the little ones are allowed out of the hovels to take the air. In London, poor families live in the cellar or in the garret of the house, often the same room houses father, mother and seven or eight children; how foul must be the air in these dwellings! The children's faces attest to it. What could be more rickety, more cadaverous than these little creatures! Their emaciation, their pale complexion, their lifeless eyes, in addition to their filthiness and the rags which cover them, offer a most piteous spectacle! I have always preferred to live in a densely populated part of town, so that each evening I found myself surrounded by the children coming out of the houses like ants out of their hills; when the streets were narrow, I would often smell a foul stench coming from the crowd of children. In winter there is no time when they can go out in the streets, and I do not know where they can go for a breath of air: unfortunate populace, you who count for nothing, with what inhumanity you are treated! The aristocracy, which have, to "take the air", their magnificent parks, their immense estates, and the entire Continent where they go to spend the money that the people earn for them; the aristocracy whose town houses, sumptuous palaces, occasional residences, occupy the finest parts of town, keep for their exclusive use the numerous squares which embellish those parts of the city;[1] whereas the poor child in cramped, close quarters dies like a dog, swollen with dropsy, in a damp cellar or a wretched garret.

I would have left London without having been able to discover an infant school, if one day, as I was speaking heatedly about the futility of my search, a Tory who happened to be present had not said to me: "You are mistaken, Madame, London has several infant schools just like yours, and if you like, I can give you the addresses of two or three." I eagerly accepted and set out at once. One of the addresses was Palmer's village, Westminster,[2] that is to say, on the opposite side of Westminster and more than several miles from the centre of town. The infant school was so little known that we had to provide ourselves with a guide, and although the boy lived in the area, it was only by asking the way at least twenty times that he finally managed to lead us to our destination; finally we arrived. We had to cross a sort of courtyard, then we came to a small low-ceilinged room with an uneven floor, furnished with an old table and two or three benches; that was where the infants stayed; there were a dozen urchins so dirty and clothed in such rags that it was painful to see. From that room we went on to another one which was larger, but

---

[1] All the squares are enclosed by iron railings, and are at the exclusive disposal of the owners of the houses around the square, although none of them ever has the time to stroll in these privileged glades.

[2] Palmer's village, founded in 1654 by Reverend J. Palmer, was apparently just south of St. James's Park, not far from Buckingham Gate (Translators).

also too low; there were fifty-two children between three and six years old, as dirty and tattered as the first; the odour they gave off was so intolerable that we were obliged to leave the room, and we observed them through the open door from the courtyard. They were being taught various things, as in our infant schools, but especially to count. The elderly woman who ran the establishment proved to be quite respectable; she gave us all the information at her command, told us that the expenses of the house were not paid by the parish, and that Mr William Smith, a Member of the House of Commons, bore the cost of it alone. This charitable gentleman had built the house, endowed it with a yearly sum of thirty pounds, plus coal and lighting for those in charge of running the school; the elderly woman, her husband and daughter had been put in charge. In addition to what the founder gives, each child must pay a penny a week; this sum, even though slight, is often beyond the means of parents who have several children to send to infant school; however, if admission is not entirely free of charge, these establishments do not wholly fulfil the purpose of their institution; but what would be a shabby and incomplete act of charity on the part of a corporation takes on a different aspect when it is done by a private individual and becomes a very noble gesture which is more likely than any other to rouse the parishes' zeal and to rekindle charity, if indeed there is any spark of charity left among the Anglican clergy, the richest in Europe. Unfortunately, in England parishes are independent, there is no central administration whose censure and supervision they have to fear.[1] In London, as everywhere else, the vestries are composed of rich people who possess a garden, a key to the square and a country house where they send their children to enjoy the wholesome air and outdoor exercise, and who show little concern for the lot of poor children.

The elderly directress of the infant school told us of another one, which also owed its existence to private charity, to the

---

[1] Since the new Poor Law, the government has felt the need to intervene in this area of parish administration in order to prevent revolting abuses, but in everything else the English parishes are as independent as the Swiss Cantons.

bounty of a venerable lady (Miss Mary Doyle).

We intrepidly followed our guide into alleys that were not even paved, and where, at every moment, our cab was in danger of breaking in two, and yet, we were in London, not far from the fashionable quarters with their splendid squares! We went down squalid, dirty streets, the like of which it would be difficult to find in any other country in Europe; most of the houses are without windows, have dirt floors, and next to the door of each one there is a hole filled with dung, dirty water and rotting filth from which arise pestiferous miasma. Moreover the names of the streets say more than any descriptions could. One is named Pond Street, another Dunghill Street, there is a Hog Lane, a Gut Lane, a Sewer Street and then streets with names like Hangedman, Slaughterman, etc.

The faces, the clothes, the language of the inhabitants of the quarter correspond to the names of the streets; although thieves and prostitutes are not in the majority; most of the inhabitants are working men with families to support, who come to live in this quarter because of the low rents. What squalor! A refuse dump is less disgusting! Ah how the poor suffer in proximity to opulence! Finally, after many twists and turns, fruitless inquiries, our guide stopped us at an alley differing from the others by a greater degree of filthiness. There we had to leave our cab which could not have got through the alleys we had to traverse; the one in which the infant school was located was interminably long, with several bends, and at every tenth step we came upon pools where rainwater was carefully conserved for the washing of clothes. The alley, a veritable sewer, is extremely dangerous for adults and must be even more so for the children going to the infant school; only after much difficulty and many precautions did we reach the house. It had rained that morning and rain and soapy water combined to make the clayey ground extremely slippery; a score of times we were in danger of falling in the pools.

A young woman of twenty or twenty-five was in charge of this infant school; she was modestly attired, soft spoken, well mannered and appeared to have been well brought up; she was a bit taken aback by our visit. "The house is in a very bad location," she said, as soon as she had greeted us, "the place is swampy, and the laundries around it make it most unhealthy. The charitable lady who founded the establishment is a friend of the poor, but she is not rich; this house was the only one she owned, and as squalid and poorly situated as it is, her generosity is none the less noble. Moreover, she deprives herself of the most necessary things to be able to pay me twenty pounds to teach the girls' class, and my father the same sum to teach the boys' class." Ah! yes, I concurred with the young woman, it is certainly a noble gesture, and I wondered if there were a single wealthy person in the United Kingdom capable of such noble generosity! The school consisted of two rooms much too small for the number of children (there were eighty of them), and so low that it was necessary at all times to leave the windows open for air; the boys' class was on the ground floor and the girls' class above. A wooden ladder gave access from one to the other; children no more than two would climb up and down clinging to a rope.

The establishment, as far as its situation, building and furnishings are concerned, was indeed extremely squalid, but all that was eclipsed by the intelligent and affectionate charity which presided over it. The children were clean, and so was their rude clothing, in which not a single tear was to be seen; the girls were especially well-groomed; the older ones were making children's clothes; each one, with the title of "mother", looked after two little ones; they washed them, combed their hair, and taught them to be neat and keep themselves clean. The children owe all these clothes too to Miss Doyle, the young woman told me. This admirable lady spends her time going to the houses of the rich to ask for donations for her children, and she clothes them with the money she is given.

These three human beings, the father, the daughter and Miss Doyle, who devoted all their time, all their means and all their faculties to alleviating the misery of the poor, were, for me, like the palm trees of the oasis rising amid the sterility of the gilded throng.

I would have returned to France firmly convinced that there was not a single infant school in the monster city, if I had not come across the notice of a society called Home and Colonial Infant School Society.

The third annual meeting of the institution was held in the Hanover Rooms, last May; it was well attended and by the most "respectable" people, which means that it was exclusively composed of the feudal aristocracy.

After the required prayers, Count Chichester addressed a few words to the assembly concerning the purpose of the society. From the content of his speech it would not appear that the social object is the development of the minds of lower-class children in order to prepare them for apprenticeship and the practice of a profession or to protect abandoned children from the dangers of the street, nothing of the sort; the sole object of the society is scriptural education, and the noble lord lashed out against those thinkers who base the principles of the education of children on nature's indications, and against the training colleges which turn out nothing but teachers of godlessness and insurrection.

Mr J. S. Reynolds, the secretary of the Society, followed the noble lord, and expounded to the gathering upon the efforts of the committee to propagate scriptural education among children. The committee feared, he said, that if the government intervenes in children's education, there will not be sufficient attention to religion, and in the name of the committee, Mr Reynolds urged the respectable members of the assembly to exert all their influence to see that Parliament has nothing to do with the education of children except in manufacturing districts, inasmuch as the society cannot expect to persuade the Chartists to adopt scriptural education for their children. The secretary ended his report with the announcement that the committee had sent teachers to Smyrna, Syria, and Egypt, in order to spread scriptural education among the Ottomans and the Arabs.

Mr V. Harcourt, after a speech worthy of a sixteenth century fanatic, called the assembly's attention to the considerable numbers of children wandering on the roads and roaming the streets of the capital without anyone's making them read the Bible, and he added that Catholics take advantage of the situation and rear homeless Protestant children free of charge in their schools, that they even provide clothing for those who have none in the hope of making converts, and that he knew of whole families converted to Catholicism in this way.

Reverend James Cumming proposed that the assembly adopt a declaration to the effect that the well-being of individuals now and for all time to come, that order within all classes of society, and that the stability of the most precious institutions of the Empire can only exist through scriptural education. He expressed his amazement that certain individuals could maintain that the Holy Scriptures are beyond the understanding of children. According to him, the baptism of new-born infants implies an obligation to initiate them in religious doctrine, and consequently to have them babbling the Scriptures as they first learn to talk. He rejects Rousseau's opinion that: "The religious education of children must not start before the age of nine or ten." He said that more than 600,000 people in London are not church goers, and that more than 900,000 have no knowledge of God or the Holy Scriptures. It is not a question, the reverend shouted, of whether children will be educated at home or in the schools, but of whether they will be educated for hell or for heaven. If the children of the masses do not receive a scriptural education, they will be brought up under one of the two powerful ideologies which war against us, they will fall into the clutches of Rome's priests or of atheists! And Reverend Cumming, carried away with a fanaticism worthy of a Luther or a Calvin, gave free rein to his hatred of Catholicism. "English children," he said, "are exposed to the greatest perils; they are on the road to perdition, because popery besieges us on every side. Catholic priests overrun the provinces, build schools and recruit Protestant children in an attempt to sway them, to dazzle them and win them away from the Anglican Church, the sole repository of truth, of 'substantiated' truth! Our unfortunate children will thus be led astray by these idolatrous priests; they will be brought up in idolatry, absurdity and all the stupid ceremonies of Catholicism; they will worship statues and paintings, and they will be taught those blasphemous words: *Ave Maria*.

"Because of the dangers which face the Protestant churches," continued Reverend Cumming, "it is imperative to establish all over Great Britain infant schools where all future children will receive a scriptural education. If Ireland had schools run on this principle it would present quite a different picture. The effects of scriptural education can be seen in Scotland where the Bible is taught from the earliest hours of infancy, whereas in Ireland the Bible is, if not altogether rejected, at least excluded from the schools."

Reverend Cumming spoke for more than two hours, and throughout his lengthy address he was fired by a holy indignation against popery. He concluded with these words: "As for myself, I do not wish it said that I furthered science, brought knowledge to my fellow citizens, distinguished myself in letters or electrified crowds hanging on my every word; I would be satisfied that I had duly fulfilled my task if a simple epitaph inscribed upon my tomb announced that I had taught just one child to utter the name of Jesus." The speech was repeatedly interrupted by applause.

Mr Labouchère, the current president of the Board of Trade, whom one would have thought either too enlightened to belong to a society whose avowed purpose is to teach the Bible to children between the ages of two and seven, or too independent not to have the courage of his opinions without stooping to court the aristocracy, was present at the session and echoed the sentiments of Reverend Cumming. Reverend J. Stratton proved more tolerant and said that he applauded the establishment of any school for the education of children. This praiseworthy philanthropy did not win the sympathy of the noble assembly.

After several other speeches, all in favour of scriptural education, the meeting was adjourned.

Truly, nowhere but in England are there still people simple enough to attempt to use Bibles for religious propaganda, and to apply logic to religion. To advocate the distribution of Bibles in order to halt the progress of Catholicism, and to teach the Bible to suckling babes is, to be sure, a most ridiculously absurd idea for such a solemn assembly! My dear Reverend Cumming, have you forgotten that the Catholic clergy in Ireland struggles along with the people and for the people, sustaining their faith and courage and sharing their poverty and suffering: that is the secret of its success! Let me remind you, Your Reverence, that in order to persuade the people one must win their affection. The Anglican clergy are extremely rich and the people do not believe in the charity of the rich priest.

In addition to the society which I have just described, there are several others supported by contributions from the aristocracy, but, in spite of all these efforts, the Anglican Church has a rough struggle before it.

XIX

Robert Owen

36. Teacher, which is the great commandment in the law?

37. Jesus said to him: You shall love the Lord your God with all your heart, and with all your soul, and with all your mind.

38. This is the great and first commandment.

39. And a second is like it, you shall love your neighbour as yourself.

40. On these two commandments depend all the law and the prophets.

MATT., CH., 22

In order that I might not be misinterpreted, I wish to make it clear that I am a disciple of neither Saint-Simon, Fourier nor Owen. If I had to pronounce an opinion on the respective value of their doctrines, I would do so according to my own point of view, after having subjected each to thorough scrutiny and compared them all in their various applications; but for the present I shall be concerned only with describing the doctrine of the English socialist, for my book is not a treatise on social theories.

During the same period, three men quite independently of one another, one in Russia, another in France and the third in

England, arrived, by separate series of facts and deductions, at a single moral truth which they demonstrated so tellingly that self-interest is powerless to deny the truth; to wit: co-operative labour alone can guarantee working men against oppression and famine, and save them from the vice and crime engendered by the organization and internal struggles of our societies. The Russian serf appears less unfortunate to Saint-Simon than the working classes of Europe, who are the slaves of hunger and ignorance, exploited by the greed and deceit of proprietors, and bled dry by those in power. Saint-Simon, as a member of the upper aristocracy, is too intimately acquainted with his class to believe in hereditary merit; he bases his hierarchy on the varying degrees of intelligence and adopts the principle of: "to each according to his ability, to each ability according to its contribution." Fourier dissects the social order, exposes all the fraud and all the injustice and all the turpitude; by induction he is led from the attraction of bodies to passionate attraction, from the harmony of sounds to the harmony of passions; harmony and attraction are the two axes of his order, and his law is a reflection of natural law. Fourier is a prophet, without aspiring to be an apostle; and taking as his point of departure the idea that the universe is reflected in all its parts, he sees in the life of man the image of the life of all humanity.

Owen has not made a study of philosophy, has not observed all the classes of European societies at the time of the upheavals of the French Revolution and, unlike Saint-Simon, he is not of a turn of mind to formulate a social order; unlike Fourier, he does not rise to the heights of the laws of the universe in order to discover in them the laws of harmony which must regulate human societies; he does none of these things. Owen is a man with a good heart and a penetrating and perceptive mind. He gained his experience in manufactories where, for thirty years, he has had a considerable number of working men under his charge, and where he has observed all the distress of the poor.

Owen's ideas are the result of a series of observations and experiences, but they do not comprise a complete theory embracing man in all his varied forms as he is found in history and in life. Concerned with the enormous influence which outside circumstances have upon us, Owen almost entirely ignores the inner man; for him, the human creature is the block of marble from which the sculptor fashions according to his whim a hero, a monster or a mere receptacle; man according to Owen is a man-made figure; I must confess that I find no trace of God's creature with his presentiments of the infinite and of his own eternal and ever progressing life. In all frankness, Owen pays too little attention to spiritual needs; but on the other hand, I find Owen admirable when he organizes material interests. He summons the vast numbers of European working men to the association; he shows them the urgent necessity for it if they wish to avoid starvation, the well-being which they would derive from it, and he shows them the way to achieve it. He demonstrates with figures and by reasoning based on experience that, through association, labour and capital would be the most productive and expenses would be the lowest in relation to the total dividends. Owen is like John the Baptist announcing the coming of Christ; he prepares the way for another who will come and finish his work, breathe life into the statue of Prometheus, add the rich hues of poetry to this materialistic life, raise the temple which the arts, with all their prestige, will beautify and where a divine harmony will lift the soul toward God and the Virgin Mary.

From Owen's writings it may be seen that he considers customs, ways of seeing and feeling, character in other words, as being the product of the order and the milieu in which man has lived; and he therefore concludes that man is not responsible. According to him, vice and crime in man are diseases to be cured. He bestows neither praise nor blame upon actions; they are the result of the moral forces which shape us and of which we are unaware. Man at birth, says Owen, is neither good nor evil. He so emphasizes the power of education, that, in the society he is shaping, he seems to assume no inequality of ability, for it is age which determines the various functions. Owen does recognize a Creator who is eternal, good and infinite: he would have man pay homage to God by loving his fellow man, but he proscribes any outward worship. Studying the laws of nature, the production of wealth and its best uses is, he says, the means of being useful to our fellow man, and it is our purpose in life.

Owen became convinced, through long experience, that the social bond can endure only through good will among men and through the love they have for one another. Yet he is accused of being un-Christian because actions alone are important to him and he is utterly indifferent to all sects alike.[1] "I shall take my place again in the Christian ranks," he replies to his detractors, "when Christianity frees itself from the errors which all and sundry feel free to heap upon it."

Never has there appeared on the world's wide stage a man more endowed than he with love of his fellow man; to find a remedy for their suffering has been Owen's goal through forty years of observation, experience and labour. God has crowned his work, and now the practical philanthropist, transformed into the apostle of the principle of love, devotes the remainder of a well spent life demonstrating to working men the advantages of brotherly union for every individual; for it is for the sake of the world's happiness that he enjoins them to love one another and to unite.

What could be more admirable than the perspicacity and sound judgement of the practical philanthropist in founding the infant school? The truth of the principles which he discovered for the education of children is self-evident. Through merely studying nature, Owen has endowed the world with a system for the mental development of young children which is superior to anything which preceded, because it introduces nothing which cannot be verified by personal observation. The energy and curiosity displayed by children at every stage of life are the two forces which Owen harnesses through kindness and gentleness; as suddenly and as vehemently as the body recoils from pain, the minds of children instinctively rebel against harsh and severe treatment and the suffering inflicted upon them. Owen blames punishment and reward for a goodly portion of the world's ills;

---

[1] At New Lanark, Owen banned all religious discussion from his mills and his school and thus re-established harmony among the sectaries of the four or five religious sects in the village.

he bans them from his school in order not to encourage lying and duplicity, in order not to give rise to envy, jealousy, false values and vanity. The natural consequences of doing right or wrong are sufficient motivation in his school: the joy expressed by others contents the author of good deeds; the child who does wrong finds himself alone, and the abuse of force is suppressed by the intervention of all. Experience has taught Owen that kindness and love have infinite power over children. Mutual acts of kindness and consideration are the foundation of his sytem of education. The gentleness and kindly disposition of the master and the pupils are in harmony with the activity and curiosity of childhood and together constitute the simple and powerful instrument, discovered by Owen, for shaping the social character of man. He masters his will through the constant exercise of kindly feelings, overcomes antisocial inclinations through the power of constant association, and acquires unlimited confidence from the authority which truth exercises upon us, for he speaks only the truth and teaches only those things whose truth illuminates the mind of the disciple.

The fundamental law of the Owenian school appeals to the constant need of love, the desire to know, that thirst for truth whereby the soul is revealed. Owen discovered that law through a series of experiments and through close study of the social principle among children and working-men. He obtains such satisfying results through the influence exercised by custom, affection and truth that it is not surprising that he has given vent to his indignation at the absurdity of persisting in antisocial modes of education which have for centuries been fruitlessly heaping line upon line and precept upon precept. The failure of theoretical pedagogy is sufficiently demonstrated, by the results of ordinary education, so that it may be taken as a proven fact that truth and ethics can have lasting influence on us only to the extent that we breathe life into them by putting them into practice. Truth and ethics must, through constant application, exercise our judgement, motivate our behaviour and shape our habits.

"It must be evident to common observers," Mr Owen has remarked, "that children may be taught, by either Dr Bell's or Mr

Lancaster's system, to read, write, account, and sew, and yet acquire the worst habits, and have their minds rendered irrational for life.[1]

"Reading and writing are merely instruments, by which knowledge, either true or false, may be imparted; and when given to children are of little comparative value, unless they are also taught how to make a proper use of them.

"When a child receives a full and fair explanation of the objects and characters around him, and when he is also taught to reason or judge correctly, so that he may learn to distinguish general truths from falsehoods, he will be much better instructed, although without the knowledge of one letter or figure, than those are who have been compelled to believe, and whose reasoning faculties have been confounded, or destroyed, by what is most erroneously termed learning.

"It is readily acknowledged, that the manner of instructing children is of importance, and deserves all the attention which it has lately received; that those who discover or introduce improvements which facilitate the acquirement of knowledge, are important benefactors to their fellow-creatures; yet the manner of giving instruction is one thing, the instruction itself another, and no objects can be more distinct. The worst manner may be employed to give the best instruction, and the best manner to give the worst instruction. Were the real importance of both to be estimated by numbers, the manner of instruction may be compared to one, and the matter of instruction to millions: the first is the means only, the last the ends to be accomplished by those means.

"If, therefore," Mr Owen adds, "in a national system of education for the poor, it be desirable to adopt the best manner, it is so much the more desirable to adopt also the best manner of instruction."

Owen has observed the development of human intelligence; he speaks to children neither of abstractions nor of the revelations of

---

[1]The quoted passages are taken from the work of Henry Grey Macnab, physician to H.R.H. the Duke of Kent.

the soul, for the simple reason that these are ideas that are beyond the understanding of the child. The first things that man learns, as well as all the means of self preservation, arise primarily from the exercise of instinct and the power of intuition on objects subjected to the perception of his senses; education must therefore begin with learning about the material world; moreover the pencil should precede the pen in the hand of a child; he must be able to draw objects before learning the combinations of conventional signs which represent their names; for once he understands the intellectual fiction which associates with different signs the memory of sounds and utterances, of words and songs, the concepts of size and number, his mind has made great progress; the world of ideas is henceforth open to him.

In the Owenian association, children are admitted to school as early as the age of two; they remain until the age of ten, and do not learn to read until they are about seven or eight. One general rule presides over instruction at the school: to teach the child nothing which is not the immediate consequence of what he already knows. Owen has too much good sense to attempt to speak of God to his young pupils before God Himself has entered their hearts; he rears them in the practice of charity, shows them that true self-interest consists in not being selfish, and relies on their feelings of satisfaction and remorse to teach them what conscience is.

Try as they might, envy, hatred, the rantings of hypocrisy could find no personal aim or ambition in Owen's designs, writings or conduct; the purest love of his fellow man motivates his life, it is reflected in everything he does, and unbeknown to him such divine charity, such superhuman mansuetude raise him to lofty heights.

In a memorandum addressed to the allied powers meeting at Aix-la-Chapelle, Owen said of himself: that he asks for nothing, has need of nothing, and has nothing to fear personally either from governments or from peoples; before taking a single step in the career be has made for himself, he weighed his life in his hand (as he expresses it); he no longer weighs it, now he considers it no more than a weightless feather in the scales compared to the enormous good that he sees can be done in the present circumstances. Obtaining that great good for his fellow man is the sole object of his concern.

Never has philanthropy appeared in a more unitarian form, never has it been so charitable as in Owen's social community: followers of Brahma, of Confucius, Jews, Christians and Moslems, children, the young and the old, rich and poor, all are united by the practical philanthropist! Tolerance is his banner; his law springs from the principle of love and brotherhood preached by Jesus; he cements the community through the power of habits of kindliness and through identifying individual interest with the interest of all.

Owen believes that the continuous labour of the sweat-shops undermines men's health, benumbs their minds, and at the same time he is convinced of the immense advantage of having the tasks of agriculture performed by groups of workers. That is why he would have these associations embrace agriculture and manufacturing. Experience has taught him that diversity of occupation, which revives the worker's zeal, is compatible with the division of labour and its efficient organization. It is clear to him that a union of workers, using perfected methods, working and living together,[1] could always offer the articles they manufactured at a lower price than could the capitalist with the assistance of the unfortunate workers whom he exploits; it is also clear to him that such an association would obtain greater credit than the manufacturer and that, finally, through the result of its labour, all the needs of the aforesaid association would be amply provided for, as would the education of the children and the pleasures of the mind.

"The adoption of the system which I propose," said Owen

---

[1] At New Lanark, Mr Owen set up for his workers stores of the necessary provisions which they could buy at cost. He set up a dining hall for workers who wished to take advantage of the lower cost of preparing food in quantity, and although the wages paid by Mr Owen were lower than in other manufactories, his workers, because of their regular habits and the savings they could accumulate, were much better off than workers in other manufactories.

"would offer enormous advantages for the poor classes, and those advantages are as susceptible of proof as a mathematical proposition."

In support of this assertion, I shall quote several passages from the report of the committee which studied Owen's proposal to organize an association according to his principles.

The committee, referring to the various resolutions and reports it adopted, and which were approved by a very large and respectable general assembly, continues to ask that it be allowed to submit the following considerations to the public:

"1. That Mr Owen has for twenty years had under his sole management, as acting partner, one of the largest manufactories in the kingdom, in which upwards of two thousand workmen are employed: that he has conducted it in a method which is very materially different from the ordinary course, and which has nevertheless been found to produce the most important advantages both to the employers and the workmen. Without entering into minute details it may be here stated, that the hours of labour have been shortened from 16 in the 24 to 10½; that upwards of 700 pounds per annum are expended by the proprietors in the education of the children of the workmen; that in the schools used for this purpose no corporal punishment is ever inflicted; that no child under ten years of age is employed at all in labour; and that a certain portion of land is kept in garden cultivation by the same persons who work in the manufactory. Under all these peculiarities, and notwithstanding the difficulties of the times which have overwhelmed so many others, this establishment has continued eminently to prosper; and, according to Mr Owen's opinion, the profits of it depend mainly upon those parts of the system of management which are peculiar to itself. On the other hand, the officers of justice have not in a single instance during the last fifteen years executed any criminal process in New Lanark. All persons agree in representing the manufactory to be in order, cleanliness, and good arrangement, inconceivably superior to the generality; and (of late years especially, and since the more perfect formation of the schools) the health, cheerfulness, intelligence, and excellent dispositions of the children, seem to have struck every one who has visited the place with pleasure and surprise.

"2. It is now proposed to form a new establishment in which agricultural and manufacturing employment shall both be used; but of which agriculture shall be the basis: Mr Owen's increased experience, and the advantage of beginning *de novo*, will enable him to make arrangements much superior to those which exist at New Lanark: he expresses the most confident opinion that the capital employed will be rapidly repaid with interest; that the labourers may be placed in a state of comfort hitherto unknown to that class: he offers to take upon himself the superintendence, at the same time that he entirely precludes himself from deriving any profit, and he is desirous to communicate in the most open and unreserved manner the whole details of his plan.

"3. Those details are before the public; and the Committee having considered them, are of opinion that to a certain extent they are not only practicable, but as sure, as human institutions can be sure, of producing the results which Mr Owen anticipates. To those who may have rejected them without examination, the Committee would suggest, that Mr Owen has already tried an union of agriculture with manufactures; that from his patience, his experience, and his success, there is every reason to suppose that he would proceed with cautious steps in arranging the proportions in which the two should exist in a new establishment; that the effect of economical arrangement in diminishing waste and saving space and time, has never been tried in agriculture and domestic economy upon so extensive a scale as that which is now proposed; that the effects of a combination of labours upon a large scale are likewise not at all known in agriculture; but that those who are acquainted with them in other departments anticipate the happiest results from them in that most important province of human exertion; and that, above all, no one can calculate the increase of power and of happiness which may be derived from a well-regulated system for the formation of moral habits and a general improvement of the character of the working classes.

"4. The Committee are aware of many objections which have

been urged against Mr Owen's system, but none of those stated have appeared to them as founded in reason or in fact.

"5. The private opinions which Mr Owen has been supposed to entertain on matters of religion form one of such objections.

"6. Several other objections rest upon a supposition that Mr Owen's plans necessarily involve a community of goods; this is a great mistake or misrepresentation. In the establishment which is now proposed there would be no community of goods, nor any deviation from the established laws of property. Mr Owen, it is true, has expressed on a former occasion some opinions in favour of a state of society in which a community of goods should exist; but he has never considered it as essential to the success of such an establishment as is now proposed, nor required it as the condition of his superintendence.

"It has also been said that these plans have a tendency to the equalization of ranks. This notion is connected with, and depends upon, the erroneous one, that they involve a community of goods.

"7. It has also been said, that injury is to be apprehended from the withdrawing of capital, now employed advantageously in other concerns. The Committee are at a loss to understand what objections will apply to the withdrawing of the necessary quantity of capital from other concerns, which will not apply to all ordinary cases of the shifting of capital.

"8. The objections, that the plan has a tendency to promote too rapid an increase of population, rest upon the same supposition of the community of goods, and that supposition being removed, fall to the ground. If the encouragement to population consists merely in the increase of comforts, which capital, thus employed, may bestow upon the labouring classes at the same time that it repays the capitalist, the Committee conceive that there can be no objection to such encouragement.

"9. A different class of objectors represent that it will destroy the independence of the peasantry, break up their domestic habits, and place them too much under the control of their employers; deaden their faculties, and convert them into mere machines. It is believed that these apprehensions have arisen almost entirely from one part of the plan, namely, that arrangements should be formed to enable the labourers and their families, in each establishment, to eat in common. Little doubt is entertained that the advantages of this plan would be so evident, that it would be generally adopted; but no sort of compulsion, or even persuasion, would be resorted to: the workmen might receive their wages in money, and the mode in which they might dispose of them would be entirely at their own option. The Committee wish to remind those who value domestic habits and independence so highly, that the domestic enjoyments of the manufacturers, who now work sixteen hours a day in the mills, cannot be very great; and that the independence of all labourers is greatly affected by the present state of the poor laws. The proposed plans, while they would afford greater comforts, would, it seems probable, afford greater opportunities of saving; and as there would be the most perfect liberty of leaving the establishment at any time, it is not easy to see how the independence of any one could be diminished. The objection, that the faculties would be deadened by a system, of which universal education and varied employment is the basis, seems to the Committee to be a singular one, the efficacy of that arrangement, as far as it can be carried into practice, in putting a stop to the brutalizing effects which have been produced by forcing the division of labour to a point at which it defeats its own object, cannot be doubted.

"10. The Committee, on the whole, submit to the public, that the present state of the poor and labouring classes cannot continue, and that some remedy must be found; that no plan can be effectual which has not for its main object the creation of moral habits and social feelings in those classes;

"That none have hitherto been proposed, of which it is so much the object as the present one; that there is at least a sufficient prospect of the proposed establishment succeeding, to warrant a trial; that no alteration of the laws is asked for; that no evil is to be apprehended, whether the Committee are right or wrong in their anticipations, but that incalculable good must follow if they are right, and that if they should succeed no further than in showing by one more example that it may be even profitable to themselves for our manufacturers to apply time, money, and attention to the improvement of the comforts, feelings, and happiness of their workmen, the whole of the money required would be well bestowed. Under these circumstances, and on these grounds, the co-operation of all who sincerely desire the welfare of all ranks of society, and especially the improvement of the general character of the labouring classes, is most earnestly solicited.

GENERAL ADVERTISEMENT OF THE COMMITTEE
London, August 11, 1819
PLAN FOR PROVIDING EMPLOYMENT FOR THE POOR

"The Committee appointed at a General Meeting, convened to consider Mr Owen's plan, held at the City of London Tavern, July 26, 1819, have proceeded under the persuasion that the public mind is fully impressed with a conviction, that the increased and increasing evils of pauperism call for some adequate remedies.

"They apprehend that such remedies will be most readily found in any plan that may provide employment for the poor, principally in agricultural labour, which, while it shall tend to secure industrious habits, may be rendered conducive to a system of training up the young in improved moral conduct.

"The Committee consider that the plan proposed by Mr Owen combines many practical results connected with the advantages above stated, and therefore are of opinion that an establishment should be formed by way of experiment, etc.

"Subscribers' names will be received by Messrs Smith, Payne, and Smith; Messrs Williams and Co.; Messrs Spooner, Attwood, and Co.; Messrs Drummond and Co., Bankers.[1]"

---

[1] In 1816 the project which the committee's report concerns was conveyed by Mr Owen to Mr Falck, the Dutch Ambassador in London. Mr Falck, who approved of Owen's ideas, submitted them to his government, and it was Owen's system that was adopted in Holland for the Labour Colonies.

Mr Owen has offered his project to the British Government several times, including the ministry of which Lord Liverpool was a member. The Cabinet would have accepted it, but on that occasion, as on all others, opposition from the Anglican clergy caused the socialist's proposition to be rejected.

In the report, which I have not given in its entirety, the committee refutes all the false accusations heaped upon the philanthropist's proposition by the rage inspired by hypocrisy, fanaticism and the aristocracy's fear of the independence that the working classes would acquire if they joined together in associations.

As early as 1819, the animosity which Owen's principles aroused was such that intrigues prevented the realization of his project. It was in vain that he called the attention of serious minds to the increase in power brought about by mechanization between 1792 and 1817, an increase which he estimated as the equivalent of the work of two hundred million men. It was in vain that he pointed out that the very same mechanical power was undergoing an immense development on the Continent, so that articles were being fabricated faster than they could be consumed, and that, in spite of England's prodigious efforts to open new markets for herself, the entire world would not provide enough of them to meet her needs.

And yet, Owen maintained, the situation continues to worsen; machines produce piles of merchandise, and mechanization progresses relentlessly; the use of manpower continually diminishes, and man's labour is so depreciated that wages are no

---

If the government had adopted Owen's plan and had pursued it as fully as the author intended, the working poor would have received professional training and been given useful employment. According to Owen, more than a hundred thousand pounds have been irrationally spent to aid indigent masses who have been corrupted by it because of the idleness in which they have been allowed to live. He maintains that the enormous expense could have been avoided and the national wealth increased by more than a hundred million pounds generated by the proper administration of the labour and industry of the settlement. Then it would not have been necessary, he says, to raise the poor rate and to require all those who were not insolvent to pay it, and thousands of individuals, among the Irish and English population, would not have been prey to famine!... and thousands of them would not have starved to death!

longer sufficient to meet the most urgent needs: it is thus a proven fact that the working classes are powerless to compete with machines; and the practical philanthropist saw the remedy for their problems in the simultaneous exploitation of agriculture and industry by associations of workmen who would be organized or managed according to his principles.

According to Owen, "The circumstances of the times render a change in our internal policy respecting the poor and working classes absolutely necessary; shall the change be effected by ignorance and prejudice, under the baleful influence of the angry and violent passions? Under the existing laws, the unemployed working classes are maintained by, and consume part of the property and produce of, the wealthy and industrious, while their powers of body and mind remain unproductive. They frequently acquire the bad habits which ignorance and idleness never fail to produce; they amalgamate with the regular poor, and become a nuisance to society.

"Most of the poor have received bad and vicious habits from their parents; and so long as the present treatment continues, those bad and vicious habits will be transmitted to their children, and through them to succeeding generations. Any plan, then, to meliorate their condition must prevent bad and vicious habits from being taught to their children, and provide the means by which only good and useful ones may be given.

"The labour of some individuals is far more valuable than that of others; and this arises principally from the training and instruction they receive. Means should therefore be devised to give the most useful training and instruction to the children of the poor.

"The same quantity and quality of labour under one direction, will produce a much more valuable result than under another. It is necessary then that the labour of the poor should be exerted under the best.

"One mode of management as to their expenditure, will create many more advantages and comforts than another. Such arrangements should therefore be made in this department as should produce the largest benefits at the smallest expense.

"Most of the vices and misery of the poor arise from their being surrounded by unnecessary temptations which they had not been trained to overcome; it would therefore be a material improvement to remove them from unnecessary temptation.

"Under this view of the subject, any plan for the melioration of the poor should combine means to prevent their children from acquiring bad habits, and to give them good ones, to provide useful training and instruction for them, to provide proper labour for the adults, to direct their labour and expenditure, so as to produce the greatest benefit to themselves and to society; and to place them under such circumstances as shall remove them from unnecessary temptations, and closely unite their interest and duty."

Unable to overcome the obstacles which religious fanatics and the aristocracy put in his path, Owen went to America, where, in 1824, he founded the New Harmony Community. The heterogeneous elements of which it was composed and the misunderstandings which the Methodists and all the sanctimonious sectaries sought to foster prevented its success; nevertheless the results were very satisfactory from the philanthropic point of view: the society which Owen founded on the 30,000 acres of land which he had acquired in the state of Indiana was subdivided into several establishments: societies of arts and crafts and of agriculture were organized, the education of children was conducted with the greatest attention and according to Owenian theory; finally the land was worked by the adults under comprehensive and intelligent direction. In all the States of the Union associations were formed on principles more or less resembling those of Owen and took the name of *Co-operative Society*. Owen encountered in the United States the same persecution as in England; for those are perhaps the only two nations in the world where fanaticism still survives in all its intolerance, in all its hypocrisy, in all its horror! He returned to Europe to rekindle the zeal of his disciples.

On his return to England Owen found that a holy league had been organized: everywhere he went he encountered committees busy organizing large meetings and promoting the dissemination of their ideas;[1] the Society had founded the *Co-operative Magazine* to be its organ.

Owen has sacrificed an immense fortune, honourably acquired, to propagate his doctrine; it is estimated that since his return from America he has made eleven or twelve hundred public speeches and that he has written for the newspapers or published elsewhere 3,000 articles addressed to various segments of the public. His travels have been perpetual, and whenever it has been a question of publicity, nothing has held him back, neither expense nor his health nor his own concerns.

There was in Manchester a society of working men under the name of *The Community*, or *The Friendly Society*; through Owen's influence and his actions in its behalf, the society has grown, and has taken the name of *The Association of All Classes, of All Nations*. The committee which governs it is presided over by Owen and numbers among its members the most distinguished men who have embraced his doctrine: Messrs John Booth, William Smith, Robert Alger, Junius Haslam, Baxter, Hanhart, George Fleming, James Braby, etc.

A number of publications have succeeded the *Co-operative Magazine* and disseminate the Society's principles: *The Star of the East*, *The Pioneer*, *The Social Reformer*, *The New Moral World*, *The Weekly Dispatch* and several others; the last named with a circulation of 40,000.

Owen having accused religions of the evils which plague human societies, the Bible sellers were all up in arms; these fanatical histrions, who live at the expense of imbeciles, took alarm, and all the mob of sermonizers who, under various denominations, contend with one another for the public's favour, launched a devious campaign of persecution against the philanthropist. They heaped calumny on him and his disciples

---

[1] In London a co-operative society had been established to which were then affiliated societies created throughout the United Kingdom, in Dublin, Brighton, Exeter, Liverpool, Huddersfield, Glasgow, Edinburgh, York, Belfast, Birmingham, Manchester, Saldfort and Derby.

and stopped at nothing in order to prejudice their private interests and to muffle the reverberations of their writings, their preaching, their brotherly actions and their universal beneficence.

The religion of the aristocracy, powerful through its immense wealth and the support of the government, did not take fright so hastily; to crush the philanthropist, it relied on the hatred of the dissident sects which play on the public's credulity.

However, Owen's followers are numerous, not only in the United Kingdom, but also in America, Germany and France. His followers take the name of *socialists*, and the association, forswearing the national hatreds fomented by the aristocracy, takes the name of the *Universal Society of Rational Religionists* and flies the banner of UNITY. A yearly council is invested with the powers of the association and governs its proceedings; it meets in one of the manufacturing cities of England, and delegates come from all the individual congresses, of which there are sixty-one. Distinct from this legislative body, there is a central committee sitting in Birmingham: it is this committee which gives a unifying impetus to the Society. Its specific task is the dissemination of their doctrine, and it sends missionaries throughout the United Kingdom and to the Continent. The missionaries receive a salary of about thirty shillings a week, in addition to travel expenses. The money required to meet these enormous expenses is furnished by individual contributions of four-pence a week.

In the principal cities, such as Manchester, Birmingham, Liverpool, Sheffield, etc., the socialists hold regular and public meetings.

Owen's followers in the United Kingdom already numbered 500,000 when the Anglican Church in turn took fright; the great sinecurists assembled; the leaders of Toryism repaired to their conciliabules and it was agreed that they would intimidate the young Queen in order to force her to proclaim in favour of persecution!

Doctor Phillpott, the Bishop of Exeter, a perfect nonentity of a man, who is nevertheless consumed with the desire of hearing his name in public, eagerly seized the opportunity and, as he could be neither a St Ambrose nor a Bossuet, reproduces in the nineteenth century the infamous role of the inquisitors of the sixteenth! He called down the severity of the law upon men devoted to the poor; he would burn at the stake true apostles who, full of love for their fellowman, say unto the working-man: "Come to us, brothers, come and unite your strength with our strength, your goodwill with our goodwill; let us work together and, by the love we have for one another, let it be known that we are religious in the TRUE SENSE. Let us be known by our DEEDS, and leave lies, hollow words and the language of hypocrisy to false prophets."

Nevertheless the good Bishop of Exeter made his denunciation; sure of a favourable reception in the House of Lords, his hatred spoke out plainly; no charitable word revealed the Christian; yet this man professes himself a member of Christianity! He claims to be a Christian bishop and yet he utters denunciation!...

The English people are still governed by medieval laws. The power of public opinion has forced the government to extend its tolerance, but the most dreadful intolerance still survives in the law. Was not Lord Brougham, that great renegade from liberty, accustomed to say in the House of Lords: "Should any Queen of England marry a Prince who does not profess the religion of Phillpott, *she would lose her right to the throne!*"

A religion richly endowed and imposed by the government, a religion professed by all the oppressors of the people, may indeed have succeeded in commanding as much respect as the law; but empty of anything which might arouse sympathy, it has necessarily had to lose some of its ascendency over the masses; for this reason thousands of sects have sprung up on English soil. Forced to tolerate them, the government has never given up the pretensions of Henry VIII, to circumscribe religious thought. The poor English people, who are told over and over again that they are governed by *the most liberal of constitutions*, would consider themselves fortunate indeed if their model constitution contained even these few articles of our charter:

Art. 1. The French are all equal before the law, whatever may otherwise be their differences of rank and station.

Art. 2. They contribute indiscriminately, in proportion to their wealth, to the expenses of the State.

Art. 3. All are equally eligible for civil and military services.

Art. 5. All profess their religion with equal freedom and enjoy the same protection for their worship.

To be sure, liberalism is found in public opinion in England; nevertheless tyranny over all is formulated in the law, and the yoke of the aristocracy is all the heavier because the English nobility is, of all the classes in the nation, the most bigoted, the most profoundly mired in prejudice, and the most ignorant. The address presented to the Queen by the Lords, calling for "repressive measures against the socialists" is the most eloquent proof of that fact. When Phillpott's factum was read, the "untoward hero" was stirred to anger and called upon all the inequities of the law to defend the existence of the aristocratic religion imperiled by the advance of socialism.

What will be the results of the persecution launched by the most honourable Lords? It will accelerate the spread of the new religion, replies the believer. The socialists, braving all dangers, will do as did the apostles of Christ; they will go about the provinces, preaching the NEW LAW! The law of brotherly association which will provide bread for all ... will dry all tears! ... Their voice will be powerful! for twenty million workmen, throughout the United Kingdom, weep and go hungry!

Sketches

I
CLUBS

In England material interests join together and form associations with wonderful alacrity; every sort of commercial venture: mining, railroad construction, colonization, etc., soon bring together a large number of individuals who require no other reason for forming an association than the profits they hope to derive from it; and as it is the amount of the profits, not the political, moral or religious utility of the venture, which is the deciding factor, with no knowledge of one another, no mutual friendship or esteem, no political or religious opinions in common, they enter their names on the roster which includes members of every party and sect, and the desire for gain is sufficient unto itself to assure the harmony of the heterogeneous mass. This spirit of association, or rather of co-operation, extends to the smallest things. The numerous London clubs are an example, those magnificent palaces where one finds under a single roof all the material advantages to be derived from community of interest.

I visited several clubs in St James, Pall Mall and Carlton Terrace. Nothing so richly decorated nor so comfortable is to be seen anywhere. The entrance to these palaces is truly regal; vast vestibules, central heating, splendid divided staircases decorated with statues and fine carpets and lit by hundreds of gas-lights. On the ground floor great dining-rooms overlook attractive gardens; upstairs are magnificent drawing-rooms fifty, sixty, eighty feet in length. Almost all of them have full length windows opening onto terraces. In summer the terraces are decorated with boxes planted with beautiful flowers. No expense has been spared in providing all possible amenities. The mirrors, which are so costly in England, are of colossal proportions; the libraries contain a selection of the most frequently read books; and finally the clubs have all the English newspapers and the latest publications, and some have French and other foreign newspapers. The cost of membership is, according to the club, eight, ten, twelve, fifteen or twenty pounds a year. A member may lunch at the club, read the papers or a novel, write letters, warm himself on his return from the Stock Exchange, and dine there as well. As is well known, for every Englishman dinner is the main thing, his reason for existence. No club which is at least moderately well appointed is without its French cook. The chef (the culinary artist retains his imposing name even beyond the Channel) is the soul of the establishment; in general one dines very well; French dishes are served in all of them; the sauterne and champagne are of the very best, and all at a very moderate price. Association brings, as you see, important material advantages; let us now inquire as to its intellectual results. What do these two or three hundred club members do? Do they sincerely strive to acquire an understanding of important social questions? Do they discuss business and politics, letters, theatre and fine arts? No. They go to their clubs to dine well, to drink good wine, to play cards and escape the boredom of married life; they come there to find a refuge from the day's trials and tribulations, not to incur the fatigue of a prolonged discussion on any subject whatsoever. And indeed, with whom could they converse? They remain strangers to one another; the status of member does not entail the obligation of speaking to one's fellow members, nor even of wishing them good day. They all walk into the drawing-rooms without removing their hats, look neither to the right nor to the left, and speak to no one. What could be more comical than seeing a hundred men or so assembled in those vast drawing-rooms like so many pieces of furniture? One man is sitting in a chair reading a recent pamphlet; another is writing at a table beside an individual to whom he has never spoken; still another is stretched out on a sofa asleep; others are strolling back and forth; so as not to disturb the sepulchral silence, there are men whispering as if in church. What possible enjoyment can these men derive from such gatherings, I wondered, as I watched them. They all appeared to be supremely bored. Amazed at such a singular mode of association, at times I fancied I was seeing a collection of automatons. I inquired of my English companion why there was so little intercourse among the members of these societies. "What," he replied. "would you have us speak to a man we do not know, about whom nothing is known; when we have no idea whether he is rich or poor, Tory, Whig or Radical; you would have us risk wounding his pride or his feelings without regard for the consequences! Only the French could be guilty of that sort of rash behaviour." "Why then", I insisted, "do you admit people you don't know?" "Because a certain number of subscriptions are necessary to cover the club's expenses, and because we are satisfied as to the respectability of the members if they have been sponsored by two members of the club and approved by the committee."

My companion's reply is a perfect example of the English mind; through association English society invariably seeks to gain some material advantage; do not expect it to associate for philosophical, sentimental or ethical reasons, for your expectations will be incomprehensible. Such impassivity, such social materialism is somehow frightening.

The English club makes men more self-centred and egoistic; it is at one and the same time a gaming room, a reading room, and a restaurant; if there were no clubs, men would be more prone to go out in society or to remain in the bosom of their families. Clubs are the source of numerous domestic disorders; husbands forsake their homes and leave their wives to dine on a joint of beef which lasts the entire week, while the gentlemen sit down to sumptuous dinners at their club, consume fine wines and lose their money at cards. When I left, there was talk of opening clubs for unmarried men, where subscribers would have bachelor rooms at their disposal...

II
POCKETS

I am firmly convinced that it is not necessary to understand the language of a country in order to understand its ways. They are revealed by every outward sign, and particularly by dress.

As opinions, manners, customs, and fashions are translated into objects and actions, and as they all have their causes from which they stem according to the laws of nature, I maintain that there is nothing pertaining to a nation which cannot be understood by alert and thoughtful observation, without the help of the written or spoken language.

When no trace subsists except in the written word, as far as we are concerned, it is as if opinions, events and things had never existed. The Obelisk of Luxor, the Arc de Triomphe, the Madeleine, the Chamber of Deputies, the fountains and the sculptures personifying the cities of France, the Tuileries, the Champs-Elysées, in short all that one sees around the Place de la Concorde is, is it not, the sign of a nation with a thirst for glory and a love of war, poetry and the arts? Surely all these things speak to us of the wonders of her history and her industry, of the discoveries of her thinkers, of the talent and genius of her artists. In contrast, the narrow, dirty, crooked streets threading their way through Paris amply attest to the fact that this is a nation more responsive to glory and great art than to material comforts.

Modes of dress are not motivated by climate, beliefs and manners alone; a host of circumstances bring additional modifications. If the *bernous*, the hooded cloak of the Arab, testifies, in a hot climate, to the nomadic ways of that people; if the constant uniformity of oriental dress attests to the immutability of its manners, beliefs and thought, one might trace in Europe the mobility of ideas and the longevity or brevity of their dominion by the duration of the fashions which reflect them.

The disappearance of the sword, the universal adoption of the cut-away proclaimed in France the triumph of equality before that principle was translated into institutions. Each phase of the revolution, war and peace, success and adversity, had its own costume, and not only do religious sects, political parties and political opinions proclaim themselves by their dress, but also clothes are indicative of the physical and moral ills which afflict a nation. The spread of cholera doubled the consumption of flannel in France, and England is the only nation in Europe where tailors make coats with pockets opening on the *inside*. I could conceive of no reason for such an inconvenient practice. Having noticed the impatience which such a peculiar fashion inspired in one Englishman, I asked him the reason for it. "What!" he replied, "isn't it obvious? If, as they do in Paris, we Londoners had our back pockets open on the outside, we would lose five or six scarves a day. Thieves have such clever hands that even so they manage to steal from us; but the precaution does spare us a great deal." I was reminded of my visit to Field Lane, and I cast about for an explanation as to why England has more thieves than any other nation of Europe.

The climate, the diet, the social atmosphere induce such a state of general torpor that, to rouse themselves from it, the English drink, indulge in every kind of excess, travel, and often do the most bizarre things. This need for strong emotions, which so often leads them to jeopardize their fortunes in a game of chance, to seek out danger, to undertake long and perilous voyages, to embrace the life of a sailor, etc., is the same which leads them to defy the law and to set themselves up, by thievery and brigandage, in opposition to society. Sloth, aversion for a never-changing task, also lead them to break the law, and, more important than any other causes, hunger and the desire to satisfy their passions are the primary motivations for both thievery and work. The moralists of antiquity, the Fathers of the Church, all preached resignation and disdain for worldly goods. In England, on the contrary, poverty is considered suspect and often treated as criminal. Luxury and debauchery abound on all sides, and honoured wealth, whatever its source, opens all doors. Is it any wonder then that wealth is a goal to be sought at any price? Under the influence of such an ethic, one might enter the *profession of thief* as one would any other. Even now, the chances of being robbed are calculated, and soon thieves and victims will be insuring themselves against risk; the former against the prosecution of the law, and the latter against theft.

III
A WORD ON ART IN ENGLAND[1]

Art does not progress in a nation until it descends into all classes of citizens, for the artist needs to be inspired by the enthusiasm he engenders; and if some are born with a love of art and with artistic discernment, almost anyone can acquire them. But how can a taste for great works of art take root in a nation where the individual is judged according to his address, his living quarters, his tailor, his servants and his spending habits? What inspiration can the artist derive from the world around him in a country where individual merit has no value, can claim no respect, if it is not accompanied by wealth? If Horace Vernet, Scheffer, Victor Hugo, George Sand, Lamennais or Mademoiselle Mars were to go to London and take lodgings in one of the little streets near Leicester Square, on the third floor of a house of modest appearance, and go about on foot or take the omnibus, people might call on them once, but not a second time. A sometime Venetian courtesan will be received with utmost courtesy if, to back up her title of Princess, she has an income of 50,000 francs, a handsome carriage and plenty of servants; but if one of our renowned artists should take a stroll down Regent Street in a threadbare coat and faded hat, people will carry rudeness to the

---

[1]In any country, art is such a vast subject that, to give an accurate idea of its present state, it would be wise to trace its history; I would have done so for English art if it had been my intention to discuss it; but in order to do so, I would have had to spend a great deal of time in England and devote an entire volume, at the very least, to so important a subject; my intent here has been merely to indicate some of the psychological causes which hamper art in England.

point of cutting him in the street. The nation has been brought up to despise poverty. Little wonder that they are so mean-souled! Their own self-esteem depends on the wealth they possess. The English have a profound repugnance for anything that smacks of poverty. The uniform, not of true poverty, but merely of limited means, is in their eyes the most dishonouring of public humiliations! That explains why England only rarely produces great artists; unlike us, they do not begin by acquiring talent. What purpose would it serve? Talent is not the primary thing, it is the means, not the end. To do so would be to reverse the direction indicated by public opinion, and to condemn oneself to be nothing but a workman forever in the pay of others. First one must strive to acquire riches, reserving the option of cultivating art at a later time, if one has any spark of vigour left remaining. Young Englishmen who become artists without having the money to make their presence felt, condemn themselves to exercise their talent abroad.

How, in such a state of affairs, can art be expected to develop in a nation? How, among a people whose every tendency is toward materialism, could art flourish? Thus it is that England is for Europe, as far as art is concerned, a veritable Siberia.

Judge for yourself what regard they have for art. Here is the quotation from the *Quarterly Journal of Agriculture* which appeared in the *Phalange* of 15 January: "Go ahead and praise, if you like, the Michael Angelos and others who fashion statues, all those artists who shape bronze and stone; but is Bakewell not also a great sculptor, a great artist? He sculpts in life, he takes cattle in place of a stone, he does not create, as others do, in the image of God; he does more, he reshapes the work of God; he does not, like the others, work with dead, inert matter devoid of reaction or resistance, but with animate limbs which must be carved from living flesh, modelled in blood, sinews, movement and strength of will."

Bakewell was endowed with a rare gift for observation, and he caused rural economy to make great strides, but only the English could compare this sort of genius with that of the artist!

Protestantism has declined to make use of any but the spoken arts for the propagation of its doctrines, and in those countries where it has taken root, the other faculties which God has bestowed on us for expressing thought have remained inactive. The imagination, in its depiction of impressions and its appeal to the emotions of others, has been confined to the language of speech. Similarly, Islamism, that great Protestantism of the sixth century, confined the rich oriental imagination to tales of adventure; the fine arts disappeared from the lands which had given them birth; soon picturesque language was no longer understood; the allegorical meaning of the forms and symbols of Greek art became as unintelligible as hieroglyphs.

I do not mean to imply that mosques are as bare, as devoid of decoration as the generality of Protestant churches; but since Islamism proscribes the representation of man and any form of animal, the Italian or Arab architects who constructed buildings in the East decorated them with foliage and delicate tracery but attached no meaning to the ornamentation. In the interior of the mosques one sees long passages from the Koran written on the walls; but aside from the crescent and the hundreds of lamps suspended from the domes, no symbol is to be found in Moslem places of worship.

The surviving monuments of the Middle Ages in England show how developed was the imaginative faculty of the time; it is still possible, with the aid of the chronicles, to read the thought behind it; whereas when we look about us at modern edifices, we encounter borrowings from every architecture, a bizarre mixture of all possible forms, totally without harmony and without thought. The constructions of public utility are of gigantic proportions and correspond perfectly well to their intended use, that is the most that can be said for them; but it would be a mistake to expect any underlying idea or historical association, any grace or thought; it is the simple dress of the Quakeress and not the elegant gown of the fashionable Parisian.

Churches, theatres, schools are now nothing but industrial speculations. England has forgotten the expression of art. In her churches harmony does not uplift the soul; no painter has transposed therein the dramas of Holy Writ nor lent eloquence to its teachings. No sculptor has erected personifications of Moses or Christ, of the Virgin Mary or Mary Magdalen, of Ambrose or Augustine or Hildebrand; in the theatres no fresco, no bas-relief evokes the costumes and manners of the ages which preceded us, nor the gods of the stage in antiquity and in modern times. The schools do not retrace in their decorations any of the great problems which engross human thought; the young have nothing to prepare their minds for the understanding of revelation, the expression of divine thought or the diversions of the stage. Mathematical reason has prevailed, has reduced all to nothing; ideas are expressed in numbers and thoughts in geometrical figures.

The Frankish language in use among the peoples of the Mediterranean, a patchwork made up of every idiom, gives some idea of the architectural *patois* one encounters in London. Should the foreigner who has not yet seen any of their national exhibitions and who is curious to know what English taste is like, what feeling they have for harmony, suddenly find himself in the midst of what is known as Trafalgar Square, at the sight of all the edifices and monuments crowding the square he will see what chaos in art can produce! The Queen's palace is mean, heavy and sombre; there is nothing original about its architecture: when one sees it for the first time, one has the impression of having seen it somewhere before. It is too small for a royal residence, and large receptions are held at the old St James's Palace. The little arch of triumph, an afterthought, completely hides the facade of the palace. It is a copy of the *Arc de Triomphe du Carroussel*. The collection in the National Gallery in Pall Mall is not extensive, but it contains paintings by the greatest masters: some Rembrandts, some extraordinarily beautiful Claude Lorrains, paintings by Leonardo da Vinci, Rubens, Teniers, Sebastiano del Piombino, Van Dyck, Poussin, an admirable Murillo, an apocryphal Raphael, and then some Hogarths, Wilkies, Lawrences and so forth.

The rich man feels the emptiness of wealth and envies the artist's exciting life and his fame. Having achieved great opulence, the English aristocracy missed the poetic thought which breathed life into their ancestors' existence, and they cast jealous eyes on Italy, Flanders and France.

Since early in the last century, the pride of lords and parvenus has outbid everyone in Europe for works of art. England is the nation with the greatest number and most precious collections of antiquities and modern masterpieces; but since they are almost always unavailable for study by artists, these masterpieces are lost as far as the progress of art is concerned.

One often encounters, in the private galleries of English gentlemen, copies, sometimes quite indifferent ones, which are nevertheless listed in the catalogue with the great names of Leonardo da Vinci, Raphael, Domenichino, Velazquez, Murillo, Le Sueur, Poussin, Rubens, Teniers, etc. The owners of the copies stubbornly insist that they are originals, and if anyone dares cast doubt on their authenticity, they take offence, whether they paid enormous sums for the daubs or inherited them from their fathers, as if they knew instinctively that an understanding of art is the true title of superiority. It is at times like these that wealth and position combined with ignorance are painful to see; one suffers for the glory of great men whose works are sequestered, deprived of the public's admiration and powerless to stimulate either enthusiasm or emulation among artists. Oh, what contempt it inspires for the wealthy, who keep genius under lock and key!

IV
A TRIP TO BRIGHTON

English stage-coaches are drawn by fine horses, are extremely light and carry almost no baggage; everything is designed to achieve the greatest speed, but in the construction no thought is given to convenience, comfort nor, I would venture to say, to the safety of travellers. I doubt that anywhere in the world there is a more disagreeable and more tiring way of travelling than in an English coach.

The inside of the coach accommodates four people, and the seats on top twelve or sixteen. The inside seats cost twice as much; they are neither better nor worse than in vehicles on the

Continent. One climbs to the upper seats by means of a ladder, and once perched on top, one must bear the full intensity of the heat or cold, be exposed to wind, fog, rain, hail, the heat of the sun, dust, and run the risk of falling off if sleep overtakes you either by day or by night. I can think of nothing so uncomfortable except riding on the back of a camel in the desert.

I have made several trips into the English countryside; I shall recount only one of them so as not to weary the reader by the monotony of my descriptions; for the landscape is overwhelming in its uniformity.

It was last year, at the end of August; the weather was sultry and threatening, and from time to time showers would fall as in France in the month of March. Toward eleven o'clock I arrived with my baggage in Piccadilly; all the trunks, bags, baskets and so forth were loaded on the coach, and then we climbed aboard. I, along with two others, had seats at the very back, and there were three people opposite me; the front seats were completely full. We prayed that our two unoccupied seats would remain empty all the way to Brighton, for we were extremely cramped. Two gentlemen arrived, but when they saw so little room, they decided not to come along. We had left London more than a mile behind us when the coach stopped in front of a pretty little house, and two ladies, one of whom was enormous, came and sat down in the empty seats. Oh my! after that I was in a position to form an accurate assessment of the charm of travelling on an English coach!

We were so crammed together that the people in the four corner seats had to sit with one leg over the little iron railing at the ends of the seats. Moreover, the boxes, bundles and baskets besieged us from every side. With each shower four umbrellas would spring open; then a concourse of spouts would add to the calamity. Nor was the sun less troublesome to ward off. It was an intolerable place to be! Yet in the front of the coach our companions were complaining even more bitterly; the wind would drive the rain into their faces and a poor lady with child was so overcome as to faint away entirely.

I vouch for the truth of what I am about to relate, even though it may seem incredible, as much for the inhumanity it presupposes as for the respect for property carried to such extremes by those who allowed it to happen.

The coach halted, and the travellers, with the help of the coachman, lifted the ailing woman down to permit her to regain her senses. We seized the opportunity to get down also; the poor lady's condition was most alarming. The coachman told us: "Inside the coach there are only two elderly ladies; they have paid for four seats, two of which are taken up by their dogs; perhaps if we asked, they might let the sick woman ride inside."

Neither the driver nor anyone else would dare to approach the two ladies, so great is the distance separating man from man in England, so much greater is respect for property than respect for humanity! One gentleman thought that if I conveyed the request to the two old ladies, I would, as a foreigner, incur less risk of being refused; the gentleman hoped that for the sake of national pride they would hesitate to show English selfishness in all its nakedness; however, the two ladies, having seen everything that happened and heard perfectly well everything that was said, had called their dogs away from the door, closed the windows and were pretending to be asleep. I had not taken my eyes off them since the beginning of the scene, and not one of their movements had escaped me. I knew perfectly well what the reply would be. Nevertheless I did not hesitate but went up and knocked on the glass: I knocked several times and quite vigorously; at length a window was lowered half-way and a voice inquired sharply what I wanted. "Madame," I replied in French, "I wonder if you would be kind enough to be of service to a poor lady who is very unwell; she is quite unable to ride safely on top of the coach; please allow her to take one of the empty seats inside with you." "Madame," she replied even more sharply, "we paid for all four seats because we did not wish to be *disturbed*, and what you are asking is quite impossible." With these words, she abruptly closed the window and hastily drew back into the coach. Everyone was indignant at such inhumanity; but everyone kept saying: "She is within her rights, she *did* pay."

Wretched people! As if the precept of charity were not above any *rights* and any *laws*! To hear them talk, one would think he was reading from one of the books of Moses: "If a man smite his servant, or his maid, with a rod, and he die under his hand, he shall not be punished for he *is* his money."[1]

The incident turned out to my benefit; for having given up my seat to the sick woman, I found myself better off in hers, although I did suffer from the cold and the wind, but at least I could stretch out my legs and lean back against a trunk, which it had been impossible for me to do in my former seat. Toward three o'clock the rain stopped, the weather turned clear and fresh, and I commanded a superb view.

The countryside in England presents an aspect of rich fertility; the trees are remarkably beautiful, the hedges dense and vigorous, the meadows wonderfully green: the thing that has always struck me is the great number of hedges which surround the fields and when seen from a certain distance, give to the countryside the appearance of a kitchen garden divided up into little beds symmetrically bordered with boxwood; I know that writers, authors of picturesque travels, have lavished praise on those verdant enclosures.

However, if one takes the trouble to analyse the impression which they produce, one will see that by their uniformity they reduce a great realm to the dimensions of a garden plot; and too, they deprive husbandry of an immense expanse of land; and in a country where wheat, food of any sort is always dear, where so many are starving, in a country where the parks of rich landowners and the feeding of their fancy horses removes a large portion of the land from cultivation, the loss of land caused by hedges strikes me as a serious error for rural economy. So it was that after some moments spent in savouring the sweet freshness that lies generally over the countryside, a freshness which is dearly bought considering the dampness of the climate, I could not help but turn my thoughts to the situation of the people in a nation where all the land is enclosed in impenetrable hedges which guard wheat, potatoes, turnips and the very grass under

---

[1] Exodus, ch. XXI v. 21

lock and key! If the people were not starving, the fields would be open, and the standing crops, as well as the stacks of wheat and hay, would be freely and fearlessly exposed to the public's honour, as is the case in France.[1]

When I travelled through the English countryside for the first time, the sight of the villages made me at first believe that they had just been built; but as I went on, I soon observed that the houses in all the villages were equally "new", and I realized that English country folk must make it a rule to have their houses whitewashed and painted every year, or at least every two years. Such neatness is very laudable, to be sure, and I applaud the attention given to walls, shutters, doors, and gates; but the result is a wearisome monotony. Seeing all those "new" houses, the traveller has the impression that he is passing through a country which goes back only twenty-five years; he says to himself: "The people who live in these villages were not born there"; and if he meets an old man bent under the weight of years, try as he might, he can see no place where the man might have been born. Besides, the tidiness of the outside of the houses is another example of "show", to which the inside is far from corresponding.

Finally, at six o'clock in the evening, we arrived in Brighton; considering all that I had had to endure, I thought of the discomfort and fatigue which must plague those who leave London at seven in the evening and do not reach Brighton until five in the morning.

V
THE IRON DIPPER

A fountain is a sign of Providence; no other creation in nature has such pleasant, graceful thoughts hovering about it; the sylvan grove has no place wherein poetic and religious inspiration makes itself so keenly felt. It refreshes the birds of the heavens and the

---

[1] Hedges are not common in France, except for enclosing gardens; they are also used in certain localities near the sea to protect fruit trees from the wind.

denizens of the forests; there the shepherd leads his flock to drink; there the young girl comes to draw water; there she first hears words of love, and there the spent old man directs his steps in hopes of finding charity. At sight of it the weary caravan goes with quickened pace to slake its burning thirst, and the water, as it courses from the fountain, repeats the name of Allah!

The Moslem bequeaths gifts to fountains; the dervish comes to pray nearby, and God assembles there all creatures made by Him; everywhere a fountain speaks of hope and happiness; why then in England does it only bring to mind the selfishness of the rich and the misfortune of the poor?

I have brought away with me from London a sound which the sight of misfortune will always set reverberating within me, a sound which recalls to my mind the poor, oppressed English working-man, ground down by the rich; the beggar furtively asking for alms and fainting from hunger in the street; in short all the creatures disinherited from heaven's gifts, all the PARIAHS who like a leprous growth are spread over this huge city with its scandalous luxury and frightful poverty.

There are in London none of those sumptuous and monumental fountains which add life to the public squares of Paris and speak to all the language of art; but one does encounter iron pumps in many streets. An iron chain is affixed to the post with a dipper of the same metal hanging from the end. This dipper is the economical goblet offered to the pauper by his lord and master, the rich man. "You see, here water costs the people nothing, they may drink at their convenience without going to draw water from the river." So speak people of the well-to-do classes, who, in London, *never* drink water.

In a nation where pure water is "very bad for one", where one must resort to the use of cordials to combat the cold and the damp, is it not the height of cruelty to put fermented beverages out of the reach of the people, through the enormous duties imposed on them? In a country where scarcely one person in twenty-five can drink wine, and one in seven drink beer, is it not ironically insulting to offer the people London water which has been dirtied by all the drains in the city? Let barley and cereals come in duty-free, put no more restrictions on wine and beer than there are in France, then and then only, O English aristocracy, will one believe in your love for the people, in your humanity; then you will be credited, your charitableness lauded, for giving *gratis* to the poor the water which they cannot buy from the company that furnishes it to the city.

One of the pumps was located not ten feet from my house; I would constantly hear the rattle of the chain and the clang of the dipper falling back against the post, and I would say to myself: "There is one of my brothers having a drink of water, a drink of that London water, so stale, so nauseating!" To be sure, not all of the water distributed in London comes from the Thames, but it is all debilitating to the stomach and often causes dysentery and fever! That harsh metallic sound pierced me to the heart! It resounded in my ears like a funeral knell! O wretched people! Will God leave you to the mercy of your lords, those lords who, without pity, watch you die that lingering and cruel death that, hour by hour and minute by minute, kills the victim vainly struggling in his agony? Oh what a terrible thought! The conqueror destroys with iron and fire, he follows the rule of war: he comes openly as the enemy, he does not hypocritically say that he has come to "protect the people" as he reduces them to slavery! But to destroy an entire people with poverty and famine! To weigh them down under the heaviest yoke that was ever borne by an enslaved population! To force them to be content with rags for clothes, with a few roots for food and water for drink, and to labour every waking hour under penalty of starvation! O lords of England, this system is the most barbaric, the most dreadful of tyrannies. God will not suffer it to endure....

Fifty years ago the people of France were setting fire to the *châteaux*, and twenty times armed Europe was powerless to prevent the triumph of their cause. Now England resounds on every side with cries of revolt and destruction. O lords, repent, beware the people's vengeance, appease their wrath and remember these words, which are as old as the world: "Vox populi, vox Dei".

www.ingramcontent.com/pod-product-compliance
Lightning Source LLC
Chambersburg PA
CBHW060833190426
43197CB00039B/2580